The Stock Option Income Generator

Founded in 1807, John Wiley & Sons is the oldest independent publishing company in the United States. With offices in North America, Europe, Australia, and Asia, Wiley is globally committed to developing and marketing print and electronic products and services for our customers' professional and personal knowledge and understanding.

The Wiley Trading series features books by traders who have survived the market's ever changing temperament and have prospered—some by reinventing systems, others by getting back to basics. Whether a novice trader, professional or somewhere in-between, these books will provide the advice and strategies needed to prosper today and well into the future.

For a list of available titles, visit our web site at www.WileyFinance.com.

The Stock Option Income Generator

How to Make Steady Profits by Renting Your Stocks

HARVEY CONRAD FRIEDENTAG

WILEY

John Wiley & Sons, Inc.

Published by John Wiley & Sons, Inc., Hoboken, New Jersey.
Published simultaneously in Canada.

For general information on our other products and services or for technical support, please contact our Customer Care Department within the United States at (800) 762-2974, outside the United States at (317) 572-3993 or via fax at (317) 572-4002.

Wiley also publishes its books in a variety of electronic formats. Some content that appears in print may not be available in electronic books. For more information about Wiley products, visit our web site at www.wiley.com.

Library of Congress Cataloging-in-Publication Data:

Friedentag, Harvey C. (Harvey Conrad)
   The stock option income generator : how to make steady profits by renting your stocks / Harvey Conrad Friedentag.
         p. cm.—(Wiley trading series)
   Includes index.
   ISBN 978-0-470-48160-8 (cloth)
   1. Stock options.   2. Investments.   3. Finance, Personal.   I. Title.
   HG6042.F737 2009
   332.63′2283—dc22
                                                            2009015534

Contents

Preface

The greatest investment experience of your life begins today. And this experience is really timely, because all the day-traders are gambling without knowing what they are doing.

Thirty-six years ago, working at my kitchen table, I started a unique endeavor for investing. Since that modest beginning, my portfolio management service has grown to be a source of personal satisfaction and income not just for me but, even better, for my clients. And this book will do the same for you.

Why? Because this book covers what I know to be the single most rewarding form of investing in existence—the covered call option.

This book is a road map. I have developed a step-by-step program to make you a successful investor, as I have made my clients successful investors. Let me lead you to the same success.

Let me open your eyes to the facts about this extraordinary investment arena. In the following pages, you will learn the basics of selecting the best stocks for covered call options.

The approach is simple. The complete strategy is easy to execute and will save you both time and money. The first chapters of the book are truly fundamental, dealing with the basics of investing. If you are already comfortable with investing, I suggest you move directly to the advanced part of the book, which tells you how to move beyond comfort to real success.

The methods discussed in this book have achieved proven results over many years. The strategies and tactics outlined will allow you to accumulate assets steadily. You can reach your investment goals within a reasonable amount of time. In studying my book you will learn:

- To heed the lessons of the past
- To invest without doubt
- To make profits in the stock market
- To profit whether the market goes up, or down, or sideways

If this is what you are looking for, read on.

When I finished my last book, *Stocks for Options Trading*, I thought I had written everything I could write about my approach for investing in the stock market. Then several things happened.

The first was a dramatic increase in my advisory business. This drove me to create, develop, try, and perfect my methods for portfolio enhancement—big words for getting more safety and income out of stock market investing in all financial climates.

Then we experienced the events of 2008. You cannot bring up the stock market these days without analyzing the events that have been taking place as I write this book. This has been one of the most unusual times I have ever experienced. I have always believed that investors should ignore the ups and downs of the market. Fortunately, the vast majority of them paid little attention to the distractions cited previously. If this is any example, very few of my clients switched to money market funds during the desperations of the period. When you sell in desperation, you always sell cheap, and truly realize your losses.

Whether it is a 508-point day or a 59-point day, and you are nervous about the stock market, you do not have to sell that day or the next. Maybe we are in a bear market and for the next two years or three years you will wish you had never heard of stocks. But the history of the stock market has been full of bear markets, not to mention recessions, and in spite of that the results are indisputable: A portfolio of stocks with covered call options will turn out to be a lot more valuable than a portfolio of bonds or CDs or money market funds. You could come out ahead of the panic-sellers, because the market will rise steadily eventually. In the end, superior companies will succeed and mediocre companies will fail, and investors in each will be rewarded accordingly.

To some, these concepts seem to defy logic, or at least they defy explanation. Not to me. They make sense. I do them every day, and so will you. I want to change the way you invest.

Every investor must be realistic. You must gather data, analyze them, and strive to come to logical conclusions, whether favorable or unfavorable. Optimism is a tonic. Pessimism is poison. You must become a realist.

This is a book about investing success. The complete strategy is easy to execute and is appropriate to save you both time and money by using tactics designed for you.

If the returns you receive from implementing my strategies seem to defy gravity, then great for you. Keep the gains. I get the satisfaction of knowing you are doing well.

As a registered investment advisor (RIA) with the United States Securities and Exchange Commission (SEC), I have been managing personal portfolios professionally since 1986. The methods discussed in this book have achieved proven results in the past. The strategies and tactics outlined here will allow you to accumulate assets steadily. You can reach your investment goals within a reasonable amount of time.

My point of view is that hindsight or rumor or case studies are only interesting if you can learn a lesson from them . . . that investing well is important, but what you get for the money you earn probably matters more . . . and that you don't have much time or tolerance for clichés, familiar faces, or formulaic advice. *Don't learn the tricks of the trade. Learn the trade.*

Before you take the plunge, consider that investing is like scuba diving: It is not for everyone. But both can be mastered by more people than have so far shown up on either scene. In both activities, it is essential that you be truly aware of exactly what you are doing, and that you are alert to the possible dangers as well as the safeguards available to protect you against them.

In the case of investing, your greatest safeguards are your constant watchfulness, a thorough awareness, and the investment of your time. You should allot part of that time to keeping abreast of outside influences, whether political, economic, or other trends that might affect the present and future of your investments.

I will share the real-life examples that bring my formulas to life. In this book, I give you all the details, methods, and techniques that I use daily to produce wealth. And then if that is not enough, I will share with you methods for serious tax reduction, wealth enhancement, and portfolio asset protection.

HARVEY CONRAD FRIEDENTAG
April 2009

Acknowledgments

A writer writes, a reader reads. As a writer, you know who you are and what the material means to you. But you cannot begin to know who the reader will be, or what background that reader will or won't bring to the page.

I have tried to write a book that will be useful and of value to both investors and prospective investors. It starts out simply and then grows in detail. It reflects my involvement over the years with the investment process. More importantly, however, it reflects some of the accumulated knowledge and experience I have gained as a veteran in the stock market.

To distill a lifetime of my experience and that of my friends and colleagues in investing into a book is a giant task and a near impossibility as well. Something is sure to be left out. Some readers may rise in protest, no matter how honorable my intentions. Yet I want to give as much knowledge as I can to my readers about this marvelous, exciting, fun, agonizing, ecstatic—and, of course, financially rewarding—way of making money called investing. Finally, I want you to enjoy investing.

This book won't make you an instant expert or give you a surefire formula for making money. But it could be an important step toward taking control of your financial future. My goal is to convince and train you to be your own portfolio manager while using a method that enables you to invest without fear.

This book is a presentation of my work and the suggestions of others, gained through broadcast, the printed word, and my face-to-face real-life experiences.

Writing a book is a formidable task that cannot be appreciated until you actually begin work on it. One must summon forth a resolve and commitment that are not normally needed in everyday life.

There are not enough words in the thesaurus to thank Hal and Martha Quiat for their assistance in desktop publishing, grammar, and making me clearly state what I meant to say. They were able to divorce their own egos and personalities from the process and concentrate on drawing me out, which they did flawlessly. Bold and merciless editing to hone the material, to be sure that only the best parts of the document were included, was matched with a stubborn determination to reject anything that did not belong. Behind their engaging and gentle exterior lies a strict discipline to prohibit excess wordage. Hal and Martha's weeding and pruning have been crucial to the presentation of this material. They gave freely of their time and talent, rearranging their workdays to accommodate mine.

Heartfelt recognition is offered to all those who let me interview them, who listened to my long-winded dissertations, and who openly shared their feelings, philosophies, and experiences about investing with me.

I have to thank some long-time friends: Stuart MacPhail got me "computerized"—or I would still be looking at a stack of indecipherable notes—edited my first drafts, corrected my grammar, helped me get my thoughts organized, and helped to get this book completed. Michael Wootan gave constant encouragement, and assisted me with the computer fundamentals and with the manuscript.

Great recognition goes to the members of the Contrarian Investment Club for using my methods and giving me their input. I thank Nate Oderberg for serving 20 years as the treasurer for the Contrarian Investment Club and spending many late-night sessions stock-picking with me. I am deeply indebted to Thomas Tolen, CPA, for helping me with the tax ramifications of covered call option investing. I also thank Guy Simone, who bounced strategies and ideas off my head, and enhanced my investment procedures.

I have to thank my friend Joyce and my family for all the long sessions when I disappeared into my office to work on this book and was not available to them.

Last but not least, my appreciation goes to Dr. Alexander Elder, who greatly facilitated getting my book to John Wiley & Sons for publishing; Meg Freeborn, my developmental editor; Kevin Commins, my editor; and Ted Bonanno, my literary agent. Thank you, all my friends.

H. C. F.

Fear and Ignorance

Fear always springs from ignorance.
—Ralph Waldo Emerson

Why must people have a fear of investing?
Why did the stock market crash in 1929?
Why was it necessary to become jobless?
Why was it necessary to become penniless?
Why was it necessary for people to leap to their deaths out of fear?
Why was it necessary to forgo the American dream?

Aren't investors by definition fearful? With little training in investing, they tend to do nothing, or they delegate investment responsibilities to stockbrokers, accountants, bank trust officers, insurance agents, relatives, or friends—often with disappointing results. After all, no one will care as much about your financial assets as you do. No one will do the job as well as you can.

It is not an easy job. There are thousands of ways to go wrong. Even the most prudent investment decisions may not work (as we know from personal experience and the tales of countless investors). The job may not be easy, but it is doable. I have learned to invest money successfully, and so can you. It takes some study and considerable personal discipline, but you will be well paid for your efforts. This book will help you get started and guide you toward rewarding accomplishments.

The best opening lesson on fear and investing is illustrated by the largest money-losing event, and worst day of fear ever seen: the stock market crash of 1929.

THE STOCK MARKET CRASH OF 1929

The tragedy of this crash is best illustrated in the many news stories of the time, as reported by the telegraphic services of the Associated Press, *New York Times, Chicago Tribune, Chicago News,* Universal International News, Consolidated Press, and the United Press.

Tuesday, October 29, 1929

Following Black Monday, October 28, 1929, newspapers ran headlines that screamed "Stocks Drop $10 to $70 a Share, Worst Break in Market History," "Billions in Value Are Swept Away by Avalanche of Sales," and "Late Rally Turns Prices Upward, Recovery Small by Comparison; Total Sales Near 16,000,000 Shares."

The greatest break in the history of the New York Stock Exchange (NYSE) continued to slash away billions of dollars in values Tuesday in the most enormous trading day in history.

Prices Seemed to Know No End   Positive assurances from the bankers and economists that the bottom had been reached Tuesday brought only a temporary respite; then the market roared downward at wide drops.

Shortly after 1:00 P.M., prices were down 1 to 50 points on both the big board and the curb exchange. New lows for the year or longer were established in many shares. The market value loss was tremendous, totaling more than $50 billion since the terrific downward movement started a few days earlier.

Rallies Were Short-Lived; Stocks Resumed Their Plunge   During the day, slight recoveries set in but these were without support; the stocks that had recovered fell back and joined the general downward rush.

All sorts of bait were dangled before the traders in an effort to revive buying. Bankers were helpless to stem the tide of reaction. They resorted to psychological methods to convince traders they were not worried about the situation.

Influential banks were said to have worked out a plan of attack for Tuesday, but it did not make itself felt in the morning. A group of representative institutions marked down the figures at which stock market loans could be made. One broker reduced commissions, and others were expected to follow. The Federal Reserve was in session, with Secretary Mellon in attendance. He was said to have conferred with President Hoover, but no statement was forthcoming.

All of the World on Selling Spree   Engulfed in the greatest selling wave in the history of the NYSE, prices were carried down Tuesday under a torrent of liquidation from every corner of the globe. Monday's losses, huge as they were, were doubled on Tuesday.

More than 13 million shares had changed hands on this record-breaking day. Stocks of all kinds crashed. In mid-afternoon, there was a rally from the lows, which brought prices back from the minimums. It still left them enormously down on the day.

A report that the Federal Reserve Board of Governors was considering closing the exchange was denied semi-officially, and it was announced that various investment trusts and banking interests were buying.

Call money, renewing at 5 percent, was advanced to 6 percent in the last hour, suggesting that the investment trusts were withdrawing funds from the call market to buy stocks. Until mid-day, every attempt to stem the tide met with failure. At the end there was a sharp rally. There has never been anything like it.

Wednesday, October 30, 1929

On Wednesday, the papers ran these headlines: "Stocks Advance $5 to $30 a Share" and "Investment Trusts Put Half Billion in Market During Rally."

The bulls staged a great demonstration in the closing minutes.

Prices were whirled up to the highs of the day, a day that had seen prices moving up regularly from the calamitous lows of Tuesday. It was a great climax, and as the closing bell rang traders and brokers shouted, cheered, and threw papers into the air in jubilation at the restoration of confidence in the market.

Investment trusts and trading corporations were heavy buyers of stock over the course of those two days, and purchases were estimated to range from $350 million to one-half billion dollars. These securities were bought outright.

The wave of hysterical selling, which had clipped more than $25 billion from the quoted value of listed securities in the New York market during the last week, subsided Wednesday, and prices rallied briskly in response to what appeared to be strong investment demand. Scores of active issues were marked up $5 to nearly $30 a share in the first hour of trading.

Developments in the Stock Market Situation   Wednesday indicated that a mobilization of the nation's leading financial forces had been undertaken to calm the wave of hysteria and restore confidence in the securities markets. John D. Rockefeller Sr., who rarely spoke for publication, authorized the statement Wednesday that he and his son for some days had been purchasing sound common stocks: "We are continuing and will continue our purchases in substantial amounts at levels which we believe represent sound investment values," he added.

Philanthropist Pledges to Help Employees Caught in Stock Crash   Julius Rosenwald, philanthropist and chairman of the board of Sears Roebuck and Company, "pledged without limit" his personal fortune to guarantee the stock market accounts of the 40,000 employees of his company. John Higgins, vice president of Sears, was delegated the duty of seeing that the employees' accounts were protected.

Higgins immediately looked up the accounts of all employees—not only in Chicago, but everywhere the company had branches. When he found an employee carrying an account in which, in the present bear market, his margin had grown too narrow for safety, Higgins communicated with the broker handling the account. "We simply put up collateral, so that our employees shall be able to weather the storm," Higgins explained. "One of the things I found out was that a great many of employees will have no need for the assistance offered. Some of them, thanks to their thrift and good judgments, are wealthy. The help Mr. Rosenwald is offering is for those who need it."

According to Higgins, Mr. Rosenwald had adopted a similar plan during the financial period depression in 1921. The sum that Mr. Rosenwald pledged was about $1,600,000, to be used as collateral for employee stock accounts. It was also revealed that Mr. Rosenwald made a gift in 1921 of $5 million worth of his own stock to the company and pledged $20 million more of his personal fortune to see the company through. It was explained that Mr. Rosenwald's 1929 offer applied to all employees' stock accounts, no matter what stocks the employees held.

A List of Stocks That Are Safe to Buy   The following information was for persons who wished to purchase sound investment issues—it was believed that the stocks named would yield good income.

Kennecot: Provided price of copper metal is held at 18 cents, Kennecot will be in a position to increase its dividend rate by the end of the year. Paying $5 a share, or better than 7 percent at current prices, Kennecot looms ahead of Anaconda as the favorite of those friendly to the copper group. 1929 range $104\frac{7}{8}$–65; Tuesday's close $65\frac{3}{4}$, down $4\frac{7}{8}$.

Pullman: Rated an A-1 investment stock, paying $4 a share, and aided by new car orders, Pullman will earn more than $5 a share this year. It is no stock to buy for trading turns, but it will do well for the investor who is willing to hold it for the long pull. 1929 range $99\frac{1}{4}$–$75\frac{1}{8}$ Tuesday's close $75\frac{1}{4}$, down 3.

American Rolling Mill: Selling at a new low for the year, Rolling Mill is an attractive buy for the long pull. Earnings for the first six months of this year were $3.26, compared with $3.07 for the entire twelve months of 1928. Stock pays a dividend of $2, plus 5 percent in stock. The company owns the valuable exclusive patent for rolling strip steel and is leasing it on a royalty basis to the biggest steel corporations in the world. 1929 range, 144 .62–72; Tuesday's close 72; down 13.

New York Central: Actually the leader of the seasoned rails, New York Central always has held its place as one of the soundest of investment issues, and has done well in price appreciation. Earnings, estimated at $16 or more this year, are steadily increasing, and the company is rich in realty. Central will never cost anyone any money in the long run. 1929 range, $256\frac{1}{2}$–175; Tuesday's close $189\frac{1}{2}$, up $3\frac{1}{2}$.

Pennsylvania: Good management is one of the required attributes of any company to the investor who is buying its stock. Pennsylvania railroad has an excellent management and never has been a market laggard. At current prices, paying a $4 dividend, it yields a little less than 5 percent. 1929 range, 110–72; Tuesday's price 82, down 8.

Underwood-Elliot-Fisher: This company has further merger possibilities, in addition to enjoying the position of the largest company in the business machine and office equipment industry. 1929 range, $181\frac{3}{4}$–91; Tuesday's close 97, down 13.

American Radiator: Mergers have often been forecast for this company, and undoubtedly they will occur in the course of time. At present, the company is a powerful unit in the industry. Dividend is $1.50 or 4.3 percent at current price. 1929 range, $55\frac{3}{8}$–28; Tuesday's close 32, up.

Thursday, October 31, 1929

"Big Buying Wave Sends Stocks Higher," "Profit Taking Fails to Wipe Out Gains Made in Early Hour," "Orders Pour In from Everywhere; Volume of Trade Heavy" were headlines that ran in the major dailies on Thursday, October 31.

The three-hour stock exchange sessions Thursday saw traders push the market forward at such a pace that $10 billion was added to the market's valuation of stock. The trading was terrific. In the short session, thousands upon thousands of shares, bargains as described by such financiers as John D. Rockefeller, were bought. The first half-hour alone was at a rate of more than 24 million shares for a full-day session.

Tickers ran an hour behind, but floor quotations just at closing time showed that stocks were up from 1 to 40 points. Buying was as frenzied Thursday as selling had been the previous Tuesday. Values came back with the vigor of the old bull market that Wall Street had declared dead just days before.

> The desire of knowledge, like the thirst of riches, increases ever with the acquisition of it.
>
> —Laurence Sterne

INVESTMENT KNOWLEDGE + STOCK MARKET = PROFITS

You can make money no matter what direction the stock market is going. You have just seen a brief insight into the 1929 crash and its aftermath. On the day of the crash, stocks were rebounding by the end of the trading day. On the following two days, the numbers were even better:

- October 29, 1929, −30.57 Dow Jones −11.73 percent
- October 30, 1929, +28.40 Dow Jones +12.34 percent

This illustrates that a lot of money can be made as a result of a market crash.

You can now see that financial hell or financial heaven may be just around the corner. I differ from many of my colleagues in my sincere belief that the prepared investor can profit when the market goes up or down. Let us emulate investors like John D. Rockefeller Sr. and Julius Rosenwald.

They say a fool and his money are soon parted. What I want to know is how he got it in the first place.

UNDERSTANDING INVESTOR BEHAVIOR

Behavioral finance attempts to provide a structure for understanding the behavior of investors and the stock markets in which they invest. This framework is complementary to the standard theory of finance, also known as the *efficient market* theory. In this latter view, investors are totally rational beings. In making decisions, they consider all available information and accurately assess its meaning. They determine the probable outcomes associated with various decisions and only take actions likely to maximize their overall wealth and minimize risk.

Under the standard theory, securities markets quickly—almost instantaneously—incorporate all known information. Market movements are based on changes in that information and reflect the collective reactions of rational investors to the new information. Securities are always accurately priced.

Behavioral finance, in contrast, holds that investors are actually not completely rational beings. They sometimes act based on imperfect or incomplete information, and they may misinterpret information or react to it in inappropriate ways. However, behaviorists believe investor behavior is not purely random or totally irrational, either. They believe that even the nonrational behavior of investors falls into patterns and may be somewhat predictable.

Mind over Matter

Market declines are a natural part of the investment process. There have always been momentous events that dampened the markets. But history has shown that markets eventually rebound. Maintaining a long-term perspective through challenging economic times isn't easy, but it can be rewarding. Throughout the history of the market, the ups generally have outweighed the downs, resulting in strong long-term growth opportunities.

> The best way to predict your future is to create it.
>
> —Abraham Lincoln

THE CRASH OF 2008

Official confirmation of the painfully obvious, that the United States entered a recession in December 2007, came from the National Bureau of Economic Research. In reflecting on the calendar year 2008, the sad state of the economy is obvious.

We saw gasoline costs go through the roof and then plummet. The Dow Jones turned into a daily roller coaster, and the $700 billion bailout took shape but did not seem to have any impact on market stability. Terms such as "mortgage meltdown" and "credit freeze" became part of the everyday financial language, and the unemployment rate rose dramatically.

It was nearly impossible to open a newspaper, turn on the television, or surf the Web without coming across a doom-and-gloom story about the economy and the financial markets. While there is no doubt that these are difficult times, this is an ideal time for investors to position themselves for long-term success.

Against the backdrop of the problems in the subprime mortgage sector, the ensuing credit crunch, and the unsteadying influence on markets, investors have been challenged to revalidate their ideas about how best to invest in a rollercoaster market. In the interest of providing context, it is important that the reader understand my investment philosophy. It is based on the tenets of broad stock portfolio diversification and linked alternative investments. We don't engage in tactical or market-timing efforts. Instead, we attempt to execute a strategic asset allocation, with targets adjusted periodically over a long time horizon.

It appears that the United States has plunged into its worst financial crisis since the 1930s. The leadership of Treasury Secretary Henry Paulson and Federal Reserve Chief Ben S. Bernanke in fighting it has been sluggish and inconsistent. The intensity of the crash will surely earn a place in financial history.

U.S. consumer bankruptcy filings jumped nearly 33 percent in 2008 amid a recession that's expected to keep filings rising in 2009.

Overall consumer filings reached over 1.5 million last year. The 2008 rate of increase fell short of the 40 percent rise recorded in 2007, and the annual total in both of those years is still short of the more than two million recorded in 2005 alone. A law that took effect in October 2005 made personal bankruptcy filings more difficult and sharply curtailed filings in 2006 to about 573,000, the lowest level since 1998.

President Obama and his Congress took the reins of the country in January 2009, but it will take time for them to develop policies to stimulate the economy and promote liquidity. What's an investor to do? Understand that when the market changes, people tend to get nervous, apprehensive, and downright uneasy.

> Neither the entrepreneurs nor the farmers nor the capitalists determine what has to be produced. The consumers do that.
>
> —Ludwig Von Mises

WHAT TO DO FIRST

First, do not dump the market by selling your quality stocks. Yes, it is the worst bear market since 2000–2002 and stocks are trading at valuations not seen in decades, but equities will come back. Panics invariably provoke investors to make the wrong moves. So resist the panicky calls from some so-called experts and many of your friends to move cash while you still have some savings left.

If you have uninvested cash, there is an almost endless choice of quality businesses trading at or near liquidation prices. The stock market is on a fire sale. Take advantage.

How patient do you have to be? How long will you have to wait? Some economists argue that it will take years to recover from the worldwide collapse we are facing. I do not agree. The United States and every other economic power know only too well the lessons of the Great Depression. Nobody will try to fight the recession by raising interest rates, or by closing the door to imports, as we did in 1930 with the Smoot-Hawley Tariff Act. We are already seeing global cooperation to prevent real disaster, such as the coordinated rate cuts made in early October 2008 by the Federal Reserve, the European Central Bank, the Bank of England, and the central banks of Canada, Sweden, and Switzerland.

It's okay, change makes everybody nervous. After all, it's more comfortable to stick with what you've always known. The truth is, a change in the market is a positive action. With the knowledge gained from this book, you will not only get the good comfortable feeling of knowing what to do, but also know how to react to anything that happens. People instantly get apprehensive if they think the changes are too big. Actually, as you will see, big changes work to your advantage. Of course, until you prove these facts to yourself, some of you are going to be just plain uneasy. I know no matter how much I tell you, the proof is going to be in the doing.

This book will show you how to prepare—not by hiding in a bomb shelter waiting for adversity to go away, but by arming yourself for battle in the financial marketplace. Take that money out of your mattress. If you do not, you will miss one of the greatest buying opportunities of your life. Times like these, when many U.S. companies are looking cheap, are the times to take action and buy.

Alarming? Not at all. The risk is surprisingly small. The rewards are great. You will learn how to use the psychology of the mob, and how to turn "nervous" into profits. You will be alerted to what it can cost you if you still believe in Santa Claus, the tooth fairy, or the good sense of brokers and bureaucrats.

Regardless of where you see the best value, most money managers agree that it's nearly impossible to predict when the markets will hit rock bottom. They recommend that investors dollar cost average into their chosen investments, regularly depositing money, so they will catch the bottom without resorting to a crystal ball.

Advised and protected by all the ideas and techniques explained to you in the following pages, you can proceed on your way and come home richer than when you started out.

> Therefore, do not repress your spirits or lose your courage. All things work according to law, and all things can be made to manifest this law.
>
> —Anonymous

MY INVESTMENT HISTORY

I just returned from a mutual fund seminar where I learned that if I had put my money with the company 56 years ago, my $10,000 would now be $10,338,589. (Total value includes reinvested dividends and capital gain distribution totaling $3,924,771 taken in shares.)

If I had participated in that scenario, I can tell you where I would really be now: I would be dead from old age. Besides, who had $10,000 56 years ago? How much would taxes have reduced the $10 million end result?

Both beginners and long-time participants dream of—and are unrealistic about—making fantastic gains in a short time. The stock market can make you a fortune, if you are willing to get rich slowly. The stock market is the place to be if your goals are to make money.

Norman, the first stockbroker I ever met socially, said to me many years ago, "Harvey, I can make you a small fortune and guarantee it." *Wow!* I thought. "Just come to me with a large fortune," he continued.

My experience in the stock market is not unique. I grew up in a poor working-class environment, where I received an appreciation for the lifestyle commonly described as the American dream.

When we are very young, we are possessors of a splendid gift—a mind that knows no limits. Faced with a new experience, our minds allow us to make discoveries, gain insights, and with time, learn something more of the world around us. If we are truly fortunate, we'll never completely let go of that early innocence that keeps us forever open to new ideas and permits us to dream.

In the United States, you have to realize that the only real limits to learning and dreaming are the ones we make for ourselves. In the United States, someone with humble beginnings can learn to earn and become a capitalist or even a tycoon.

> I've been rich and I've been poor. Rich is better.
>
> —Sophie Tucker

For many families today, simple economic survival is a problem. If you are able to invest, you must operate as a businessperson to be successful.

Intelligent businesspeople must have the ability to learn or understand from their own and others' experiences. They need to know how to buy and sell products and services with a profit motive, in an efficient and methodical manner. Using the knowledge thus gained, one can become a successful investor.

No one I knew as a child . . . family or extended family . . . owned stocks. The first time the notion of fear of stocks expressed itself was when I was warned never to buy any stock, *ever*, because some people had jumped from rooftops when the market crashed in 1929. I was afraid, but I thought, *Didn't all rich people have stock?* "If I ever buy stock I will never go on a roof," I decided.

I never worked for a bank or brokerage house, nor did I take any stock investment courses in school. I happened upon the stock market in 1957 because of my business as a commercial photographer. I dealt with companies and corporations, and began to see what American business and industry were all about.

On assignments, I visited factories where I took pictures of the manufacturing process, from raw materials to the finished products. I was working with sales managers, advertising directors, and chief executive officers (CEOs) to create photographs for annual reports and advertising.

Many of these executives would tell me about their companies and suggest that I buy some stock. I was working with my hobby, photography, doing what I loved to do, and getting paid at the same time. I enjoyed my work and made a living, but I never made any real money.

My First Stock Purchase

My first buy in 1962, with the few hundred dollars that I'd managed to accumulate, was in a major theme park to be built outside Denver. This was a new issue, and the broker even said I would not have to pay a commission. What a deal! I did not do any research, just looked at some pretty photographs (which I had produced) and turned over my money. I did not know Denver was starting a fledgling industry in penny stocks, and I was an early customer. I bought my first stock . . . and lost it all. Boy, did I learn a lesson.

Insider Trading

A short time later, I had a friend who was a principal in a company that wanted to expand its business. I bought in with the understanding that whenever he was selling his shares, he would let me know, allowing me to get out also. About two years later, I received my first communication, which stated that the company had failed and was bankrupt. I called my friend and he told me he forgot to tell me he was getting out so that I could sell! Then and there, I decided this was my first and last time to use insider trading. I had lost again, but I resolved that I would become an informed investor in the future.

> Experience is not what happens to a man; it is what a man does with what happens to him.
>
> —Aldous Huxley

Mutual Funds

Next, I decided that when it comes to investing, you should let someone who knows do it for you. "Yes, certainly!" shouts the mutual fund industry, and its success in getting that message across has been one of the last decade's most remarkable marketing stories. I picked a no-load growth stock mutual fund with a long track record and invested... and lost my growth (although I kept my principal).

Mutual funds are the third-biggest financial industry in America, behind only the banks and insurance companies. As recently as 1980, there were fewer than 600 funds. Today, the country has more than 10,000. This explosive growth is not justified, if you judge by the ability of the average fund to beat the market. None were up in 2008. None were down less than 10 percent, and the average performance was –43 percent. I didn't know that the unmanaged Dow Jones Industrial Average advanced more than half again as much as the typical stock mutual fund.

Why did I go with a mutual fund? First, because I was frightened and baffled by the volatility of the markets, I had become convinced that a fund portfolio manager could handle my money better than I could. Second, slick advertising dazzled me with claims that were extravagant and deceptive to an innocent, novice investor.

Self-Management: A Better Way

Realizing that I was going nowhere with the fund, I decided to manage a small portfolio myself. I divided my investment money, leaving one part in a "growth mutual fund." The second part I supervised. Then I watched which of my investments did better. My portfolio won handily. It was not only good for my pocketbook; it was good for my ego. Besides, I thought, why should someone else have all the fun with my money? I withdrew all my money from the fund and have since managed it myself.

Why did I win? My holdings outperformed the heavily advertised "professional management" of the mutual fund, because I stuck with a diversified portfolio of quality stocks, and they didn't.

The best of prophets of the future is the past.

—George Gordon, Lord Byron

SUMMARY

Today, a growing number of people are entranced with the subject of investing without having any basic know-how. Within these growing numbers, most become amateur investors; many find themselves caught in a poor deal and are afraid to invest again. Only a few become successful.

Making the leap from serious investor to successful investor to a professional registered investment advisor (RIA), while seemingly a simple and evolutionary step, is quite complex. In my case, I got into it by sheer drive, the sort of urge that starts in the soles of one's feet and grows into a burning desire until it becomes an all-consuming way of life. As in professional photography, this competitiveness becomes more evident when you compare the number of amateurs to the number of pros. The success of the professional in any competitive environment is due to this burning desire, and a certain amount of glamour and romance is associated with it.

The proliferation of stockbrokers, investment counselors, and salespeople (along with their advice) induces many to invest with inadequate knowledge. This results in creating fear in many investors and leaves the opportunity for profit purely up to luck and chance.

Many make investment decisions influenced by prejudice, social injustice, pollution, or anything else that is real to them. When investing, the only thing on your mind should be making a profit. If you don't want money, don't invest. Making a political statement does not belong in the investment arena, and should not be any part of your investment decisions. If a company offends you, write letters, make a placard, and go picket the social injustices that you see happening. Emotions that make you boycott a stock do not hurt the company.

Then there are the engineers and technical people, who spend their days producing charts and graphs. They do not read their financial media or the Internet to select stocks. They look at patterns from the past and expect to see them duplicated today. Many of them do it very successfully.

Astrologers have entered the stock market arena, gazing at stars and the planets' alignment to foretell the future. No doubt a few crystal balls are in use today. You would do as well to put your "lucky" pet on the financial pages and use its first dropping to mark the pick of the day.

Regardless of what you paid for a stock, you will find, as I have, that the only realism is the ticker tape. It tells you what a stock is selling for right now, not what you wish it was or what it will be. Trying to apply reason, logic, or any other sane intelligent thought process is meaningless. Why? Because the market is irrational!

The desire to become a successful investor can be strong. With it comes the task of developing an investment strategy. What you do to support your interest usually sparks the jump from casual to successful investor. Even if you are not going to become a professional investor, you have to think and invest like one. When you learn this, you are on your way.

With this book, I intend to provoke your thoughts and challenge your beliefs; my goal is for you to understand and know how to invest. I have worked hard, sifting my experiences to offer you accurate, meaningful, and vital information that you will need. I wish to prepare you, as simply and completely as I can, to face the main investment challenges that await you.

Take fast hold of instruction; let her not go; keep her; for she is thy life.
—Proverbs 4:13

Education does not mean teaching people to know what they do not know; it means teaching them to behave as they do not behave.
—John Ruskin

CHAPTER 2

Invest with Confidence

October. This is one of the peculiarly dangerous months to speculate in stocks. The others are July, January, September, April, November, May, March, June, December, August, and February.

—Mark Twain

*I*nvesting means using capital with the expectation of growth or income. The challenge is to make this happen despite the hazards, some of which affect even supposedly safe investments such as bank accounts. Such risks include inflation, volatility, taxes, the trauma of adverse news events, the solvency of the enterprise or sponsor, and the damage sometimes done by our emotions or flawed knowledge.

Many fear the recessions and depressions that have occurred many times throughout history. Although these adverse periods bring fear and uncertainty, they are a natural part of the business cycle. There are a lot of myths surrounding market cycles; I want to help you understand them, so that we can look beyond these myths. Let us examine recession and depression, how they work, and what they really mean for investors.

First, let us look at recessions. A recession is defined as two consecutive quarters of negative economic growth, or a significant decline in national economic activity that lasts longer than just a few months.

Our economy rests upon the balance between production and consumption of goods and services. As the economy grows, so do incomes and consumer spending; this continues the cycle of growth. Since the world is not perfect, at some point the economy has to slow. This slowdown could be caused by oversupply: The manufacturers make too many goods, or

15

imports fuel the oversupply of goods. When this happens, demand for goods will drop. This causes earnings to slow, incomes to drop, and then financial markets to fall.

Since the 1850s, the United States has had 32 recessions. Most have varied in length, with the average recession lasting 10 months. The shortest recession lasted for six months, from January 1980 to July 1980. Two long recessions lasted for 16 months: the recessions of November 1973 to March 1975 and July 1981 to November 1982.

Depressions are a severe economic disaster in which real gross domestic product (GDP) falls at least 10 percent. Depressions are more severe than recessions, and the effects of a depression can last for years. A depression causes serious declines in banking, trade, and manufacturing, as well as falling prices, very tight credit, low investment, rising bankruptcies, and high unemployment. Getting through a depression is a challenge for both consumers and businesses.

Depressions happen when a number of factors occur simultaneously: Sales drop, causing overproduction followed by fear as businesses and investors panic. The combination of excess supply and fear causes business spending and investments to fall. The economy slows, unemployment rises, and wages and jobs drop. The falling wages and loss of employment cause consumers to cut back on spending. This combination starts a business cycle in which the purchasing power of consumers is battered severely, making them unable to pay down their mortgages and consumer debts; in response, banks tighten their lending standards, which leads to bankruptcies.

There are several examples of depressions. The most well-known is the Great Depression of the 1930s. From October 1929 to March 1933 GDP growth declined by 33 percent.

We can learn from these recessions and depressions; they illustrate for us both the negatives and positives, which we can use to gain an understanding of how recessions and depressions work and how to overcome them.

There are four negatives inherent in recessions and depressions:

1. Rising unemployment is a classic sign of both. As consumers curtail their spending, businesses cut payrolls to cope with falling earnings. The unemployment rate is less in a recession (5 to 11 percent) than in the Great Depression, during which unemployment increased from 3 percent to 25 percent by 1933.

2. Recessions and depressions cause a massive unwinding in the economy. During times of growth, businesses keep increasing production to meet the consumer demands, but at some point there will be too

much supply in the marketplace. When this occurs, the economy slows as demand drops. Recessions and depressions allow us to use up the excesses, but the process is painful and many suffer during this time.

3. Fear is produced by recessions and depressions. As the economy slows and unemployment rises, many consumers, fearful that things will not improve any time soon, cut back on spending, which causes the economy to slow even more.

4. Values of homes, businesses, and the stock markets recede in recessions and depressions because earnings slow along with the economy. The falling prices also slow investment for expansion and affect asset values for many businesses and people.

All is not doom and gloom, however; there are three positives too:

1. During recessions and depressions, excesses are erased. Inventories drop to normal levels, allowing businesses to experience growth once demand increases for products and services.

2. Economic growth is balanced by recessions and depressions. If the economy grows unchecked, it could lead to uncontrolled inflation. Recessions and depressions force consumers to reduce their purchases in response to falling wages. The falling purchases force prices to drop, creating a situation in which the economy can grow at normal levels, avoiding inflation.

3. Poor economic times create huge buying opportunities for every asset class: homes, businesses, and the stock markets. The downturn gives investors an excellent opportunity to make money as these asset classes return back to normal.

Hardships, economic and other, create a change in the minds of consumers. I still remember well my parents and their friends discussing their lives during the Great Depression, selling apples and standing in soup lines. As consumers stop living above their means, they are forced to live within the income they have. This change in behavior makes the savings rate rise and enables investments in the economy to increase once again. Eventually, the recovery can lead to us having and enjoying the great society we once had.

Both recessions and depressions affect the overall economy. To survive and thrive in these environments, you must understand what causes them. By carefully studying recessions and depressions, we can learn how to identify them and protect our investments from them.

> One secret of success in life is for a man to be ready for his opportunity when it comes.
>
> —Benjamin Disraeli

First, a precaution: Before investing, you should provide for emergencies. You should have adequate savings and life insurance. The stock market is not for your first dollars. Provide for today first, then invest for your tomorrow.

WHAT IS INVESTING?

Countless millions of dollars are spent on books, seminars, newsletters, and so on by people trying to find the surefire formula for making money. Unfortunately, many followers of these wealth-promising Pied Pipers end up poorer than when they started.

Countless millions of dollars are lost by investors who rely on the tens of thousands of brokers, financial planners, money managers, newsletter writers, and so on operating in the financial sector. Over the long period, only a very small minority of these investors end up winners. Experiences like those outlined in Chapter 1 keep people from further investing. It is not just the money, but the fear of loss that prevents their further actions toward future financial independence.

For individuals who face decisions about their investments, there is good news and bad news. The good news is that they can now choose from a vast array of investment alternatives. The bad news is that they can now choose from a vast array of investment alternatives.

There are many new avenues for investing. Investors can benefit from new ideas to help them formulate investment strategies and new vehicles for deploying their funds. No one has learned to forecast tomorrow's stock and bond prices, nor has anyone managed to obtain additional returns without facing additional risks.

ASSET ALLOCATION

The first decision an investor should make is how to allocate his assets among stocks, bonds, cash, and other investment categories. Only after completing that task is an investor ready for the second decision, which is how to allocate the equity portion among industries that seem attractive and distribute funds within other asset classes.

Only then can an investor start to choose individual securities. Never mind the eternal quest for a good stock tip. A solid long-term investment strategy is almost certain to be more productive for one's financial future than a constant search for the next hot investment idea.

> The trick is to shed much of the risk while shedding only a little of the return.
>
> —Wendell Dunn

RISK VERSUS REWARD: FINDING YOUR BALANCE

Successful investors learn to take as few risks as possible and to make sure that the risks they take are in keeping with the probable return. They are always asking "What if?" questions. They make sure that the amount at risk is small if the potential returns are small, and risk larger amounts for probable larger returns. If the "What if?" answers don't look too attractive, they look elsewhere.

Investors have always recognized that there is investment risk (e.g., the risk of an investment doing poorly because the circumstances of the company change). They are also growing aware of inflation risk, the risk that an investment may turn out to be safe but will fail to keep pace with long-term inflation rates. This will result in a loss of purchasing power, no less real than if the investment had fallen in value.

Managing risk is a matter of understanding the calculation of risk and reward. Investors need to learn to minimize unnecessary risk and to balance risk and return. The successful investor does not take unnecessary risks.

A long-term goal for some investors is to retire at 55 on a tidy monthly income. Achieving this goal would require a moderately aggressive 8 percent to 10 percent annual after-tax return on investments. The problem is that many investors panic about any investment riskier than a money market account. This fear of risk, despite a good income, will leave them short of their ambitious early retirement plans.

The source of many investors' timidity is a succession of poor investments that lost money. The experience leads to a drop in their portfolio and a bitter taste for financial risk. The principles set forth in this book will help debrief shellshocked investors regarding the idea of risk.

Learn Your Risk Tolerances

As any seasoned veteran investor knows, capital appreciation is linked to risk. Usually, the greater the investment risk, the greater the potential reward. Most of us have a risk tolerance, influenced by who we are, what we do, and what we have experienced.

Think about the *long-term* risk for any financial investment. Don't agonize by looking at the price quotes every day or even weekly. Make a long-term commitment and live with it.

There are two factors to consider when assessing your monetary risk tolerance:

1. *Capacity to invest:* Your job, age, marital status, children, and short- and long-term objectives.
2. *Risk personality:* Your willingness to accept uncertainty and sometimes loss of principal.

Understanding the Risk Factors

The key to living with and even profiting from investment uncertainty is to be able to accept it. There are several varieties of investment risk:

- *Market risk* is always present. It is possible that your investment won't appreciate at a satisfying rate and may even depreciate. Over the long term, dramatic price swings could produce hefty profitable returns if sold high. This kind of "know when to hold them, know when to fold them" skill takes considerable judgment and experience. Investments exposed to this risk include stocks, bonds, many mutual funds, real estate, collectibles, and gold.
- *Inflation risk* reduces the purchasing power of your assets over time. Inflation is highest when the economy is growing and lowest during a recession. Investments that are exposed to this risk include savings accounts and certificates of deposit. If you put too much of your assets in such cautious investments, you are losing money.
- *Interest-rate risk* occurs when interest rates rise and the prices of bonds and their fixed-income investments fall. Investors locked into fixed-rates miss the potential for maximum gain. When rates fall, those who maintain cash in savings accounts and money market funds

suffer. Investors with dividends or rollovers from CDs will be faced with reinvesting at rates lower than they previously enjoyed.

- *Business risk* presents the unpleasant prospect that a security issuer cannot make interest or dividend payments if business conditions are poor. Investments exposed to this risk include corporate and municipal bonds and dividend-paying stocks.

Monetary Risk Tolerance

There are several ways of increasing risk tolerance while maintaining a safe portfolio:

- *Diversification* is distributing your assets. Because financial markets gain and lose popularity at different times, you can take advantage of these market swings by diversification.
- *Liquidity* will enable you to get in and out quickly if assets are soaring or declining. Liquid investments are stocks, bonds, and mutual funds. Nonliquid investments include real estate, annuities, and limited partnerships.
- *Market volatility* is the rapid and extreme fluctuation of stock prices. This instability increases your risk exposure. Buying into the market a little at a time maintains a systematic investment plan, which helps lower this risk.

For those of us who had begun to underestimate the impact volatility can have on managing investment portfolios, the events of 2007 and 2008 have been a sobering reminder. Volatility can savage investment discipline as investors panic and wish to retreat at the worst possible time. It can sap an investor's confidence when the most securely constructed portfolios waver; in such an environment, investors question every decision they make. When the investing environment becomes unpredictable, we all have to face down our worst fears. A *long-term view* is at least a five-year time span. Never panic when your net investment value goes down; most losses can be recovered by patience. Use the market downs for adding to positions.

Assessing Risk

What is your attitude to investment loss? How have you reacted to investment loss in the past? Note that I am not mentioning risk tolerance. While attempting to determine your risk tolerance is an informative exercise, we are more concerned now about how you react to losses.

Much of behavioral finance literature suggests that investors experience more extreme negative emotions when they suffer investment losses than they do positive emotions when they enjoy investment gains. While investors will always reserve the right to panic during a bout of market losses and bail out at precisely the wrong time, it is the investor's responsibility to estimate his or her breaking point and design a portfolio that will test this breaking point on the downside.

If we can foster reasonable market expectations from the outset and convince the investor that volatility is normal and to be expected, we will have gone a long way toward setting reasonable investing ground rules.

Since risk is relative, you must have some standard by which to compare the return versus risk on any given investment. The place to start is with the truly risk-free investment.

In this country, the closest you can get to a risk-free investment is the 91-day U.S. Treasury bill. The U.S. Treasury has never defaulted and, unless the country completely collapses, will never default on paying the interest on its obligations. (If the government defaults, it won't matter which investment you own.)

You can consider the risk on a 91-day U.S. Treasury bill as essentially zero. Everything else will have some degree of risk associated with it. So any investment you undertake should give you a higher rate of return than the current U.S. Treasury bill.

Some investors think concepts like *risk management* and *investment strategy* are too much bother. In fact, anyone who invests has a strategy. The important thing is to shape that strategy to reflect your risk tolerance and your willingness to participate.

> Know thyself.
> —Inscription in the forecourt of Apollo's Temple at Delphi

THE THREE STRATEGIC FACTORS

There are three strategic factors to investing with confidence:

1. *Understand why you are investing.* It's important to establish an investment goal because that helps you select appropriate investments.
2. *Understand rewards entail risk.* Keep in mind what particular investments can and cannot do, and match your selections to your short-term and long-term goals.

3. *Understand your comfort level with different degrees of risk.* Investments should suit your nervous system and your financial profile. If volatile prices keep you awake at night, never mind what the experts say about owning growth stocks. If trading fascinates you and you can afford to be an active investor, give some economic value to the fun you are having.

The stock market is unscientific and illogical. Can you train yourself to follow an investment program and stick to it? A carefully developed strategy is essential, but it must be an ongoing process. Changing personal needs and changing markets demand periodic adjustments of your investment strategy.

Map out your strategy. Careful investors have an opportunity to reach any reasonable goal in today's financial markets. To capitalize on the opportunities offered, you not only need to understand the markets, you also have to know your goals and objectives.

STOCKS: THE LONG-TERM CORE

Shares of stock in corporations should be the core part of investment portfolios. Over the long term, the best way to participate in the growth of the U.S. economy is through a diversified portfolio of common stocks. In the past, stocks have been the hands-down winner over the long haul.

> Doing little things well is a step toward doing big things better.
>
> —Anonymous

Data shows that $100 invested in common stocks in 1925, using the Standard & Poor's (S&P) 500 index as representative and investing all dividends, produced an end value of over $81,000 as of the end of 2007—a compounded growth rate of about 10 percent per year. Similarly, $100 in U.S. Treasury bills (or banks or savings and loans) produced an end value of $1,266, for a growth rate of 3.6 percent per year.

During the same period, the cost of living increased by a factor of more than seven, for a compounded rate of 3.1 percent per year. Strip this inflation effect out of the preceding numbers to figure out relative buying power in 2000. The result for stocks would have been $6,311 instead of $81,000 and for U.S. Treasury bills (T-bills) about $337 instead of $1,266.

If past history was all there was to the game, the richest people would be librarians.

—Warren Buffett

Because of the additional bite of taxes, an investor in T-bills, banks, or savings and loans (S&Ls) could have ended with less buying power than he started with after having spent all those years in safe investments. History shows that yields in fixed-income investments generally exceed inflation by only a small amount, and that taxes can take away this excess and more. Still, stocks during the same period produced a better return than any other major investment vehicle, including real estate. Stocks have the additional feature of certain liquidity.

Stocks are generally superior performers, because they are the only investment medium tied to general growth of the gross national product (GNP). Corporations are the major participants in business activity in the United States. Since corporations issue stock, it is no surprise that stock values should grow as the economy grows.

History shows that stocks have been profitable over the long term, in spite of recessions, depressions, inflation, wars, economic and political shocks, deficits, and foreign competition.

Most People Cannot Afford to Avoid the Stock Market

An abundance of excellent books has been written about the stock market. I encourage you to read and study the books listed in the Resources section. There is no one perfect book, because investors vary greatly in their experience, goals, amount of capital, and philosophies.

Many investors don't learn from their everyday mistakes; thus, they commit those mistakes repeatedly. Making mistakes will happen; continuing to make the same mistakes is unforgivable.

14 Investment Fables to Rationalize Stock Prices

The biggest mistake a potential investor can make is to believe in investment fables. These are traditional stories of apparently historical content, whose origins are lost or changed in the telling. Fables are fictional, imaginary, and unreal as compared to actual, real, and genuine.

When stock markets go up, people find ingenious explanations for why the stock should keep going up, and they buy. When stocks are really low, they rarely find reasons to buy (and usually find reasons to sell). Their rationalizations and justifications sound sensible at the time. Acting on them, however, often has undesirable results.

Unfortunately, these investment fables prevent many people from enjoying the benefits that common stock investing, managed correctly, has to offer. I hope to dismiss 14 fables.

1. *The stock market is for gamblers.*

Gambling? The stock market is not gambling, because you have control. At a horse race, you can bet on the favorite; when the bell rings, all you can do is watch the race, win or lose. You are locked in. It's the same with dice—once they leave your hand, it is win or lose. In the stock market you can, whenever you wish, get off your pick if it is losing and get on the winner. You certainly can't do that with games of chance.

More than any other, the gambling fable closes the door to opportunity and profit for many. The truth is that the stock market is primarily for investors, not gamblers. While there is an element of risk in it, it's far from gambling. Do your homework, follow sound investment principles, and have patience. In the long term, the stock market can be the best available way to increase your wealth.

2. *Buy low and sell high to get rich.*

The fable title is true, but achieving this is practically impossible. What is the low? What is the high?

Most people who try to get rich this way usually end up generating commissions for their broker and little profit for themselves. You must be very lucky. Most investors who believe in the first fable do so because they tried and failed with the second.

3. *The stock market is for those who have money to lose.*

A variation of the first fable, this one implies you should have money to lose to be in the stock market. This is not true. Everyone can benefit from common stock investing if it is done the right way. This includes individuals who can only afford to invest a small amount each month.

The stock market is for anyone who wants a return on their money that, over the long term, keeps up with or beats the rate of inflation. The market is not an exact science. Your portfolio will have many ups and downs. It will require study, knowledge, hard work ... and patience.

4. *Individual investors cannot compete with the professionals.*

This is utter nonsense. Individual investors not only can compete with professionals, but often can outperform them. You have an advantage over professionals, who only have a given amount of time in a day to keep track of many stocks for several clients. You have the opportunity to complete a more in-depth study of your stocks. Taking note of companies close to home and tracking their management is a good start. If it's possible, try out those companies' products and services. Remember, you can gather as much relevant investment information on a company as professionals can, and perhaps more.

5. *The stock has gone down so much that it has to be a good buy now. What can you lose?*

Maybe a lot more. If the stock price has gone down dramatically, there has to be a reason. If the reason is poor fundamentals or discouraging prospects for the future, the stock may be far from a good buy at any price. Don't send good money after bad just because the price is lower. Study the fundamentals, and if things have changed for the worse, admit the mistake. Then consider what your money could be doing in another investment.

Keep in mind that a stock that drops in price is not automatically a loser. It could drop for reasons that have little to do with the company's underlying value. When a stock moves contrary to the market or its industry, try to find out why.

6. *I'll wait until I break even before I get out.*

This could be a big mistake. You may never get out. Don't hesitate to remove losers from your portfolio. Everyone has them, and it doesn't mean that you are doing a poor job of investing. If you are right 80 percent of the time, you will be a successful investor. Admit your errors and go on. Consider: Will your money grow faster in a stock with excellent prospects, or in the dog you made a mistake buying? You will lose opportunity and time trying to break even.

7. *It takes a lot of money to invest in stocks.*

It doesn't take a lot of money; it takes a lot of time. Whatever sum of money you choose to invest in the stock market regularly, through good times and bad, can lead to unbelievable results over long periods of time. The biggest mistake for many people is not realizing the magic of compounding and the reinvestment of dividends.

Purchase of an *odd lot* (less than 100 shares) costs a little more. For most issues, you will pay an additional fee to odd-lot brokers for trading a small amount of stock. Beyond that, brokers generally do not charge higher commissions for such trades. A small odd lot of stock may run up against the minimum commission at many brokerage houses. If you are buying shares that you plan to hold for five years, the total effect of a slightly higher price will be small.

Some brokerage houses offer a monthly investment plan in which you can start investing. Once you purchase the initial shares, you can add to them at regular intervals. Your money plus dividends will buy more shares. Many heartwarming investment stories have come from people who built their wealth this way.

8. *Don't buy during a bear market.*

This big mistake is made by amateurs and professionals alike. A bear market can be the best time to buy good quality stocks at bargain prices. If, after studying a stock, you find it has good fundamentals, a bear market will ensure that it represents a good purchase value as well. Many investors rely on a contrarian strategy; during out-of-favor time periods, they buy the undervalued shares that appear low in price compared to the worth of the company's assets. Then they wait for other investors to recognize the stocks' true worth and bid up their stock prices. That is the basis of sound value investing.

9. *You can't go broke taking a profit.*

No, but you sure can miss the top dollars. The greatest investment success stories come from investors who have bought and held, keeping stock in companies that have continued to grow year after year, market cycle after market cycle, sometimes for decades. If you only hold your stocks for the short term and then sell, you might limit your profits. While short-term profits range from 5 to 25 percent, holding for the long term could earn two, three, or four times the price paid for the stock.

In addition, those who sell have to pay taxes on the profits . . . and they have to find another place to invest their money. If they don't reinvest successfully, they may lose their original profit.

10. *What my stocks are doing daily is important.*

This fable is the reason that the current Dow Jones Industrial Average (DJIA) has such prominence in daily newspapers and on the nightly news report. Yes, it is important to keep up-to-date on the stocks in your portfolio. But when the price dips next Tuesday, you needn't panic. When you are holding for the long term, the daily rises and falls of the stock market should be of no more than passing interest to you.

More important are the fundamentals underlying the stocks in your portfolio. Are they still strong? What are the company's plans? Is there anything on the positive or negative side that may change your outlook? Read the annual report and other various sources to keep current on what the company is doing. There is little in the daily news that is significant to the wealth you can accumulate over the long term.

11. *If interest rates go down, stocks have to go up.*

When the federal discount rate is cut, stocks have to go up because savers are pulling their money out of low-interest savings accounts and looking for something better. I hear people say, "I'm not happy with the interest rate I'm getting at the bank, so I'm going to buy stocks." This change will not help if the fundamentals of the stocks in your portfolio are not strong.

12. *Stocks are scarce.*

All a company needs to create more stock is a printing press.

13. *Soaring profits are just around the corner.*

What if the future earnings don't happen? In a really bullish market, that is no problem. Last year, an analyst said a stock was low-priced at $15, a mere 40 times the 88 cents a share it was going to earn. The company's earnings turned out to be minus $2.61. Don't give it a thought, the analyst said: "The loss was from a write-off, and write-offs don't matter. The stock is now at $17 and is cheap against this year's earnings." There is always a gap between forecasts and reality. Don't bet on what analysts think might happen in the future.

14. *The stock market is rational.*

If this fable were true, then investors could buy blindly, knowing that any company's price on Wall Street accurately reflected its prospects and risks.

What can a rational investor do? Buy stocks when interest rates are high and all the experts say, "Stocks just can't compete with bonds." But did you have the guts to buy in those days? If you didn't, you shouldn't be buying stocks today.

Now, dispel those fables. The old-fashioned reality is that the stock market is based on long-term fundamentals. Undoubtedly, stocks do move too fast, both up and down, because of the instant widespread distribution of facts, rumors, and false information. Yet, when stocks are cheap ... not just looking cheap, but truly are cheap, based on a comparison with the company's earnings, cash flow, equity values, and dividends ... they should be bought.

Facts do not cease to exist because they are ignored.

—Aldous Huxley

DEFINING *INVESTING* AND *FEAR*

Investment is the use of capital to create more money, either through income-producing vehicles or through more risk-oriented ventures designed to result in capital gains.

No matter what your strategy, stock selection demands three things: fundamental knowledge, time to analyze companies, and the capital to support a large-enough portfolio. These criteria will enable you to diversify among several stocks for safety. If you lack any of these, you may find investing in a growth and income stock mutual fund more suitable.

To *fear* is to be afraid, uneasy, anxious, or doubtful, to panic and to dread. A frantic, unreasoning fear often spreads quickly and leads to irrational, aimless action.

Often fears and anxieties are used to describe the same thing. Fear causes mental tension due to a specific, external reason, such as when your car skids out of control on ice. The fear of losing money in the stock market is mildly depressing, absolutely maddening, or no big deal, depending upon one's psychological makeup.

Anxiety is as much a part of life as eating and sleeping. Under the right circumstances, it is beneficial. It heightens alertness and readies the body for action. A person faced with an unfamiliar challenge often is driven by anxiety to prepare for the upcoming event. For example, many people practice speeches and study for tests because of mild anxiety. Both anxiety and fear can be protection from danger.

In the words of President Franklin D. Roosevelt in his first inaugural address on March 4, 1933, "The only thing we have to fear is fear itself."

To help relieve your fear, I offer a bit of history: What you see today in the economy of our country and in the stock market has happened before and will occur again. You can learn by understanding some stock market economic conditions and their meanings.

- A *stock cycle* is a period of expansion (recovery) and contraction (recession) in economic activity that affects inflation, growth, employment, and prices of stocks.
- A *bull market* is a period of prolonged rise in the prices of stocks, bonds, or commodities. Bull markets usually last a few months and are characterized by high trading volume.
- A *bear market*, in contrast, is a prolonged period of falling prices. A bear market in stocks is usually brought on by the anticipation of declining economic activity.

In the short 240-year U.S. history of securities trading, a series of important stock market bottoms appear in a 60-year stock cycle pattern—1800, 1860, 1920, 1980, and 2008. What makes the cycle pertinent is that each bull market that followed these bottoms was followed in turn, by a significant bear market collapse about a decade later.

The most dramatic market setback was the 1929 to 1932 crash, which saw the DJIA drop nearly 90 percent. Prior to that, there was a crash in 1869; after reaching a record high, stock prices crashed following the failure of Jay Gould and Jim Fisk to corner the gold market.

Fisk and Gould's experiences serve as an example of how fortunes and legends were made in battles over gold, railroads, and other highly capitalized investments. In 1867 James Fisk, Jr. and Jay Gould successfully maintained control of the Erie Railroad in the face of a determined challenge from Cornelius Vanderbilt, who had tried to buy the line to eliminate its competition with his New York Central Railroad. Gould and his cohorts secretly created and released to the market watered stock (stock representing ownership of overvalued assets, the total worth of which was less than the invested capital) for Vanderbilt to purchase. As a result of their scheme, they collected millions of dollars.

Because of this and similar schemes, stricter market standards were adopted. All shares of listed companies were to be registered at some satisfactory agency. The registrar was responsible for ensuring that all transactions were recorded by the transfer agent. The number of shares issued to the purchaser equaled the number of canceled certificates from the seller. The registrar's task was to ensure that the total numbers of shares issued were within the authorization granted to the corporation.

Such regulation could do little to prevent fraud or to control major market operators such as Gould and Fisk. When they collaborated in an attempt to corner (take control of) the gold market and thus make a fortune from the rise in price as the metal became scarce, the U.S. government sold some of its gold supplies and the price of gold plummeted, ruining many speculators. This triggered the sharp price break of securities on September 24, 1869, a day that became known as Black Friday.

Over the ensuing three years, the economy managed to avoid recession and resumed its growth. It was a weak prosperity, built on mountains of debt accumulated during the Civil War and heavy borrowing from overseas to finance a real estate and railroad boom. The United States' international debt exploded. Yet stocks managed to recoup nearly all their post-1869 losses. What happened next was even more unnerving. Following a bank panic in 1873, the U.S. economy sank into a four-year depression. Stock prices plummeted, losing half their value.

The eventual recovery took the market to a new high. However, on October 29, 1929, Black Tuesday struck, resulting in a depression that lasted until the start of World War II. As it had before, recovery from the Great Depression took the market to another new high.

MARKET MADNESS: BLACK MONDAY, OCTOBER 19, 1987

The market's volatility around Black Monday created general anxiety. The day saw an accelerated stock market decline that turned the investment community upside down. Buying back shares was one recourse companies took in the sliding stock market. The action raised the price of the stock by spreading the value over fewer outstanding shares. This represented a vote of confidence from the company that the stock's value would remain high. It also protected companies from takeover moves, which become a threat when stock prices decline.

Companies that are not cash-rich typically rely on their stock for collateral, against which they borrow money to finance expansion or major product development projects.

Spending volume changes somewhat in a recession. Consumers will start to question whether they need a new car or another TV or they can make do with what they have right now.

If you had only bought that stock on Monday, October 19, this is how you would have profited in just two days:

Company	Oct. 19	Oct. 21	Net Gain
AT&T	23.62	29.50	5.87
IBM	103.25	122.75	19.50
Bell South	33.75	39.50	5.75

Years later, after the 1987 crash, circuit breakers were installed to prevent large-scale, rapid one-day market swings. Today, we also have the Federal Reserve System, poised to head off any starting panic. Also, there is now a large service sector that is less exposed to swings in the economic cycle. Finally, government spending and social programs appear larger and are a shock absorber to jolts in the general economy.

Some financial numbers:

October 19, 1987	−508 Dow Jones	−22.61% change
October 21, 1987	+186 Dow Jones	+10.15% change

Alas, human nature never changes. Fear follows greed as surely as night follows day. This is what creates cycles. Remember the words of Santayana: "Those who cannot remember the past are condemned to repeat it."

MARKET ANXIETY IS CAUSED BY MANY FACTORS

When the DJIA is near its all-time high, luring speculators into the market, the "buy now before it goes up further!" mentality is prevalent. When this occurs, other factors in the economy are affected as well.

When inflation is very high, it destroys the integrity of the dollar and dollar-sensitive investments. Inflation causes people to lose confidence in the currency and put their assets in real estate or gold. Inflation is a hidden tax we all pay.

When interest rates are very high, the cost of using money will be high. Business expansion will be curtailed, and consumer spending will go down.

When inflation is low, growth in the U.S. economy will be low, affecting consumer spending and confidence. This will result in fewer job opportunities as companies cut back, lowering production and services.

As of December 17, 2008, with the fear of recession (and possibly depression) growing, the effect is falling prices, reduced purchasing, rising unemployment, increased inventories, deflation, and closing of factories. When business and personal debt are costly, more people will default on their loans. Corporate and personal taxes will be very high, causing the real return on investment and disposable income to go down.

When the size of government and its spending is very high, it causes taxes to rise, making inflation spiral upward, and prices rise, affecting our export business.

When business and savings are low, consumer confidence falls. The money available for investment is scarce, which makes interest rates rise.

When international uncertainties are growing (e.g., threats of war, OPEC oil price increases, threats to our industries by foreign competition, pollution and waste disposal), there will be a corresponding growth in unemployment, minority unrest, social insecurity, and crime.

YEAR 2008: THE COLLAPSE OF THE STOCK MARKET

Now is not the time to sell. Bear markets separate the speculators from the real investors. An average speculator is many times more interested in the stock price than in the underlying business. Bear markets shake the speculators out of stocks and, in contrast, encourage real investors to gather up the available bargains to hold them for years, creating real wealth. Real investors, who do not try to time the market, get most of the rewards.

This is the second terrible year for stocks in this century. We are all hurting, speculators and real investors alike. Look at the great American companies and how they have declined. These are companies with histories of great success. In just months, their values have been drastically lowered:

- Citigroup, the world's largest bank, is down 90 percent.
- Gannett, the publisher of *USA Today*, is down 80 percent.
- Bank of America, a leading bank, is down 72 percent.
- Microsoft, the software giant, is down 47 percent.
- Disney, home of Mickey Mouse, is down 37 percent.

Presently, the world's stock markets are a graveyard of broken dreams and hopes. During times of market anxiety, there will be:

- A drop in stock prices
- Low incentive to invest in common stock
- Low reward-to-risk ratios

During times of market euphoria, there will be:

- A rise in stock prices
- High incentive to invest in common stock
- High reward-to-risk ratios

There are two ways to learn anything: the hard way, through harsh experience, or the comfortable way, by studying. In reading about the experiences of others, we can learn from their mistakes and profit from their accomplishments. Your success in the stock market depends on acquiring adequate knowledge and then using it.

One who knows, and knows that they know, is a master.
One who knows, and does not know that they know, needs a teacher.
One who does not know, and knows that they do not know, needs love.
One who does not know, and does not know that they do not know, is lost.
—Ancient proverb

INVESTING AND GAMBLING

I am not very covetous; I do not crave a lot.
The things I want are limited; To what I haven't got!

—Richard Armour

As a young man I served in the United States Air Force. After duty hours, we would try to recycle our monthly pay. The barracks hosted a continuous poker game.

The boys were eager for action and loved the occasional big win. Thus, they would violate the elementary rules of odds, drawing to inside straights and other hopeless propositions. Meanwhile, hour after hour, the sergeants methodically raked in the winnings. Being of an analytical bent, I eventually joined in the game, having memorized a table of odds that I got from a book. So it was that I learned about poker and investing. You make money on the difference between playing the true odds and the opponent's disregard of the odds. In other words, investment opportunity is the difference between reality and perception.

On a more elegant level, bridge players call a hand with no face cards a *Yarborough* after Lord Yarborough. He gave odds of 1,000-to-1 that one would not get dealt such a hand. Since the true odds are about 1,600-to-1, he did well with his wager. His lordship exploited this truth.

Today, the willingness of otherwise sane persons to get involved in commodity programs, or in low-priced, high-risk stocks of unknown prospects, enables the Yarborough philosophy to continue.

In investing, we want the odds to be as favorable as possible. Frequently, an investor is averse to anything with a taint—a couple of down quarters, a lawsuit, or a skipped dividend—though the depressed market price more than reflects the problem (with improved odds). Thus, one successful investment technique capitalizes on the public's low tolerance for discomfort. Some investors make money, year in and year out, buying in companies that are under a temporary cloud, while others are selling out.

The more savvy investors invest for both capital gains and cash flow.

The reciprocal psychology shows up when investors pay too much to avoid discomfort. They buy the winners that have already appreciated and appear to be very safe. This is comfort investing—taking a lower-than-necessary return simply to avoid fuss and worry. Bond investor programs seem to fall into this category.

No stock market investment is without chance and risk. Stocks are bought with the thought of income or profit. We know that stocks can vary in price daily; some will go up handsomely and some will lose severely, while others have little fluctuation.

Stock prices are influenced by rumors, the general economic cycle, rumors, interest rates, rumors, Federal Reserve policy, and perhaps most importantly, *rumors*.

Stock markets can become overbought and sell off; oversold and go up; overvalued so they decline; undervalued so they rise. These occurrences happen without any change in the basic true worth of the company in which you have an equity position.

INVESTMENT POLICY STATEMENT

A written *Investment Policy Statement* is a prerequisite to successfully managing a portfolio. It defines objectives; establishes a disciplined and coherent approach; and provides rules, guidelines, and restrictions to be followed. It serves as the conceptual guide for the management of one's portfolio. It is a reference against which the portfolio activities ultimately are measured. It should specify targets for expected return and for risk. It should specify the asset categories to be included and any limitations on the number of securities to be employed. It should address possible contingencies and provide guidelines to reduce the likelihood of unreasoned, emotional responses to future events. It should provide a rational discipline for the investing process. It should provide a framework within which the portfolio will be managed, with actual security selection and timing left to the investor as a separate activity.

DISCIPLINE CAN BE REALLY GOOD FOR YOU

Self-control, self-mastery, and willpower are the indispensable elements of discipline.

When it comes to investing, self-discipline is absolutely essential! It's going to take some independence of mind and the exercise of your willpower. Can you handle it? Sure you can. Reading this book will prove it to you.

I offer to you a simple approach and method that has served me well for 21 years of professional investing. I present all the techniques, strategies, and attitudes in this book. There have been boom times, as well as the great crash of 2008, and my procedures worked through both. Only those who are willing to exercise the necessary discipline and patience required by my investing philosophy will be able to successfully accomplish this.

> Sir, I have found you an argument; but I am not obliged to find you an understanding.
>
> —Dr. Samuel Johnson

I encourage you to evaluate my methods and, after you understand them, form your own conclusions. Until you have a thorough understanding, do not attempt to use them in the marketplace. I believe that wishing, hoping, or praying is not an optimal financial strategy.

> We can easily represent things as we wish them to be.
>
> —Aesop

CHAPTER 3

An Overview of How to Invest

If you bet on a horse, that's gambling. If you bet you can make three spades, that's entertainment. If you bet cotton will go up three points, that's business. See the difference?

—Blackie Sherrod

L et's begin with some cautionary words:

- The stock market is not for your first or last dollars.
- You should provide for emergencies and have adequate insurance and savings for everyday needs.
- Provide first for today. Investing is for tomorrow.
- Security investing is tomorrow's security.

The first step in establishing an investment plan is to have an emergency fund adequate enough to cover a minimum of three to six months of living expenses. You should accumulate this money in a savings or money market account, or in a checking account that pays interest. These forms of savings vehicles are liquid, which means you can withdraw your money from them whenever you need it without paying a penalty for the withdrawal. Once you have this base covered, you can move on to more sophisticated investments.

One of the biggest causes of losses in stocks is having to sell because you need the invested sums. Money invested in the stock market may not be ready for you to take out when you must have it. Stock market investments are long-term, usually a five-year time commitment.

When it comes to making investment decisions, the first line of defense is a skeptical investor. As the old adage goes, "If it sounds too good to be true, it probably is."

In preparing your investment plan, you need to reflect on your income and growth objectives, your tolerance for risk, and your personal investment preference. Some investments do more for your money than others. And obviously, some investments do less for your money than others—sometimes dramatically less.

Most low-risk investments lock you in or limit you to a fixed rate of return. Higher-risk investments offer possible higher returns. There are money market funds, annuities, mutual funds, government securities, government agencies, certificates of deposit, Treasury bills (T-bills), growth stocks, high-yield stocks, blue chip stocks, corporate bonds, convertible bonds, discount bonds, high-yield bonds, options, corporate income trusts, real estate limited partnerships, and so on. Every day, it seems, someone is calling me with yet another investment opportunity.

Reading this book and putting in practice the strategies described will open new vistas of investment opportunities for your money. In fact, there are more opportunities than you have money. The aim of this book is to explain why the best of these choices is owning corporate stock in American companies. You will find joy and confidence in investing and make your money grow faster. Remember, over time, stocks always outperform other investments . . . so be patient!

INFLATION

Good growth-oriented stocks can outpace inflation by three to five percentage points per year and should be your most important resource. That three- to five-point real return can make an enormous difference in your future financial plans. Because inflation always remains a threat, you should keep your money in good stocks with prospects for earnings growth of 5 percent or more per year.

> If you've always wanted to live in a $1 million house, you may get your wish without even moving.
>
> —Harvey Friedentag

One insurance company has, for years, featured an advertisement that in 1940 read, "How I retired on $150 a month." By 1950, this had changed to read, "How I retired on $250 a month." By 1960 it read, "How I retired on $350 a month." By 1970 it read, "How I retired on $550 a month." By 1980 it read, "How I retired on $950 a month." By 1990, the advertisement was no longer being run. I suppose the insurance company went out of business, or the ad doesn't work these days.

As bad as taxes are, inflation is still your most treacherous enemy. At 5.4 percent nominal inflation, today's $20,000 car will cost you $32,382 in just 10 years and more than $55,000 in 20 years. Today's $100,000 condo will jump in price to more than $276,000 in the next two decades (taxes on that condo will climb even faster). Long-term care now costs $30,000 per year, per person. In 10 years it will have jumped to $97,145 per year. How long will your nest egg hold up to that rise?

I hope you can see now that investing in debt instruments is a loser. The only way to capital growth is through equity investments in good companies, by buying their stocks and owning a piece of their business.

> The value of all things depends on the use we make of them.
>
> —Anonymous

The deadly sins of stock investing are:

- *Impatience* . . . wanting to make money quickly
- *Greed* . . . always wanting more
- *Emotionalism* . . . worrying about day-to-day market swings
- *Fear* . . . growing afraid due to tales of others who "lost it all"
- *Underdiversification* . . . increasing your risk
- *Buying low quality* . . . purchasing stocks of unknown, unproven companies

INVESTING IN STOCKS

In the stock market, you make your money on how closely you trade; look for bargains. You don't make your money selling; you make your money on how well you buy.

Investing in stocks is misleading. We are investing in a business by purchasing a share of that company. Each shareholder is a part owner in the company. The extent of ownership depends upon the number of shares owned and the number of shares outstanding. Remember, a share of stock is not a lottery ticket. It is a part ownership of a business.

The stock certificate is a dispassionate piece of paper representing ownership in a business. The certificates are usually printed on high-quality paper, with a watermark to discourage forgery. Some stock certificates, such as those from Playboy and Disney, are works of art, and there are collectors who buy a single share solely for framing.

The stock exchanges are striving to become a paper-free financial market. They are developing a trading system that will completely computerize the transfer and settlement of stocks. Eliminating paperwork will lower administrative costs, reduce the risk of clerical error, and speed up stock transfers. Japan and several other countries have dispensed with certificates altogether. This is an idea whose time has come, even if it means the end of the stock art collectors.

Large traders, banks, life insurance companies, mutual funds, and institutional investors are buying stocks for their portfolios. It is widely believed that the little guy doesn't have a chance. On the contrary, many smaller investors have found it possible to prosper handsomely in this challenging stock market. No matter whether the stock prices are going up, down, or sideways, there are opportunities for profits.

Let me say that again. No matter whether the stock prices are going *up, down,* or *sideways,* there are opportunities for profits. An informed investor with common sense and great portfolio flexibility still has the upper hand.

Also note the words "great portfolio flexibility." The big portfolio managers have to buy and sell large blocks of stocks to get in and out of their large holdings, which affects the stock prices because they must pay more to acquire . . . and will receive less when they sell. Rapidly dumping a huge block of a corporate stock is the sort of utter stupidity that one should not expect from big block holders, but it happens. It sometimes produces a spectacular plummet in the stock's price that day, and a headline the next day that usually produces a continuing downward action. Don't be unduly alarmed at spectacular price movements occasionally produced by big blockheads.

Every business day, millions of shares of stock are bought and sold in thousands of companies. What a difficult task, looking at thousands of companies. In later chapters, I will show you how to make this task manageable.

The average investor dealing in smaller amounts can buy or sell stocks at any time without affecting the market price. In today's stock market, the small investor represents what liquidity and real pulse remains, and he shouldn't panic at the super price changes momentarily produced by sophisticated money managers. There is just no way, other than a stunning discovery of fraud or a bombshell bankruptcy that can make a share of stock worth $40 at the beginning of the day and only $30 at the close. Most certainly, a stock will seldom stay worth exactly what you paid for it. More often than not, it is worth more, if it was soundly purchased in the first place. There is no realized loss or profit until the stock is sold.

Clearly profits are important to everyone involved with stock. Without profits, new products and services would not be sold. Factories would not be built. More workers would be looking for jobs. The tax collector would not receive his revenues. Speaking of which, taxes are of utmost importance. Your real return and profit are what you have left after paying them.

Diversification

For your investment plan to have relative safety, it is essential to diversify. Don't put all your eggs in one basket. Some stocks are like chicken eggs and others are like tennis balls. When the market falls, most stocks fall. We all know that when an egg falls it crashes, breaks, and leaves you with a mess. When the tennis ball falls, it will bounce right back, not as high as before, but it will bounce. It's our goal to avoid the eggs and find the tennis balls.

Many a market sector drifts in and out of fashion: autos, drugs, technology, banking, and so on. There are about 30 core industries, and they take turns being in favor. Put your tennis balls in several baskets. We do know that a mixture of stock market industries will provide good returns, with less uncertainty than a single investment.

Diversification means different things to different people. One of the most popular approaches of late is called "asset allocation."

Financial planners look at asset diversification in broad terms that include cash, fixed income, stocks, real estate, gold, and so on.

Insurance salespeople push insurance and annuities as good investments.

Real estate salespeople sell income property. The largest asset of most people is the equity in their home. This value cannot be included in asset allocation.

List your investments in two categories:

1. Investments you directly control.
2. Retirement assets (IRAs, Keoghs, 401(k)s, etc.).

Many people forget that their retirement assets are an integral part of their investment program.

Investment plans should be refined according to your objectives. For instance, if your investment objective is *income*, then you might own utility stocks. If it is *total return*, you would be less interested in high-dividend return from your stocks. Buying growth stocks would imply that dividends would not be of importance.

Once you have determined what your asset allocation is and whether you are happy with the current mix, you need to monitor it regularly. After stocks are selected, they must be watched over and cared for.

This popular form of diversifying risk (asset allocation) seems to make sense for most people. If you knew exactly which asset was going to hit its high each year and which its low, then you would shift accordingly—particularly in your retirement plan, where there is no tax implication. Since the ultimate goal for many is to increase their wealth each year, this is a good approach.

Diversification to people selling on Wall Street means dividing your investments among stocks, bonds, and cash. A leading brokerage firm makes it more simple than that. It only divides between stocks and bonds.

Most investors like to own both stocks and bonds. The stocks provide the action and the promise of greater wealth in the future. The bonds give them a feeling of stability and an appealing flow of income. But does it really make sense to hold bonds in an investment portfolio?

We know that bonds show inferior returns to stocks, and we also see that they aren't a very good hedge against declines in the stock market. So who needs bonds if stocks are usually moving up? No one wants an asset that provides lower returns than an alternative.

The thought that bonds are less risky is little justification for including them in a portfolio. There are better ways to hedge the risk in owning equities than by holding bonds; hedge your risks in the market by using options. You can use a contrarian move, selling stocks as they go up, and buying stocks as they go back down.

There is also a little-noticed influence at work: Bonds are contracts that pay the same income, year in and year out, until they mature. Stocks are claims on uncertain cash flows that investors buy because they expect higher dividend income in the future. Optimism or pessimism about dividend growth play an essential role in the interaction of bond and stock returns. When investors are more pessimistic about future dividends, bonds are in favor. When investors are optimistic about dividend growth, stocks tend to outperform bonds, because investors build higher expectations into stock prices, but bonds don't benefit from the changed expectations.

The long-term record tells us that bonds have a lower total return (income plus capital growth) than stocks. Since 1925, stocks yielded a compound annual return of more than 10 percent, bonds a bit under 5 percent—a two-to-one advantage in stocks. I see no reason to hold bonds either as a hedge or for capital gains.

All Assets Invested in Stocks

At the risk of inviting controversy, my approach to asset allocation requires that all assets should be invested in stocks. It is important to stay fully invested and to use the three investment objectives: growth, total return, and income.

The market was low on March 10, 2008, and though it has moved up substantially to record highs, compared to most categories of investments, some good-grade common stocks are very much on the bargain counter.

If you had stayed fully invested, you would have done about two to three times as well in stocks as in money market funds or long-term bonds. You would have done better than in collectibles, and often better than trading in your worldly possessions for bags of gold, as some leading gurus of the gloom-and-doom set recommended at the time.

A bear market is a buying opportunity. When the market goes down, most stocks go down, the good and the bad together. However, when the market goes up, most stocks go up, the good and the bad together. This is a selling opportunity, a bull market.

Nobody, as far as I know, has ever guessed consistently which way the market was going, when, or by how much. If they could, they would be the wealthiest investors alive, just from the sale of investment advisory newsletters alone. There are about 2,000 newsletters for sale right now, some of which have published valuable advice. But their research is not designed to meet your specific investment plan. Also, if anyone truly knew consistently which way the market was going and when, surely that investor would keep such information top secret! I know these advisers are making their money selling the newsletters, not by investing in the market.

Because we don't know when the market will change direction, I always stay fully invested in shares of good companies with earnings and revenues that are growing at an accelerating rate. You should be able to verify the companies' track records over many years. This philosophy has helped true professional investors establish an outstanding performance over the years. I believe a down market presents an excellent opportunity for investors to buy more shares of stock for their money, therefore giving them a better position when the market comes back. I also believe that an up market gives investors an excellent opportunity to sell shares of overvalued stocks for more money, giving them a better position when the market goes back down. Be in the right position for the market swings.

The Stocks of the Stock Market

There are four levels of stocks in the market:

1. *Blue chip stocks*, the elite of American industry; the companies with the longest track records, dividend payments, and financial strength.
2. *Secondary stocks*, the solid well-established companies that have a little less investor confidence and are listed on exchanges.
3. *Growth stocks*, the younger companies, in newer industries, with growth potential and a higher degree of risk.

4. *Penny stocks*, the long shots, companies with almost no true value other than their speculative future success.

The stock market is one of the best investments available anywhere. In the years since 1926, the stock market has been up approximately twice as many years as it has been down. When it has been up, its total returns have roughly doubled the returns for the minus years. In other words, success is more a function of time *in* the market than of timing the market.

Over the years, the Standard & Poor's (S&P) 500 index, an unmanaged index, has outperformed corporate bonds, U.S. bonds, and T-bills. Over time, the risk of losing purchasing power due to inflation is much lower in stock equities than it is in money markets, CDs, or bonds. And the potential for gains in the stock market is much greater.

Stock Market on Sale

In Denver, there is a store that has a ski sale every year. The store's customers line up the night before waiting for a bargain. My wife runs to the supermarket or other stores when they have a sale and fights the crowds. Many people panic and want to get out of the market when it's low, but rush in when it's high, thus missing the "sale."

Why, on October 19, 1987, was I one of the few who were happy, delighted, and thrilled to be buying when the stock market was on sale? And buying I was! "Companies that are doing well are selling for one-third to one-half off what they were selling for yesterday. I can't buy their products for such markdowns, but today I can buy into the company at these markdown prices," I said on a television broadcast that very day.

There were many who were happy, delighted, and thrilled to be buying when the stock market was on sale. In one day, 604 million shares were traded. For a share to be sold, a share had to be bought, or there would or could not be a trade. The press proclaimed, "Worst day ever on the stock market." I, looking at the same news, would have said, "Best day ever; the stock market is on sale!" Of course I didn't know when it was coming back or how severe it would be, but I was ready for it—and most importantly, I took advantage of the buying opportunity.

Keep in mind that this approach does not guarantee a profit. If you have to sell at the bottom of the market, no investment strategy is going to give you a gain. Remember, too, that someone's loss can be your gain. Ask yourself, "Would I rather buy high or low?" Or "Would I rather sell low or high?" You've got to have the mental and financial resources to ride out the lows. Be persistent and consistent, and your strategy will work.

What Is a Stock Worth?

On Wall Street, a stock sells for what someone is willing to pay. In reality, a stock is worth its true value. Some stocks sell for more than they are worth, and some stocks sell for less than they are worth.

A stock does not have a fixed, objective value. When many people buy a stock, they act like bettors at the race track. They bet that other people are going to buy that stock also and that the price will go up as a result, giving them a winner. In the stock market, as at the race track, the betting itself influences the outcome. If many bettors bet on ABC stock, making it a favorite, the price of ABC stock will rise. The stock will become a higher-priced stock simply because many people thought it would.

An investor watches the companies very carefully, since the value of shares should be directly related to how well the company is doing and not only to the price of the stock.

What do we mean by value? Investors do not agree, although everybody wants value. Many money managers, for instance, declare their style of business to be "finding undervalued stocks." Will we ever hear one say he is trying to buy overvalued stocks? Simple as it seems, the word *value* describes a philosophy of investing. Someone who looks for stocks that are priced low in relation to their earnings or their assets is probably a value seeker. Someone who looks to high-priced favorite stocks, aiming for quick, extraordinary growth, fads, or glamour, is not.

A value investor is patient and builds expectations on long-term trends rather than on recent events and rumors. He or she does not buy the argument that all stock prices are always rational. Indeed, irrationality is everywhere:

- Companies trading at one price one day and half that price another, without any change in the fundamentals.
- Stocks trading at unbelievable multiples of their price-earnings (P/E) ratio and dividend yield.

Two stock market terms used to appraise stocks are *price-earnings (P/E) ratio* and *dividend yield*. They are easily understood.

Price-Earnings Ratio

The P/E ratio simply describes the relationship between the stock price and the earnings per share. It is easily calculated by dividing the price of the stock by the earnings per share figure. For example, if the price of the share is $10 and the annual earnings per share are $1.00, the P/E ratio is 10 ($10 divided by $1.00 per share). If earnings improve, the annual earnings per share are $2.00, and the price of the stock is still at $10, the P/E ratio will be 5 ($10 divided by $2.00 per share).

Individual P/E ratios and average P/E ratios can be found in the financial pages daily. This number gives investors an idea of how much they are paying for a company's earnings. The higher the P/E, the more investors are paying, the more earnings growth they are expecting, and the more it is like picking the favorites at the track.

The P/E ratio is a critical piece of information because it shows the value of a stock in terms of company earnings, rather than the selling price. Remember, there is no perfect P/E ratio. Some stocks that have lower earnings will have higher P/Es; these are usually the growth stocks. An income stock that pays higher dividends will tend to have a lower P/E.

Dividend Yield

The dividend yield, often called yield, represents the annual percent return that the dividend provides. The yield of a stock is calculated by dividing the annual cash dividend per share by the price of the stock. For example, if a company pays its stockholders an annual cash dividend of $0.50 per share and the stock price is $10, the return, or dividend yield, is 5.0 percent ($0.50 per share divided by $10).

Low P/E Investing

There is a strategy that has worked well over time, and has provided investors with superior returns, though it rarely gives spectacular ones. This is called *low P/E investing*, buying stocks with price-earnings multiples below the stock market's average. For instance, the S&P 500 is trading at 15 times last year's earnings. If your stock sells for 10 times earnings or less, you have a low P/E stock.

Research studies from the 1930s up to now have validated the strategy of buying low P/E stocks. These low-priced stocks yield both higher dividend income and better capital gains. Who said you can't have them both? That dividend return helps prop up the prices of stocks in bear markets. It makes them more attractive because of the yield.

Low P/E value investing is generally the best strategy for all seasons, and the long-term results are impressive. A commentator on television recently asked, "Aren't such companies out of favor with good reason? You have to wait forever for a turnaround." A good question, and one that has been asked of me many times. My reply is that you rarely have to wait "forever." True, one should have the patience to wait, but markets make the wins come a lot faster than you might think, thanks to rapid changes in investor knowledge.

If the performance record is no secret, why doesn't everybody follow this method? Because most money managers and analysts believe earnings fit stock prices over time. Therefore, they favor stocks that look as if they will enjoy rapidly growing earnings for years to come and think the price of the stock will skyrocket to the stratosphere.

That kind of future-gazing is dangerous, because *past* performance has nothing to do with future performance. Past earnings growth is almost useless in predicting future earnings growth. The future is unpredictable, yet most analysts estimate based on the past, fearlessly forecasting what the future will be. Since they lean on such an undependable method, we should expect a high rate of error, especially when the forecasts are for extraordinary gains. Guess what? A high rate of error is what you will find. And remember whose money they are using: yours!

If you follow the market closely, you will find plenty of stocks that looked good but faltered badly. The more successful a company becomes (products or services), the more competition, government controls, and market saturation will restrain its returns. Costs rise and cannot be passed on. Winning products or services are suddenly displaced by new technology, marketing programs, political or economic shocks, an energy crisis, or rapid inflation.

When investors are disappointed by high P/E stocks, they tend to overreact, dump their holdings, and drop the price, because of fear. Low P/E stocks are already cheap, so bad news puts little pressure on them.

One delight of low P/E stocks is that they are so far down that just coming up to average creates substantial profits in them. If they go on from merely average to selling at a premium, the profits can be sensational.

An occasional freebie that comes with the low P/E strategy is the takeover play. Corporate treasurers on the hunt for value often find it precisely in this type of stock.

I do not claim that the low P/E strategy is the only market strategy that works. I do say that it produces above-average results on a consistent basis and at times can yield a good deal of excitement as well. Low P/E is not synonymous with dull.

The low P/E investor must learn to exercise discipline. He must discount rumors, hot tips, and fad stocks, and put out of his mind the rocketship-high P/E stocks that he wishes he had or could have bought.

Low P/E value investing does not give you a crystal ball to predict market turns. The informed investors act according to a consistent notion of underlying values.

To their disadvantage, some people avoid stocks. There are always reasons to put off investing in stocks. These include uncertainty about the usual unpredictables: What will stock prices do? When will the economy change? What will interest rates do? Which way will politics go? Where will international developments lead? Trying to make such predictions is an exercise in futility.

Yet above-average stock market results have been obtained by many investors who focus in a disciplined way on longer-range trends and ideas, many of which are predictable. The population will continue to grow. More people will need more goods and services. Research and free enterprise will create and market new products. Improved productivity and lower prices will stimulate demand. Well-managed companies in the right businesses will continue to make progress in revenue, earnings, and dividend payments.

Those who never buy stocks at all are the ones that say, "How are you doing playing the market?" Or "The stock market is gambling." My answer is always, "I am very seriously investing in the market, and I am not playing with the money I have at risk."

CONTRARIAN INVESTING

Go against the crowd. Be a contrarian: Buy when others are selling, and sell when others are buying. When selling pressures are extreme, a contrarian buys, and when buying pressures are extreme, a contrarian sells. The October 1987 crash proved that point, even when it took some time to do so. Slowly, the idea of contrarian investing sank into the minds of investors, both institutional and individual—though individual investors did not trust their stock-picking ability; they would participate via mutual funds.

The crash of 1987 was a clear example of the new trading rule, which is to buy when others are stampeding to sell. That selling stampede was over in less than a few hours, a combination of late Friday afternoon and Monday morning. Therefore, what took place appears as a small blip on a long-term chart, and perhaps historians will have a difficult time knowing what really happened.

GROWTH STOCK INVESTING

Everyone dreams of finding a stock that appreciates by five to ten times the original investment. Few have succeeded, because they insist on investing for the home run. They seek the inside tip or the hot rumor, or they just trust stock selection to plain luck. Investing can be profitable, but, like every other method of making money, it takes dedication, discipline, and hard work. Remember, what makes a stock go up is more buyers than sellers!

At the basis of selecting stocks for growth is the discipline of maintaining a strict listing of financial and operating requirements. Once a stock is analyzed using the requirement screens, it may qualify for serious attention and possibly purchase. The eight criteria discussed in the following section should be used in screening potential stock purchase candidates. It would be rare for a stock to show favorably in all eight categories. At this point, your good judgment becomes the determining factor regarding purchase.

COMMON-SENSE STOCK SELECTION

Common-sense stock selection starts with assessing the following eight factors:

1. *Rising unit sales volume:* Leader or laggard? Is the company in a young industry, such as biotech, or in an aged one still making the equivalent of buggy whips? Look for new products and services being marketed. Over the past three years, the stock's price should have increased by a greater amount (total percent) than did inflation, as measured by the Consumer Price Index (CPI) in the same period.

2. *Rising pretax profit margin:* There should be a rising trend in pretax margins over the past five years.

3. *Return on stockholder equity:* Does the company have the potential for an annual return of 15 percent on average stockholders' equity within the next two years? If the answer to this question is no, your money should be invested elsewhere.

4. *Relative earnings per share growth:* Over the past three years, the company's earnings per share should have advanced by a larger percentage increase than the calculated per-share earnings of the Dow Jones Industrials.

5. *Dividends:* The company must pay a dividend, and the dividend trend over the past five years should have risen steadily.

6. *Debt structure:* The company's long-term debt should be below 35 percent of stockholders' equity. Debt above 50 percent of stockholders' equity is a danger sign and means the stock should be avoided.

7. *Institutional holdings:* Institutions should not own more than 10 percent of the outstanding shares if the company is less than five years old. Ideally, in older companies, ownership will range between 10 percent and 30 percent. If more than 40 percent of ownership is institutional, the stock has been overexploited.

8. *Price-earnings multiple:* A basic tool in evaluating earnings is the price-earnings multiple, or P/E ratio, an indication of what investors are willing to pay for a dollar of earnings. P/E multiples are important, since appreciation in a growth stock results not only from the steadily increasing per share earnings, but also through a rising P/E ratio. The P/E should relate to the rate of growth. A good rule of thumb is that the P/E should normally not exceed the projected growth rate of earnings.

I recommend that the stock candidate show favorably in at least five of the eight categories.

DIVIDEND INCOME STOCK INVESTING

Selecting stocks for dependable current and rising dividend income requires different techniques than those for growth investing. While earnings per share continue to be important, increased emphasis is placed on the dividend record and financial stability.

A minimum of four selection criteria should be used.

1. The company should have a record of uninterrupted dividend payments for at least 10 years.
2. Dividends should have increased in at least five of the past 10 years.
3. Quality of the company and its stock should be above average. It should be rated A– or better by Standard & Poor's.
4. The stock should have sufficient size and liquidity in the marketplace for ease of trading. A minimum of 10 million common shares outstanding with capitalization of at least $500 million is required. The larger the capitalization, the more secure the stock.

KEEP IN MIND

Some investors will pay $20 for an investment worth $10, because it seems sure to go to $30 soon. (Usually they are heeding a tip or a rumor, since no one could know for sure.) This logic is used by otherwise rational people who overpay because they are confident someone will pay still more (the greater fool theory). It is also the thinking of new-issue buyers. Most new issues are lousy long-term investments.

Don't let the tail wag the dog. Having chosen investments for their value, you can arrange your investments to minimize taxes. Don't let beating the tax collector push you into an investment without proper underlying value. Investing and paying your taxes are of equal importance in this business. The money left is your true return.

Seek and you will find is the motto for stock selection. Use the vast quantity and quality of information at your disposal to guide your decisions. You will have a head full of useful facts—and a head start on most of your competition.

First, a warning: Safety, safety, safety! Better safe than sorry. All common stocks that you will buy or hold should stress safety. Once you have built up a portfolio, you can take some prudent risk.

Penny stocks are dangerous! The vast majority of these stocks sell for small amounts because that is precisely what they are worth—on their best days. Sometimes the companies that issue penny stocks aren't even viable, going concerns. They are just fronts for security swindlers. Remember, buyer beware. This type of investment is not what I mean by prudent risk.

Buy stock in large companies. Ignore those clowns who tell you that the only stocks to own are small-company stocks. Large companies suffer less accounting gimmickry than smaller companies, and results are spotted more quickly.

To properly diversify your portfolio, you should own stock in at least 10 different companies and own no more than two companies in one industry. Consider dividend yields a strong plus. A dividend yield is not all, but it is an important contributor to total return. A yield also supports the stock in bad markets. The dividend is an excellent indicator of the stock. An increase or decrease tells you how the company is doing.

Scout for low P/E companies. Try to distinguish those that are in a long-term downtrend from those merely suffering temporary setbacks. Sell a stock when the P/E greatly exceeds the market average, and replace it with another low P/E stock. Be like a child flying a kite; let out the string and enjoy the soaring. Be wary though—when the updraft is over, pull in the kite string and sell.

Buy companies that are financially strong enough to sail through the rough weather they may encounter. Look for high financial soundness and a low debt-to-equity ratio. A low debt-to-equity ratio suggests conservative financing and low risk.

Look for high book value. Book value can be a guide in selecting underpriced stocks. Remember, the emphasis is on upward price movement for security and good earnings trends. Remember the child with the kite. Don't try to fly a kite unless the wind is blowing correctly.

Finally, be patient. In low P/E investing, you have a lot going for you, but it won't produce fast results. Nobody knows it all. Some know more than others. You are not attempting to be flawless in the stock market, just to make a decent average profit. "Know thyself." Can you resist going with the crowd? Can you train yourself to follow an investment program and stick to it?

There is a problem with over-diversification. If you have a harem of 40 women, you will never get to know any of them very well.

—Billy Rose

The safest way to double your money is to fold it over once and put it in your pocket.

—Kin Hubbard

CHAPTER 4

Stock Picking, Research, and Annual Reports

When everyone is bearish, there are only potential buyers.

When everyone is bullish, there are only potential sellers.

—Jason Trennert, ISI Group

Knowledge born from actual experience is the answer to why one profits; lack of it is the reason one loses.

—Gerald M. Loeb

I bought stocks like they were going out of style. And they were.

—Anonymous

Stock picking is Wall Street's term for figuring out, case by case, which stocks are most likely to rise. It is based on how well the individual company is doing in business, not on general stock market conditions. Put away your darts and pull the stock page from the wall. (To show that an unmanaged, no-study system could work, the editors of *Forbes* magazine once did throw darts to make stock selections. These chance selections actually outperformed some professionally managed funds.)

No one invests in a vacuum. We act on some type of information, whether it is a tip from a friend, advice from a banker, a broker's recommendation, a newspaper report, a magazine article, or a financial web site.

Not knowing which of many sources of information to rely upon, individual investors have a difficult time.

Most investors don't take the time to research a stock in depth before making their investment decision. They have a business life, a family life, and a social life, and the time remaining from these pursuits, if any, is likely to be very limited. For the small investor, investment selection becomes a hit-or-miss operation. This is why 90 percent of small investors lose their money. You have to devote as much time to investing your money as you did in earning it in the first place, or you will be spending the time reearning it. If you saved money from working, the funds remaining after taxes are what you will have to earn to reinvest. Think of it as a loss not just in money, but also in time.

QUESTIONS FOR INVESTMENT DECISIONS

Ideally, the smart investor should ask and obtain answers to many questions, but here are a few to start with:

- What is the state of business and the economy? Where are we in the business cycle? Is the boom likely to top out? Are we in a recession? Answers in this area will vary with the stage of the business cycle.
- What is the state of the market? Are we in the early stages of a bull market? Has the low point of a bear market been reached? Is the bull market about to top out? Answers will vary with the stage of the market.
- If answers to the preceding questions seem favorable, then what industries are likely to grow most rapidly? Are there any special factors that favor a particular industry?
- Which company or companies within the industry are likely to do best? Which companies are to be avoided because of poor prospects?

Educated investors are aware that good stock-picking research takes effort and knowledge. When the bull market is roaring, you can do well in the stock market by throwing darts at a stock page and buying whatever you hit. The reason? The buying frenzy generally sends most stocks higher, including those of weak companies. The odds (gambling?) are that random selection would give you more winners than losers. Because bull markets send bad stocks up too, it masks many stock-picking sins. Even in poor markets, some stocks go up because they were so low they had no other way to go.

Bottom fishing is based on a notion that stocks can go only so low. Some rise because something sets them apart: a turnaround, a well-known name, a popular industry, or an attractive dividend.

To arrive at an investment decision, the average small investor must devote the time, using one or more sources of information, to answer all the preceding questions in depth.

Past experience should be a guidepost, not a hitching post.

—Anonymous

SOURCES OF INVESTMENT INFORMATION

"Where do I go from here?" Good question. The key to wise investing is being well informed. As a smart investor, you will want to research the security you are thinking of buying. While this will take time and requires work on your part, the good news is that the data you need is readily available through a variety of sources, and much of it is available for free.

Today, most investors use the Internet as a source for some of their research. The Internet is easy to access, most of the downloaded information is free, and the news is mostly current, since financial sites are updated frequently. Some of these sites are Yahoo! Finance, CBS Market Watch, CNNMoney.com, *Money* magazine, *Barron's* Online, *BusinessWeek*, *Kiplinger's Personal Finance*, Reuters, ABC News, Fox News, Nightly Business Report, U.S. News/Associated Press, Dogs of the Day, TickerSpy. com, SmartMoney.com, Worth.com, and the *Wall Street Journal*, to name a few.

Both online and brokerage firms offer web sites to their customers. The sites offer quotes and information about specific strategies, as well as recommendations and analysis. Though Standard & Poor's and Value Line are the two most common sources of commercial sites, they are just a starting point. There are many other information sites, and you will have to use your judgment to decide whether their information and analyses are reliable and worth their cost.

Choosing from the army of financial periodicals assaulting your mailbox and wallet these days can be tougher than picking a penny stock, and the list just keeps growing. For the average investor, who just wants general information, *Money* magazine and *Kiplinger's Personal Finance* are the sources to read. If you are a little more sophisticated, the information found in *Forbes, BusinessWeek, Financial World,* and *Fortune* magazines is more in-depth.

Two publications, the *Wall Street Journal* and *Investor's Business Daily,* keep readers abreast of what's going on in the world and in business. They both print the stock tables, but *Investor's* has a few more useful pieces of information and data.

Caution: Opening the stock listings in the financial section is like walking into a jungle of long, incomprehensible numbers for the uninitiated.

It is important to read the business stories on the financial pages. The information presented is extremely valuable and may include, for example, dividends, earnings reports, new products and services, takeovers, and selling of assets. The business press publishes abbreviated press releases before the companies mail annual or quarterly reports to investors. A newspaper's story contains the meat of a company's quarterly performance. Frequently they add the insight of Wall Street analysts, who follow a company to decide its potential investment value.

Worth magazine is a well-written and -illustrated bimonthly that covers investing topics in a varied and delightful way.

When, in the daily press, information about a stock catches my attention or, as a customer, I like a company, its products, or its services, the first thing I do is open my *Standard & Poor's Stock Guide.* The *Stock Guide,* published monthly, is an excellent starting point, and covers more than 9,000 companies. Perhaps the only thing you know about a stock is its name. By using this guide, you will find out if the company is publicly traded (it may be a privately owned company), if it is optionable, its stock symbol, its main line of business, and the S&P rating. Also included will be the company's high and low price history during the past decade, the previous year, the current year so far, and the past month.

Value Line, published weekly, covers 8,000 stocks. The Value Line Investment Survey in its summary and index presents the publication's up-to-date rankings for price performance, timeliness, and investment safety. The stocks are rated from 1 (highest) down to 5 (lowest). In addition, each of the stocks is the subject of a comprehensive new full-page Rating and Report at least every three months. It also carries analyses of interesting industries to review.

Barron's, published weekly, is another exceptional source of investment data and lists the last reported earnings of a company. In the *Wall Street Journal* and *Investor's Business Daily,* earnings as announced by a company are reported only once.

Many investors choose to use *Standard & Poor's* and *Value Line* as their primary sources for evaluation and then use other sources for additional background information to aid their judgment. Before you spend time on studying any single stock, use *Value Line* and read the general discussion of the industry, which will give you a good overview. Then read the discussion of particular stocks in that industry. You will spend less time studying a stock only to find out later that another stock in the industry was better.

Forbes (published biweekly) and *BusinessWeek* (published weekly) are two of my favorite magazines. They contain an enormous amount of ideas on companies and the economic climate. *Forbes'* editorials and investigative reporting are wonderful reading, and the magazine's investment philosophy has influenced my thinking and beliefs immensely and profitably. *Forbes* annually rates companies within industries, comparing and contrasting profitability and performance. *BusinessWeek* reports timely and useful business news in depth. Both magazines have mail-in cards to request annual reports from companies in which you may have an interest.

TRADE PRESS

One of the very best sources of information known is the trade press, which encompasses journals of considerable value. For anyone concerned with the wide world of investments, these narrow-band periodicals can often be worth their weight in gold. The intense focus on an industry or slice of business provides information that rarely makes the dailies or newsweeklies. When it does, it is long after such information appears in the trade press. If you're looking into a particular industry, such as the medical field, it is a good idea to pick up a medical journal and page through it.

If you had read *American Banker* during the late 1990s and early 2000s, you would have known in advance of the problems and disasters that have struck the banking industry.

Since the computer and all its peripherals are actively represented in the stock lists, I have made *Electronic News* part of my perusal routine. *Occupational Hazards*, the magazine of safety, health, and environmental management, keeps me posted on matters in this important industry. *AV Video Production and Presentation Technology*, *InformationWeek*, writes on matters of interest to their industry. Through it, I find companies that are the leaders in that fast-developing field.

Following the trade press is one of my most important methods of finding the "up-and-comers" in industries about which I know nothing. Reading their editorials and their industry concerns gives me the inside information that I need. The advertisements give me the names of companies to consider. I send for their annual reports and study them. I ask people in those fields personal questions about their products. Ask your doctor, lawyer, tradesman, and friends which products they like and use in their respective occupations. The list can be endless. Are you getting the idea?

The sources listed previously, and many others, should be available at your public library. Many people are afraid to ask for help, but the business librarian is there for that purpose.

> Always listen to experts. They'll tell you what can't be done and why. Then do it.
>
> —Robert A. Heinlein

INVESTMENT CLUBS

The investment club is a somewhat safe and reliable method of investing money in stocks that enables you to learn by doing. You should inquire of friends and at the library to find a club in your area.

Investment clubs give guidance in the selection of securities and the management of an investment portfolio through their membership. Some hold classes in your locale. Investment clubs do permit people to put small amounts of money into the stock market, some clubs as little as $10 per month. The average portfolio of a club is about $100,000, or $8,000 a person, and has about 12 members.

Joining an investment club is a way to learn and a way to earn. The clubs will expect some sweat equity from you. Each member may be responsible for finding information about a company and recommending whether to invest in that stock. Meetings are held once a month. Once you join a club, it should be a long-term commitment. The best part of the meeting is discussing the club's portfolio and whether to buy, sell, or hold the different stock investments.

Investment clubs work. Mark Hulbert, writing in *Forbes* on November 25, 1991, stated that groups of individuals have done much better than the professional investors. Many clubs, using a long-term approach and investment savvy, have beaten the market.

Because we live in a world of daily financial decisions, investment education is a lifelong process. Many individuals get their first successful stock investment experience in an investment club. As an investment professional, I belong to such a club, because the monthly meetings with a group of individuals interested in stocks builds investment exposure. The club helps me follow the latest stock market trends and opens the door to likely investment opportunities. More minds and more people of different backgrounds and interests provide a wealth of investment ideas.

I have been a member and President of the Contrarian Investment Club, Denver, Colorado for 20 years, and I thoroughly enjoy it. I wish I had known about investment clubs when I, as a beginner, first started investing. The cost of investing through the group is low. The club teaches how to buy stocks with low or no commissions, as well as how to participate in, and general education on, finding undervalued stocks that will outperform the market. There are hundreds of companies whose stocks can be purchased directly, overriding the beginner's hurdle of high commission costs for buying a few shares.

> Forget the past; no company has yet backed into success.
>
> —Anonymous
>
> In the short run, the market is a voting machine—reflecting a voter-registration test that requires only money, not intelligence or emotional stability—but in the long run, the market is a weighing machine.
>
> —Benjamin Graham

READING THE ANNUAL REPORT

A company's annual report is its progress report to the owners of the company, the shareholders. Companies listed on the New York Stock Exchange (NYSE) must submit an annual report to each shareholder. The report provides valuable information on the state of the business in the past year and the outlook for the future. It's better than the grapevine, news releases, or rumors. The research begins with the financial statements contained in the annual report. Annual reports are an investor's window to a company. They are as revealing for what they don't say as what they do. Lacking a financial background, most investors tend to concentrate on the letter from the chairman, browse through the feature articles, and look at the photographs. The annual report contains all the data and much additional information. It is the place to begin reviewing and studying a corporation. It doesn't take much effort, and you can save yourself possible future problems and losses.

Annual reports are filed 90 days after a company reports its year-ends. They often include a letter from the chairman of the board to shareholders, balance sheets, income statements, and discussions of the yearly performance results.

Certain pieces of information in the report are more important than others. Cut through the promotional material and get to the essentials. Start from the end. This is where all the numbers and fine print are.

Remember, the big type giveth, and the small type taketh away. The small type is where you'll find the report from an independent auditing firm whose task it is to look over everything. They make sure that the annual report is honest, thorough, and accurate in recording its business and financial transactions.

Look at the *accountant's opinion statement*. Since financial reporting involves considerable discretion, the accountant's opinion is an important assurance to the investor. If there is a "qualified" opinion, it signals concerns and warrants further investigation. Throw away the annual report that has a qualified opinion, and save your time and money to spend elsewhere. There are more good companies to invest in than your finances will permit.

Understand that accounting practices require the financial report be based on guidelines published by the Financial Accounting Standards Board (FASB). Where clear guidelines are nonexistent, accountants must rely on their professional body of knowledge and the practices prevalent at the time the decision is made. These interpretations, guidelines, and judgments are customarily termed *generally accepted accounting principles*. You have to be sure that the auditor's report gives the company a "clean" opinion with no reservations.

The *income statement* is the vital piece of information. It shows how much the company made or lost in the past year by adding up sources of income and deducting expenses. The earnings result is net income, which is often translated into earnings per share. Earnings per share are what savvy investors look for. They show how well a company's core business did. Beware of onetime gains, such as when a company sells some real estate. The windfall may boost the earnings, but it does not tell you how well the company is being run.

Check what portion of the corporation's earnings per share goes toward paying cash dividends. Growing companies probably will pay out little or no dividends because earnings are frequently being reinvested in the company. A utility will commonly allocate more than half its earnings toward dividends. If a company is paying out an increasing portion of earnings to sustain dividends, this could be a sign that the business is having some financial difficulty.

Check the footnotes for possible changes in accounting policies during the year. A change (e.g., inventory, depreciation, etc.) can have the effect of raising flat or declining earnings. The footnotes also contain litigation sections. Financial time bombs can be hidden here.

A more detailed picture of how a company is doing shows up in its filings with the Securities and Exchange Commission (SEC). Particularly revealing is the Form 10-K, an expanded annual report that details the company's history, its property, its competition, and its industry outlook. These are available upon request from the company's investor relations department.

Check to see whether earnings increased because of higher operating profits or because the company sold some assets, such as a plant, securities, or even one of its businesses. Compare both operating and pretax income to sales for several years to detect variances.

Extraordinary means an event or transaction during the year that is considerably different from normal activities. What is considered extraordinary? It can be a substantial gain or loss on the sale of a business or asset. A gain could come from the recovery of property or money through a court settlement. You will find extraordinary items explained in detail in the *notes to consolidated financial statements.*

Check the company's *statement of accounting policies* to find whether the corporation is capitalizing money spent for research and development, engineering, or training. By deferring those charges over several years, the earnings can look better this year. But those items represent deferred costs and are not assets.

Check to see if the ratio of *accounts receivable* to sales is growing. If so, revenues are not coming in like they should. This can suggest poor credit practices.

Inventories are a mixture of raw materials, goods in the manufacturing process, and finished products ready to ship to the customers. Check to see if inventories are increasing. This can suggest poor purchasing practices or lack of sales aggressiveness.

The *balance sheet* is an accounting statement showing the company's financial condition. It is broken into two parts: assets and liabilities.

1. *Assets* are the resources of a company. They are employed by the management of a company to produce products, services, and sales. Assets usually are divided into current assets and noncurrent or other assets. Current assets are classified as such because they can be turned into cash, usually within one year.

2. *Liabilities* are debts owed to others. Current liabilities are debts due within one year. Short-term debt is the portion of long-term debt that must be paid within the year. Accounts payable are the amounts due to suppliers who have extended credit to the company.

Liabilities can be either short- or long-term financial obligations. Subtract total liabilities from total assets to get shareholder equity, the portion of the company owned by investors. Shareholder equity typically grows at well-run companies, because remaining profits after dividends are reinvested into the company.

Compare long-term debt to shareholder equity. This is a measure of leverage, the use of borrowed money to enhance the return on shareowner's equity. The stockholders should have more invested in the company than the lenders do.

The *balance sheet* shows the position of a company's assets, liabilities, and shareholder equity.

There are some basic questions you will want to ask when looking at the balance sheet. What would the company be worth if the business were liquidated or sold? How much current debt is there, compared to assets? Have there been any large changes in the items listed?

Cash is king; it needs no explanation.

Accounts receivable are unpaid bills of customers to whom finished goods or services have been supplied. It is normal for businesses to extend credit to customers and receive credit from suppliers. Be sure that there is an allowance for bad debts, since a possibility always exists that customers will not pay their bills. That allowance is based on the total receivables and is generally a percentage applied by the accountants. In a difficult economic climate, the percentage is usually higher than when the economy is good.

Other *current accounts* usually include prepaid expenses, such as insurance, rent, and other items.

Property, plant, and equipment is the depreciated value of those fixed assets. This is the investment that management uses to produce, distribute, and sell its products. The amount shown represents the net plant investment after deducting the depreciation allowed by the IRS.

These items, included in the *book value* of a company, may vary significantly from market value. The equipment or supplies on hand used to make a discontinued product may be worth less than indicated in the books. Conversely, buildings and plants may be depreciated on the books, but can be worth a great deal more than the book figures.

Book value is a guide for rating under- and overpriced stocks. *Patents and other intangibles* include the patents acquired to produce certain products, trademarks, or goodwill. Goodwill could be the excess over book value paid for an acquisition of another company (Did they pay too much? Does it fit in with their present businesses?) These assets have no physical existence, yet still have a value to the company.

Accrued payrolls and *accrued pensions* are part of the money the company owes: salaries and wages to its employees. In addition, these employees have earned credit toward a pension to which the company contributes. Such debts are shown under these headings.

Income taxes payable usually are stated separately; these are owed, but not payable until later.

Long-term debt and *deferred income taxes* are debts that fall due beyond one year. A fast check will show the assets and liabilities. The difference is the shareholder's equity, or the stockholder's ownership. The total shareowner's equity figure is the corporation's net worth, after subtracting all liabilities from the total assets.

Par value is an arbitrary figure and has no relationship to stock value. *Paid-in-capital* is capital received from investors for stock in the company, as distinguished from capital generated by earnings. *Additional paid-in-capital* is the amount paid in by shareholders over the par value of each share. It may be donated stock, contributed capital, or property.

Retained earnings can be called surplus earnings. They are the accumulated amount of profit left in the business after the payment of dividends.

Footnotes are an integral part of financial statements. They *must* be read to understand the entire financial report (they are also where items can be hidden).

Changes in financial condition shows how much money a company has to work with and identifies sources of cash and disbursements.

The Little Type Taketh and the Big Type Giveth

Now that you have done all the important studying, you can continue browsing toward the front of the annual report. Go through all the fancy color graphs, photographs, and charts on expensive paper . . . to the opening page finding the chief executive officer's (CEO's) color picture and ask, "Why is this man smiling?" You can answer the question: "Because he has done an excellent job."

Sometimes you can tell a company by its cover. In teaching investing, one of my most popular sessions is to scatter a pile of annual reports, and ask the students to look at the covers and decide if the company had a good year or a bad year. Those companies with quantitative items on the front usually had solid years. Those with modern art and non-business related subjects on the cover tend to have had a poor year.

Beware of being taken. Nobody expects an annual report to trumpet where management went wrong. Read those footnotes and the phrasing of the accountant's letter. They can often tell quite a revealing story.

First the idea is created that there are earnings curves that can rise in unbroken lines. Investors put a premium on such curves and ignore companies whose curves run flat or follow a fluctuating course. Those without the right curve are hit where it hurts, right in the P/E ratios. A cyclical company, no matter how good it is, is lucky to get 10 times earnings in the market. Those with sweeping up-curves go for 20, 30, even 50 times earnings. What this does to stock prices, options, merger possibilities, even to corporate prestige, is all too apparent.

Imaginative companies start doing things with their books, making it appear to investors that they too have those attractive curves, even if they really don't. Even sound, businesslike managements do this. Their very existence is threatened by companies who know how to use high P/E stocks to take over low P/E companies.

Today, most annual reports must be studied skeptically. Many are outright deceptive. Only a minority are truly honest, despite opinions handed down by the American Institute of Certified Public Accountants (AICPA), despite rulings by the SEC, and despite so-called full disclosure by management. The annual report has deteriorated to such a degree that one has little confidence in its contents.

The following rules cover only some of the cases where confusing and sometimes misleading reporting is freely used. Once there was faith in the famous two paragraphs:

"We have examined the consolidated balance sheet of The ABC Co. and subsidiaries as of December 31, and the related statements of income, retained earnings, and capital surplus, and the statement of source and application of funds for the year just ended. Our examination was made according to generally accepted auditing procedures that are considered necessary in the circumstances.

"In our opinion, the accompanying consolidated financial statements present fairly the financial position of The ABC Co. and subsidiaries at December 31, and the results of their operations for the year then ended, in conformity with generally accepted accounting principles which have been applied on a basis consistent with that of the preceding year."

To the ordinary investor and to many professionals, these two paragraphs meant that auditors had checked the figures and found them sound. Then came the scandals. The public learned that the two paragraphs gave no guarantee of the facts upon which the figures were based. Now the accountants are more careful. For those willing investors who make the effort, annual reports have begun to have more of a between-the-lines meaning.

Now the fairly common phrase "subject to" is often included in an audited statement. The subject is usually specified in a footnote to the report. It means that the auditor is in serious disagreement with the company about its disclosure or lack of disclosure, concerning an important area.

A "subject to" can suggest that assets and earnings are as indicated only if inventories or other assets, like investments, are really worth what the company claims. This claim is one the auditors do not certify. What this bluntly means is, "Here are the figures, but we won't swear by them."

Examples "In our opinion, subject to the realization of work-in-progress inventories and accounts receivable described in Note 3, the statements mentioned above present fairly, except for the change in accounting for administrative and general expenses and independent research and development costs described in Note 2."

"The change in accounting in Note 1 increased earnings by $44 million out of a total of $88 million reported."

Do not think that you can skip the footnotes just because the company receives no accountant's objection. Sometimes the only way to understand a company's annual report is to compare it with another report in the same line of business. For example, Ford Motor Company's annual report makes more sense when read concurrently with that of General Motors.

This does not suggest that every company is curving or cooking its books. Many companies—DuPont, Eastman Kodak, IBM, and Corning Glass are among them—still keep conservative books.

As a potential investor, however, you need to learn the meaning of the quality of earnings. Two companies each report earning $4 per share; that does not mean that both of them are equally profitable. On a strictly comparative basis, one of them might only be earning $3.50 per share and the other closer to $4.50, depending on their accounting procedures. High-quality earnings also are more stable earnings. By borrowing, in effect, from the future, the less-conservative company runs the risk of a severe downturn when business weakens. The more conservative company, by contrast, has built-in stability.

Though numbers are still the investment community's best and brightest yardstick of performance, numbers do not always paint the entire picture. They can be stretched, shrunk, and shaped to fit into almost any mold via artwork and visuals.

Charts, Graphs, and Photographs

I caution everyone to verify any visuals provided in the annual report by returning to the numbers in the back of the annual report. Numbers don't lie, but pretty visuals such as charts, graphs, and photographs are not above bending the truth.

Despite their apparent innocence, charts, especially those advanced as a portrait of a company's financial stability, require the closest inspection.

Usually, financial figures are provided by people who have something to gain by their interpretation. While companies are legally required to furnish accurate figures, how accurately they portray the company in visuals is often a matter of perspective.

Change the scale of a chart or a graph. Use a wide-angle lens for a photograph. What is really a financial free-fall suddenly looks like nothing more than a harmless, subtle dip.

Maybe investors, not to mention businesspeople who bought companies based on exaggerated figures, should have paid more attention to the footnotes and the accounting changes in the first place.

The chairman's letter will give you an impression of the company. What happened this year, and why? What is the chairman's insight on economic and political trends? Make certain that the chairman's letter is "up front" in more ways than one. While you're there, check out the financial review that describes how the operating groups and their divisions fared over the most recent three years.

THE QUARTERLY REPORT

I make use of quarterly earnings as a thermometer to keep tabs on corporate health. Daily headlines about specific companies' quarterly earnings being up or down from the same quarter a year ago usually have an immediate impact on their stock prices.

If three-month profits are way up or down, it can be for any number of reasons: currency fluctuations, one-time windfall or cost-cutting write-offs, high start-up costs for new products or plants. Some special reasons that could make a quarterly report's results go down should, if properly understood, send a stock price upwards. The bottom-line results are not the sole criterion for judging corporate value and corporate prospects. It's the figuring behind the results that gives them true meaning.

It's up to us to try to dig out the whole story and to clarify why a quarterly earnings report isn't the whole story. Many managements who conduct quarterly financial press reporting take to juggling, managing, overemphasizing, and window-dressing the figures. They need to look good, often at the cost of long-range planning for capital investment, research, and development. The quarterly reports are unaudited.

CHANGING THE RULES

Imagine two 30-year-old millionaires. One made a fortune by building a company from scratch. The other inherited it from a wealthy uncle. Which do you think will be more financially successful 10 years from now?

Of course, there is no way to know for sure. When it comes to projecting future success, what you have is frequently less important than how you got it. That is the reasoning behind one approach to measuring corporate performance.

> Remember that money is of the prolific, generating nature. Money can beget money, and its offspring can beget more, and so on.
>
> —Benjamin Franklin

The factors driving value in companies today are quality, service, cycle time, innovation, and continuous improvement. You must measure not only financial value, but also the elements that create that value.

Instead of concentrating on *lagging indicators*, such as return on investment and earnings per share, look at *leading indicators*: customer perspective, business processes, financial perspective, and organizational planning.

Measure such factors as customer satisfaction, on-time delivery, development cost, time to market, profitability per employee, and percent of sales from products less than one year old. The measures are expressed as corporate goals and objectives linked to the organization's vision and strategy.

For most serious investors, the main purpose of reading financial reports is to glean some basic historical knowledge about a company, not to discover the next Wal-Mart. Look at the company's annual reports over the last three years to get a feel for how realistic their forecasts have been. Certainly a corporation's past performance is no guarantee of future results. A company whose forecasts have been reached is a good company. Such well-grounded forecasts could make the company's stock a big winner.

The reality is, you can study the numbers and find a financially sound company, but that doesn't mean its stock is going anywhere. Be mindful of market perceptions, as well as actual company performance, when looking for promising stocks.

Where do you go from here? You now understand the key elements in the annual report. If this objective has been achieved, then you can explore the annual report in depth. Go ahead... you will find it interesting and informative reading.

ANNUAL MEETINGS

Even more interesting, if the opportunity presents itself, would be to attend an annual meeting. This is the annual gathering of a corporation's directors, officers, and shareholders. At this time, new directors are elected, shareholder resolutions are passed or defeated, and the past fiscal year's operating and financial results are discussed.

Most of these meetings are very matter of fact and conducted in a very businesslike atmosphere. Occasionally, the CEO is put under pressure while honestly answering shareholder questions and explaining the company's business direction.

I attended an annual meeting of a public utility that was doing poorly; I wanted to see what would be reported at the meeting to the shareholders.

The CEO opened the meeting. "Good morning, ladies and gentlemen, thank you for coming. The first thing I would like to say is, 'The dividend is secure.'" The audience reacted favorably and cheered the good news.

I waited patiently to the question-and-answer part of the meeting. "Sir," I said, "Would it not be more prudent to forget the dividend, rather than borrow more money to pay the dividend?" Well, 250 shareholders started booing and hissing me. The meeting was being held on the second floor of the hotel, and I felt that if they threw me out of the windows, I would survive.

Another memorable annual meeting for me was when an investor encouraged the CEO to get rid of the *re-* words. Every annual meeting the shareholder had attended recently included talk of *re*evaluating the company, *re*structuring it, *re*vitalizing the workforce, *re*assessing the marketplace, and *re*directing resources. Next year, the shareholder suggested that the *re-* word be *re*ality.

Of course if the company is *re*ally doing that poorly, the investor should *re*tire from that company by *re*deeming the shares held in that corporation, and *re*investing the money elsewhere.

STOCK SELECTION SUMMARY

Stock selection is the art and science of finding good stocks. Selection depends on how much risk you are willing to tolerate. Risk is the possibility of losing, or of not gaining value. Below are three long-term stock picking strategies.

1. *Earnings growth:* In the long run, nothing determines a stock's price more surely than its earnings. Over time, the stock prices of companies with the fastest growing earnings will grow the most rapidly. Don't chase a stock. If a stock in which you have an interest starts going up rapidly and you missed buying at the price that you wanted to pay ... let it go. Watch it, and when it dips in price, buy.

    Look for a company that dominates a fast growing market or market niche. Beware of reliance on heavy debt, shrinking profit margins amid high-income growth, and net income growth that lags behind operating income growth. Beware also of stocks with P/E ratios that greatly exceed earnings growth rates. Diversify with several stocks; only one or two need to really take off to give your portfolio good gains.

2. *Total return:* There are two ways to make money in the stock market: price gains and dividends. Dividends are the part of earnings paid to the share owners. Adding dividends to price gains gives you a stock's total return. Total return is a useful stock-picking focus for the informed investor.

Look for a company with a long history of dividend payments that is also in many different market environments, to protect yourself against unforeseeable industry swings. A company that is in different markets will be safer. Look for evidence of the company's ability to operate in good and bad times and its commitment to sharing the wealth with shareholders. You want earnings growth and dividend growth. Avoid stocks such as utilities, which pay the highest dividends but often lack growth potential.

3. *Bottom fishing:* Picking solid companies whose stocks have been so badly beaten down that they have nowhere to go but up promises the greatest possible rewards. Look through a trash heap for treasures, rather than picking favored stocks that have already made their move and are at the top. Buying at the top is expensive, and the stocks could drop in price from their lofty heights. I am a bottom trash picker and have done very well.

Look for a company on the bottom that is solid but caught in a guilty-by-association downdraft, a company in a cyclical slump because a similar company hit investors with unexpected troubles, or a company that is simply out of favor. Look at what put the company on the bottom in the first place.

Check the stock price for signs that it has stopped falling, for sometimes beaten stocks can languish on the bottom. Study the company for clues to internal trouble: high debt, shrinking market share, operational problems, heavy insider selling, and sudden management changes. Don't catch a falling knife.

And with all thy getting get understanding.

—Proverbs 4:7

Investigate before you invest.

—United States Securities and Exchange Commission

CHAPTER 5

How to Read the Financial News

You can either be squirrel food or the seed of a mighty tree.

—Paul Richey

Stock prices are quoted in most daily newspapers, with emphasis on the news of local companies. For extensive market information, the financial press (special business publications), such as the *Wall Street Journal, Investor's Business Daily,* and *Barron's,* have even more detailed information. Kindly get a copy of one of these publications, and I shall guide you through all of the elements listed.

Your daily newspaper will not have all the information provided by those mentioned above but probably will still give the important facts you need. Most daily newspapers have gone to an online edition of the business pages.

Stock prices will be shown for the listed and unlisted stocks. Listed stocks are those traded on a stock exchange. The major stock exchanges are the New York Stock Exchange (NYSE), the American Stock Exchange, and the NASDAQ (National Association of Securities Dealers Automated Quotation System). Stocks not listed on an exchange are traded OTC (over the counter), which lists the largest number of stocks.

The information on a stock page shows:

- *The 52-week high/low*: This is for the preceding 52 weeks, not for the calendar year. During this period, the stock traded for these prices, and there was always a buyer and seller.

- *Stock*: The stock name is always abbreviated and listed alphabetically. After you start watching a stock regularly, you can find it very quickly.
- *Symbol*: The identifying letters used for companies whose stock is publicly traded. The symbols do not appear in all papers.
- *Dividend*: The actual cash amount paid annually to shareholders of part of the company's profit. Where no figure is shown, the stock does not pay a dividend. Based on today's price for a stock, most dividends don't appear very exciting. But if you had held the stock for some years, the dividend would represent a large return on your original investment. Also, you would have received dividends throughout the years and would have an appreciated value on your investment. *Total return* is all dividends received and the capital appreciation on your original investment.
- *Yield*: Yield is the amount of the dividend expressed as a percentage of the current price of the stock.
- *P/E (price-earnings ratio)*: If there is none shown, that means the company did not earn a profit in the preceding 12 months. It should be noted that the P/E ratio will fluctuate whenever the stock price or earnings per share rises or declines.
- *Volume 100s*: Sales in 100s shows how many shares were traded. Volume or stock market activity is important. Investors should not be concerned if a particular stock is or is not on the most active list. Stocks can also rise or fall on low volume.
- *High, low, close*: Three columns showing the high, low, and closing price for that day. Usually, the differences are small.
- *Net change*: Shows the change in price from the previous day.

Stocks are traded by 100 shares, a round lot. Investors who trade in less than round lots may have to pay a differential charge for odd lots. (An odd lot broker's business is to break up round lots). You can save this fee if your order is placed before the market opens in the morning.

The prices for which stocks trade are based on the decimal system (e.g., one cent, nickel, dime, quarter, half-dollar, and dollar).

OTC stocks are usually reported in the same manner as the major exchange stocks. Generally, they are smaller companies that do not meet the listing requirements of the larger exchanges. Some companies prefer to stay on the OTC because the financial reporting requirements are not as stringent.

Separate tables highlight the 10 most actively traded stocks for the day, showing the volume of shares traded, the closing price, and the net change.

Periodically, the earnings of companies are reported in the newspaper. These reports are based on the company's quarterly or annual reports. *Earning reports* are usually made available a few weeks after the quarter ends. Generally, a company issues three interim quarterly reports and one annual report. Earnings can be better or worse than the investors expected: "The company didn't lose as much as we feared," or "The company didn't make as much as we hoped." Talk like this has an immediate reaction on the stock price. It can make good news trigger a negative reaction and bad news a positive one. Long-term traders do not react to these earning reports. They always know the true worth of their company, because such investors stay informed.

Dividends in cash or stock are declared at the quarterly meetings of the company's board of directors. At the same time, a date of record is set, which means stockholders of record on or before that date are entitled to the dividend. The next day, after the date of record, the stock is traded ex-dividend (xd), and the stock market price is usually reduced by the amount of the dividend.

When the company is doing well, the directors can raise the cash dividend or declare an extra cash dividend. When the company is not doing well, the directors can cut the dividend or omit one entirely. You can find stories on dividends in a column called *corporate dividends* in the newspaper.

Another form of dividend offered is in stock instead of cash; this type is known as *stock dividends*. Stock dividends are given when the directors wish to save cash for the business, but still want to give a dividend. A shareholder with 100 shares of stock who receives a 5 percent stock dividend would then own 105 shares. You really didn't get anything, because the value of your 105 shares equals the value of your original 100 shares.

A *stock split* means that the stockholder receives additional shares based on a percentage of his holdings. If, for example, you owned 100 shares of a stock on a two-for-one split where the stock was $20 per share, you would now have 200 shares valued at $10 per share. The pie has been cut into smaller pieces; you have more pieces, but their value equals the value of what you had previously. The NYSE has found that companies that have a stock split, usually increased their dividends more than twice as often as non-splitters."

Many investors feel that a stock split lowers the cost per share and therefore makes the stock more desirable to the investing public. This is true, because investors try to buy in round lots of 100 shares. Stock splits probably do attract smaller investors, who are likely to hold on to the shares for long-term investment. The small investor gets an advantage towards attaining a round lot.

Many investors also feel that 1,000 shares of a $10 stock will go up faster than 500 shares of a $20 stock. Other investors see a company that they have looked at previously now selling for a lower price (post-split), which is their primary reason for buying. They fail to realize that the true value per share is the same before and after the split. Their actions create an unrealistic short-term price for the stock.

In identifying split candidates, look for one or more of the following factors:

- A sharply higher market price.
- A history of stock splits or large stock dividends.
- A limited number of shareholders.

Usually, when a company announces a stock split, the newspapers give all the details. Until the new shares are traded and the old ones dropped, the stock is traded *when issued* (wi), and the shares are outstanding, though not yet issued. The split shares on the financial page are shown by an *s* after the stock name.

A reverse stock split may be initiated by companies that wish to raise the price of outstanding shares, usually to meet the requirements of the exchange or to attract investors who avoid low-priced stocks. Many mutual funds and large financial organizations will not trade stocks selling for prices under $10.

GUIDE TO THE ECONOMY AND THE STOCK MARKET

By reading the financial pages of the newspaper daily, an investor can be well informed. He should focus on four fundamental news subjects: the business cycle, inflation, liquidity, and interest rates. These key indicators will help investors understand economic influences on the stock market.

1. The *business cycle* describes the expansion or contraction of the economy as a whole; it has an important influence on the earning's trends of most companies. The business cycle affects profitability and cash flow, which is a key in corporate dividend policy and is an element influencing the fluctuation of the inflation rate. Thus the business cycle affects the return on investment.

2. *Inflation* is the hidden tax we all pay because of the dwindling purchasing power of our dollar. Inflation causes prices to rise and is generally caused by excessive government spending. Inflation should be monitored, because it is tied to the business cycle. Inflation has a direct

impact on investing. A rising or falling inflation rate affects the shift of cash between stocks, bonds, or other alternative investments.

Economists have studied the relationship between the inflation rate and the stock market over long periods of time. They have discovered that the two tend to seek a norm of 20, obtained by adding the market's P/E ratio to the current inflation rate.

When the combination of P/E and the rate of inflation exceeds or is less than the norm of 20, it suggests that there will be an adjustment in the market.

3. *Monetary policy,* mainly through the Federal Reserve Board decisions on the money supply liquidity, can make the economy grow faster or put a brake on economic growth.

There are several indicators of money supply, but the most useful one for investors to follow is *M2,* the amount of money in savings and checking accounts. Liquidity and the stock market tend to move together. When M2 grows faster than the economy, stock prices rise. As an example, in the early 1980s the economy declined sharply, the money supply surged, and the stock market took off.

4. *Interest rates* and the stock market move in opposite directions. When interest rates decline, the market does well. When the interest rates rise, stock prices tend to decline. You can always find winning stocks, but it's dangerous to move against the relationship of stocks and interest rates.

How do investors know which direction interest rates are headed? Look at the Federal Reserve Board (the Fed); it monitors and directs the interest rates in the American economy. Look for major turning points in Fed policy, such as the continued discount or interest rate cuts, like those we saw in 2008. Don't concern yourself about the minor midcourse adjustments.

Inflation and the markets' P/E add up to approximately 30. That means that any rise in inflation could send the market downward. A further drop in the inflation rate could give the market an upward bias.

Liquidity is positive. If the money-supply growth rate accelerates, stocks could move even higher. Still, if it declines, investors should expect stocks to drop from their current lofty levels.

Federal Reserve Board Chairman Ben S. Bernanke has in the past moved several times to bring interest rates down. The stock market attracts more investors due to the current interest rate. Investors have to keep informed by reading the newspapers and stay tuned to the direction of any major Fed policy. This is how they work today.

Common stocks would move lower if the economy slipped back even further and stock earnings declined. If the worst is behind us, and the economy is indeed turning around, higher earnings could be ahead.

Certainly, market cycles are different. The extent to which current events will affect the stock market remains to be seen.

Being informed of the four major market indicators and knowing what they mean will help investors through the years ahead. But the unknowns (politics) are enough to keep things very interesting.

> What lies behind us and what lies before us are tiny matters compared to what lies within us.
>
> —Ralph Waldo Emerson

YOUR WALLET CAN BE A LEADING ECONOMIC INDICATOR

Consumers account for two-thirds of America's spending, and it's easy to understand why it is worth listening to us. Our plans to spend, to save, and to invest are shaping economic trends. This knowledge will help you forecast changes in the economy.

In 2008, the Consumer Expectations Index documented a drop in consumer confidence that reached a low point. Now the economy was in a recession. Consumer expectations and confidence forecast fell for the long recession before the official onset of the economic recovery in December 2008.

Why is consumer confidence so reliable a forecast? It's because we, as consumers, rely on personal experience. We are the ones who have to balance our checkbooks every month. We see what is happening to interest rates when our CDs mature. It's not the prime rate we care about; it's the mortgage rate. It's not the national unemployment figures that affect us; it's whether we lose our jobs, or anyone in our immediate families or neighborhoods loses theirs. These factors are much more important to consumers than the abstract figures reported in the newspapers.

In early 2009, it's clear that consumers are increasingly concerned about the economy. It seems that we are hoping the worst is over, and we are expecting improvement in the year ahead. But we don't anticipate a roaring recovery. We are paying off debts, saving a little more, and spending a little less.

Reading the financial pages will keep you aware of unusual opportunities for profit. You can buy or sell against the emotions of the crowd.

The hardest thing about making money last is making it first.

—Anonymous

There are more things in life to worry about than just money ... how to get hold of it, for example.

—Anonymous

CHAPTER 6

The Art of Investing, Risk, and Reward

I have to be wrong a certain number of times in order to be right a certain number of times. However, in order to be either, I must first make a decision.
—Elbert Hubbard

Managing a portfolio properly requires a dedicated amount of time and effort. You should be willing to put in as much time managing your money as you did to earn it. Guess what? If you lose your money, you must spend time to earn it again before you can invest.

Time is an extremely important factor to an individual investor. Pension funds live and are invested for perpetuity, while an individual investor only has several years to accumulate wealth. If a financial goal is 10 years away, an investment that fails to provide results within a year effectively eats up one-tenth of the investment life of the individual. Each lost period increases pressure for higher returns and risk in the future, ultimately, a failure to meet goals. Worse yet, allowing a small irritating loss to grow into a major loss in principal will dramatically extend the time needed to reach financial goals.

In reality, the loss of substantial principal is all too common, as individuals rationalize that their stock or the market will come back. Certain stocks may or may not regain their previous value. But where does one borrow the extra years needed to resume progress within the natural time limits we all must face?

The stock market is dominated by institutional investors (banks, mutual funds, insurance companies, etc.), and it is their time frames and objectives that influence the market. The institutions have objectives that stress low risk and short time frames. Their performance is evaluated weekly, monthly, quarterly, or annually. The institutional and professional investors must conform to performance standards over the short term.

The institutions must have funds available on short notice to permit withdrawals. When the requests are larger than the cash reserves, securities have to be sold—and quickly. This creates an opportunity for the small long-term investor. He can buy undervalued stocks when they become available, as prices are forced down by the institutional and professional investors.

It is a big mistake to have a short time frame. You must take time to let the investment work. The time is critical, because what is best for the short term may not be best for the long term.

Long term in this case means five years. No one should start a long-term investment strategy if they are going to need their monies returned in less time.

Having to get out of the stock market at any time, because of the need for your money, is a terrible error. You may need to get out at the bottom of a business cycle, which will result in a loss . . . or when it is still going up, which means you miss the opportunity to gain. Taking money out of the stock market at the wrong time can seriously impair your long-term strategy. *Don't do what the big players have to do.*

More money is invested by individuals in T-bills, bonds, CDs, bank accounts, and real estate than in the stock market. There is a mystery and challenge to the stock market, and while the returns are high, volatility creates fear. Let us remember the investors who jumped from rooftops.

STOCKS OR BONDS?

History provides some guidance, but it must be used with a degree of caution. Remember the seminar I spoke about at the beginning of the book? If I had followed that scenario, I would be dead, but my estate would be worth a fortune. For most of this century, yields on stocks were ahead of bonds. This is appropriate; stocks are riskier, so stocks should continue to do better.

The old rules were thrown out the window during the bull market, after the crash of 2008. The Standard & Poor's 500 (S&P 500) pays about double what safe treasury bonds are paying. Since 1934, a stock portfolio, after allowing for inflation (if all the dividends were reinvested) would have been a terrific investment, averaging about 6.6 percent a year. Treasuries have averaged little more than 1 percent per year. Historically, stocks have been the best investment vehicle.

When inflation comes quickly, as it did in the 1970s, it murders bond portfolios. Interest rates rocket up, and bond prices go down. That is why Treasury bill holders fell behind. Now lenders have gotten wise; they insist on being compensated for accepting principal paid with dollars that are worth less and less. Anticipated inflation is factored into bond yields.

What about dividend growth? While bond principal is being eaten away by inflation, stock prices and dividends are keeping up with inflation. Dividends have grown modestly in real terms, upward at a 1.3 percent annual rate since 1934. Now we can make a realistic comparison between stocks and bonds.

Think of each investment in terms of the real return by which it can grow. If corporate America can continue its record of dividend growth, you could count on a 3.8 percent cash yield on an average portfolio of stocks. Also, the proceeds from a small amount of capital gain 1.3 percent every year.

Are stocks or bonds a better investment? They are both equally predictable. Over the short term, stocks can crash faster. Over the long term, bonds are riskier.

The market could crash, making your portfolio worth half, but your dividend stream would hold reasonably well. The market could double tomorrow. Your dividends wouldn't be any higher, and it would be a mistake to use the paper gains to live better. It would be more prudent to leave those gains invested as a hedge against future market crashes or to let them continue to grow on the upswing.

Remember, no one knows how high is high or how low is low. Don't become a psychoanalytical investor and try to analyze the irrational market.

MARKET TIMING

Can the smart investor get rich by catching these wild swings between the high and the lows? Can the smart investor buy cheap and sell dear? A few really have, and many lie about it, but more have lost money trying to time the market.

The market is represented by the unmanaged Dow Jones Industrial Average (DJIA) and transports and utilities indexes. You can do better than "Average" if you truly manage your portfolio, not just buy and hold as the average investor has done.

Market timing is trying to catch those wild swings. Market timing fails more often than it succeeds. Too many investors continue to look for a system that will help them beat the market. They want to convert to cash before stock prices slump, and want to hop back into the market near the low to catch the next rise.

The long-term trend of stock prices is upward, paralleling the growth of earnings and dividends. The market rises two years out of three. So whenever an investor holds much cash, he is betting against 2-to-1 odds.

It is true that major market advances and declines are caused by broad shifts in valuation. Historically, when stocks are high-priced relative to earnings, dividends, and asset values (book value), they are vulnerable to decline. On the other hand, when stocks measured by those yardsticks are low-priced, they are ripe for advance.

Always, major shifts in the market away from unusually high or low valuations, have been started by a triggering event. Almost always, those events have been unpredictable.

Investors' mood swings are often extreme. Good news feeds on itself and so does bad news. As usual, these extreme mood swings keep the market timing folks from doing what they were trying to do—that is, to sell high and buy low. It's extremely hard to sell when everyone is enthusiastic and buy when everyone is in despair.

The subject has been studied and the results are in: Market timing is just as foolish a quest as trying to find a system for consistently beating the odds at the racetrack. The allure of trying to outguess the market because of the tremendous profits that would result if you could do that successfully is more than many investors can resist.

Any Time Is a Good Time to Start an Investment Portfolio

If you had invested $1,000 a year for the past 20 years on the worst possible day each year, the day the market peaked, your average annual rate of return would be 14.27 percent. If you had made the same investments on the best possible day each year, the day the market hit bottom, your average annual rate of return would be 16.05 percent. So, either way, you still would have done very well.

AVOID COMMON INVESTMENT RISKS

Risk capital is money at risk. No matter how conservative the investment, money is still at risk. Let's look at the most common kinds of risks most investors face and how to avoid them.

Do you currently have investments that you do not understand and never did? That is the most common indicator of *adviser risk*, and results from acting on the advice of the person selling to you. Rely more on yourself and less on the advice of salesmen.

Do you keep putting off doing something with your money? *Procrastination risk* results from lack of understanding the facts necessary to remove fear and lack of self-confidence.

Reading and understanding this book will keep you ahead of the herd. When it comes time to buy, shop around and ask questions. That is the only way you can gather necessary information.

Do you buy "government-guaranteed" bond funds? You are suffering from *it-doesn't-exist risk*. There is no such thing as a government-guaranteed bond fund. There are mutual funds that invest in government-guaranteed bonds, but the funds are not guaranteed.

Do you invest in stocks directly? Investing in individual stocks is supposed to be the American dream. I just want to point out the risk of investing in an individual stock, including the stock of your employer. In doing this, you are taking on *nondiversification risk*, the risk of having too many of your eggs in one basket.

Do not put all your eggs in one basket.

> Put all your eggs in one basket and watch that basket.
>
> —Bernard Baruch

RISK BREEDS FEAR

I have known firsthand what it's like to be almost paralyzed by fear, to distrust my own stock market indicators, to feel incapable of making financial decisions. All these situations create unmanageable fears. If I wanted to stay in the investment business, I had to make my fears manageable.

I became fascinated by the stock market when I was in my teens. Since my "investments" at that time were only on paper, I was completely fearless.

Several years later, after I had started my first business, I put some of my meager earnings into stocks. After my first losses, fear became a regular companion . . . rarely intense, but always there.

> Fear is actually lowest when people see it as the greatest; and when most think of it as absent, it is actually the highest.

In 1965, I launched my investing program and also got involved in money management. To fear the loss of hard-earned savings, and to fear missing out on stock market gains by playing it too safe, is absolutely normal.

So it seems neither realistic nor even desirable to try to eliminate fear from investing. My goal is to make fear manageable, to see that it plays a constructive rather than destructive role. Here are some steps I've taken.

The first thing I had to do was to set my priorities and rules and not waver from them, no matter what.

The top priority, above everything else, was to accept, deep down, that the stock market is irrational and that the prices of stocks will fluctuate.

Accepting this, I reached the following decision: to be fully invested in the stock market at all times. I prefer to hold too much stock in a rising market than have too much uninvested cash. If I appear foolish at such times by being in the market, I can live with that, because I am being true to my risk-avoidance priorities.

The worst investment mistakes I've made came from distrusting my market indicators. That is what can happen when fear takes over, like a pilot distrusting his compass. But I've learned my lesson. I trust my priorities, not my emotions.

I've spent 46 years developing these priorities and rules. They're not perfect, but they are by far the most reliable guide to market timing. I do not try to predict future stock market moves. Remember, the stock market is irrational.

My goal is to be in stocks during big market advances and during big declines. This is the surest road to riches. Trying to catch absolute market tops and bottoms, besides producing extreme anxiety, is an utter waste of time.

Understanding and minimizing risk and fear is an important goal of this book ... as is informed investing. Risk ... what is it? Risk is the likelihood that your investment will be worth less after a time period than it was when you originally invested. This definition should be modified to take inflation into account by stating that risk is the possibility that your investment will be worth less in real dollars after a time period than it was when you originally invested it.

The more bang for the buck, the higher the risk, as in gambling and lotteries. The tradeoff is between risk and reward. Investments decisions must be stated in terms of both risk and return, and depend on the risk the investor is willing to take.

Risk and reward change depending on the time period involved. The risk and return will be different for a six-month holding period than for a five-year holding period. Generally, risk declines as the holding period extends.

Diversification reduces risk. Value, supply, and demand of a stock are determined by the investors' perspective of the companies and movements in the general market trends. The stock market is irrational. To avoid being caught by irrationality, you have to diversify.

By diversifying your investments among several different companies in different industries, you spread out the risk. The odds (measurable risk) of all industries going down at once and all the stocks you bought going down at once are greatly reduced by diversification.

An investor with all his tennis balls in one basket is taking on a 100 percent risk of loss. An investor with ten baskets is taking on less risk of loss by diversifying. An investor with one conservative stock is taking more risk than the investor with ten growth stocks. The conservative investor is getting a lower return, since they are in a lower-risk, lower-return situation. A diversified portfolio of growth stocks gives a higher return and lowers the risk factor.

GENERAL INVESTMENT STRATEGIES

Many different approaches can be used to invest, but most are under five broad categories:

1. Buy and Hold
2. Momentum Investing
3. Technical Analysis
4. Fundamental Analysis
5. Contrarian Investing

Buy and Hold

This strategy calls for accumulating stocks over the years and requires minimal time and attention. This approach allows for favorable long-term capital gains tax treatment when applicable. The buy and hold approach will outperform the market over the long term (for example, total return).

Long-term investors not only do well, they also sleep well. Over the years, equity investors who own shares of strong successful companies, who don't try to jump in and out of stocks with every change of the wind, are a lot calmer and more confident about their portfolios than those who are trying to time the market.

Momentum Investing

This strategy tries to hitch a ride on stocks that are accelerating in price because the companies are growing at a double-digit rate. The flip side is that at the slightest hint of stiffer competition, production snags or slower sales can cause nearly instantaneous markdowns in the stock prices.

Severe industry problems push down the prices of strong companies' stocks as well as weak companies' stocks. This process creates wonderful opportunities to buy into the strong companies if the industry is not going to be permanently in difficulty.

Technical Analysis

This strategy tries to predict the future price of a stock or the future direction of the stock market based on past price and volume changes. The strategy is based on the concept that stock prices and the markets follow clear trends. Practitioners of this strategy know they can predict future returns if the patterns are identified early.

I have a friend, Jim, who did this all the time—just substitute the words "horse" and "track" for the words "stock" and "market." Jim played the horses, and like the horse track, the stock market has its share of "gurus" touting the future of the races. Most academic studies show investing entirely by technical analysis like the racing form does not work. Many successful investors still use technical analysis in combination with fundamental analysis.

Technical analysis practitioners are called *technicians*. They believe that by looking at the past history of a stock's price movements, one can predict future prices, despite today's economic reports and company news. Technicians and their computers scan graphs or charts of a company's stock prices and trading volumes. They are searching to find patterns that can be projected into the future. "Everything cycles," they will tell you, "and these cycles repeat themselves if you know how to look."

While technical analysis has many uses, investors who blindly follow chart patterns or other tools of technical analysis often find themselves buying after the market has moved up substantially (when there is not much profit potential left). Just as often, they sell after the market has come down substantially and their losses have already begun to pile up.

Technical analysis sounds like black magic to some. Maybe it is, but the fact remains that some technicians do very well predicting market and stock moves. But, like the fundamental analysts, some technicians have success and others do not. Although there is undoubtedly validity in technical market analysis, it does not have all the answers.

Fundamental Analysis

This strategy is mainly concerned with value. Appraise a company's financial condition and management and an industry's competitive position. Examine factors that decide a firm's expected future earnings and dividends. Put a value on the stock accordingly. Look for stocks to buy that are undervalued—for example, stocks that are selling low in relation to their perceived value. The stock market will recognize them later and bid the price higher. Fundamental analysis shows which stocks are overvalued in relation to their perceived value. This is a signal to not buy them ... or to sell them, if owned.

The cornerstone of fundamental analysis is the P/E ratio, price divided by earnings. Over the years, the average P/E ratio for stocks that make up the DJIA has been around 14. Many analysts recommend that investors do not buy stocks with a ratio that is higher than half the average P/E. If the P/E ratio for all stocks on the NYSE is 20, one should pay no more than a P/E ratio of 10 for any given stock.

The return on equity is the amount of money a corporation earns relative to the amount it has invested in plant and equipment. A company should have a return on equity of at least 15 percent for the last 5 years to be considered for investment purposes.

The ultimate value of a company boils down to net sales and profit margins. Of these two, the most important is an accelerating rate of net sales. Management can control expenses or improve the efficiency of the operation. However, sales growth of 10 percent for the last 5 years is what you should look for in a stock candidate.

If you, as an investor, feel generally favorable about the stock market and the industry group into which your stock candidate fits, and you have looked into the above fundamental factors, your chances of having a sound investment are very high. Unfortunately, every other astute investor is looking for this stock as well, and they do not occur often. Usually, the fundamentals are mixed, with some items favorable and others unfavorable.

Pure fundamental analysis has two problems. First, there are many ways of interpreting data, and three stock analysts evaluating the same company may come up with three different conclusions. Second, and more importantly, the price of the stock may not reflect the underlying fundamentals. There are no guaranteed systems.

Contrarian Investing

Contrarian investing is my approach to stock selection, and I swear by it. If you want to make money, do what no one else is doing. Buy when everyone else is selling and hold until everyone else is buying. This is not merely a catchy slogan; it is the very essence of successful investing. Contrary investing is probably the most powerful, simplest, sanest, and most reliable money-making technique ever devised. Contrary investing will enable you to buy low and sell high for maximum profit. It works in any market, from gold and silver to stocks, bonds, currencies, real estate, and collectibles.

Why? Human nature is the same everywhere. You don't need special academic training to profit from it. All you need is an independent mind and an ounce of courage.

Buying on bad news and selling on good news goes against most people's grain. When a company omits its dividends or fires its president, or a chemical factory accidentally leaks tons of poisonous gas into a teeming city, investors tend to become afraid about the prospects for the stock. They're inclined to sell. If you want to make money, your attitude ought to be just the opposite: *Buy.*

As prices go down, you should become more cheerful, and as prices go up you should become more concerned. Why? As prices go down, the stock by definition is closer to the ultimate bottom. When prices go up, you should become more concerned, because the ultimate peak is approaching.

If you want to buy low and sell high, as all of us presumably want to do, you must train yourself to buy when everybody, including yourself, is feeling discouraged, depressed, and full of fear. Buy when the news is all bad; that is likely to be the bottom. Sell when everyone is euphoric and the news is excitingly good, because that is likely to be the top.

Unfortunately, too many people do just the opposite: they buy high and sell low. They're trend followers or, to put it more bluntly, they're crowd followers. They are less fearful when prices are at the top, and that is when they buy ... every time.

The successful investor is a trendsetter, not a trend follower. He or she gets in, and out, ahead of the crowd. To do this, you must think for yourself. Yes, learn from other people, by all means. Don't be pigheaded. Being a contrarian doesn't mean you think you're always right and everybody else is always wrong. Even practicing contrarians make blunders.

When you are listening to other people, though, take what you hear with a grain of salt. Be a skeptic. Never give up your sacred right to judge for yourself whether someone is talking sense or nonsense. It's your money. It's your decision. Nobody else is going to take your losses for you. If you're going to take control of your investments, take control of your emotions first.

THE TOOLS OF CONTRARIAN INVESTING

The simplest and best tools a contrary investor can work with are literally under your nose. They are books, magazines, newspapers, and television (especially the news and financial programs).

If you read *Time, Newsweek, BusinessWeek*, the *Wall Street Journal*, the *New York Times*, or your local newspapers, you'll develop a feel for what the great mass of people are thinking. For the most part, these major magazines and newspapers merely repeat the opinions of the crowd.

You don't need to be a sophisticated investment analyst to interpret what the mass media is reporting. Just look for extreme or hysterical predictions by respected establishment economists and investment professionals.

Don't waste time in trying to figure out what a stock *should be* doing, but look and see what it *is* doing. It is not important to know why a stock is moving up or down (in fact, this is probably unknowable). Instead, concentrate on what happened to the stock in the past when it was in a similar setting.

CLASSIC STOCK MARKET STATEMENTS

At market peaks and bottoms, you'll hear certain types of comments in newspapers, in magazines, or on TV. These phrases recur so often that it's a mystery why people don't try to catch themselves before they make such careless statements:

No end in sight. At just about the top of a stock market boom, a newspaper headline will read, "Stocks Soar; Analysts Say No End In Sight." That was the end; an emotionally tinged comment like "no end in sight" means it is the end. Similar outbursts occur near market bottoms, but the "no end in sight" rhetoric is a classic warning of a top.

Correction someday, but not now. This type of statement is heard at most major market turning points, up or down.

A new standard of value; old values have become obsolete. Analysts and brokers will say, "Well, the price seems crazy, but we're in a new standard. The old parameters don't work anymore."

No buyers to be found. Remember to buy when everyone else is selling. If you buy when the advisors are telling you there are no buyers to be found, you will come pretty close to catching the absolute bottom.

Worst market in years (or decades or ever). At the bottom of the 1987 Black Monday, and after the stock market took its terrible plunge in 2008, within a day or two, respected commentators in the *Wall Street Journal* were quoted as saying, "This is the worst market in 50 years." (Alas, history does repeat itself.) When you hear that note of fear, take courage: the bottom has arrived. You'll also see picturesque metaphors thrown around like bloody, scarred, or battered to describe how badly the market has behaved.

Selling climax. At almost every stock market bottom, some establishment advisor will predict a selling climax. When the Wall Street technicians call for a selling climax, it usually means that the heaviest selling has already occurred and the market is ready to turn around. The climax that everyone fears, a massive liquidation of stock 1987-style, seldom happens.

No buyers. When a market is approaching the bottom, many analysts see the bargains waiting to be grabbed. But nobody has the courage to buy. The resulting general paralysis leaves the crowd too dazed to act; the contrary investor buys with both hands.

MADNESS OF CROWDS

Beg, borrow, or steal the book *Extraordinary Popular Delusions and the Madness of Crowds* by Charles Mackay. It was originally published in 1841 but is still in print.

This is a case study of human folly throughout the ages. This landmark study of the crowd psychology and mass mania throughout history includes accounts of classic scams, grand-scale madness, and deceptions. Described in detail are the Mississippi Scheme that swept France in 1720 and the South Sea Bubble that ruined thousands in England. A must-read saga of the Tulipmania of Holland recounts that fortunes were made and lost on single tulip bulbs.

This book has confirmed for me the madness of crowds that I still see today in the stock market. Bernard Baruch wrote, "I have always thought that if in 1929 we had all continuously repeated 'two and two still makes four,' much of the evil might have been averted."

Madness of Crowds in 1994

Looking back 15 years, we saw many billions of dollars (nobody is sure how much) flowing out of low-paying money market funds, certificates of deposit, and bank accounts. The money was landing with a roar in the stock market, which was then at a new record all-time high. The assets of money market funds decreased $17.9 billion in December 1991, with much of the money being placed in the hot stock market.

The economy hadn't improved, despite repeated cuts in interest rates by the Federal Reserve. Corporate profits were still expected to be bad for many months. President Clinton's popularity had not become significantly better or worse.

Some people did believe that Fed Chairman Alan Greenspan's biggest rate cut of all would finally turn the economy around. Many others were alarmed that lower borrowing costs hadn't, and wouldn't, do the job. Even the Federal Reserve admitted that the economy was lackluster.

Most of the money flowed to Wall Street simply because the new investors, people who never bought stocks before, were reacting to the expectation that stocks would earn more money than investments like certificates of deposit. Such money comes into the market because the return is better than any other.

Wall Street, naturally, was happy about its good fortune. The stock market didn't mind that it won the investment war by default. Money, after all, is money. New investors thought that compared with banks, money market funds, and Treasury bills, the stock market seemed a better place to go. That was good enough to keep stock prices from collapsing.

You might remember that the stock market had placed its hopes on an economic recovery from the successful Persian Gulf War. That had Wall Street smiling, and the new investors kept bringing their money into the stock market. (Especially the darling defense stocks with all those wonder weapons).

Except in the imagination of Washington, the recovery never arrived. Consumers, the backbone of the economy, were just too scared to spend.

The big questions are these: Were there legitimate reasons for buying stocks even though they were well into record territory? If there weren't good reasons to purchase stocks at this time, would the economy provide the justification later?

When stock prices stop climbing, new investors will stop being lured into the market. That is when the deluge of cash, which has been keeping the stock market at record breaking levels, will suddenly stop.

Right then, new investors thought stocks were the only sure thing. All sure things have an end. One market strategist put it best: "I wake up every morning and I'm afraid to be in the market and I'm afraid to be out of it."

The Madness Continues, 2008

Imagine the Federal Reserve Chairman, for example, going on television and saying, "We don't care if Chase Manhattan and Citibank go broke because of their subprime home loans. We don't care if the whole banking system goes down the drain. Let them sink or swim by themselves."

Imagine the Feds releasing the unemployment and GNP figures and not keeping open their right to readjust these figures later.

Obviously, these are impossible happenings.

A cautious mentality prevails in the investment community. Most analysts at the bigger institutions would rather be wrong and respected by their colleagues than be right and regarded as part of the lunatic fringe.

The mentality of most institutions almost guarantees that they will not purchase the truly great long-term investments. Using a bank, pension fund manager, or other institutional investor to manage your investments will produce mediocrity in most cases.

In fact, the performance of stocks recommended by 10 large brokerage firms in the 12 months ended December 31, 2008 all resulted in losses. The *Wall Street Journal* periodically assembles different groups of so-called experts to select timely investments. The experts' recommendations were judged against a portfolio selected by randomly throwing darts at a list of stocks. The darts usually won. Get the point?

Typically, people at the big brokerage firms and the large banks will hedge on what they say to the press. Once in a while, at a major market turning point, they will blow their cool and will make extreme or hysterical predictions that turn up in your morning news.

In addition, you will hear, at important turning points, a chorus of advisors predicting the same thing. (Please note that I'm not arguing that the majority is always wrong. This is an often misunderstood aspect of contrary thinking.)

"Is the market correctly anticipating the economic recovery this time? Or is this the final fake-out that will trap many desperate investors in the lower rung of the price pyramid?"

The majority can be right for some time. But the majority is wrong when it becomes unanimous and hysterical. When you see that such a majority has formed, you can safely conclude that an important turning point is near.

TAKE ADVANTAGE OF THE PROS

There ways of exploiting the knowledge that most professionals won't beat the market. Consider, for example, the professional's cash-to-asset ratio. This shows whether the pro is bearish (holding above-average amounts of cash) or bullish (holding below-average cash). The overwhelming conclusion of extensive studies on this indicator: Do the opposite of the professionals. Turn bullish as the cash-to-assets ratio rises to very high levels, and bearish when it falls to particularly low levels.

Among large mutual funds, for example, favorite issues that appear in many portfolios include Procter & Gamble, IBM, General Electric, ITT, General Motors, Texaco, and Wal-Mart, for example.

When you think of innovation and growth, does this list fit the bill? Large investors are required to favor some criteria above all others, such as predictability, market dominance, and financial strength. Does the above list now fit the bill?

Yes. The big institutions must invest predominately in companies with large numbers of shares issued. When billions of dollars are invested, the liquid assets provided by large capitalization stocks are essential. But this often leads to mediocre performance.

Also, take advantage of window-dressing—the professional's habit, before each quarter's end, of dumping stocks that have been losers. Excellent long-term holdings can be purchased at bargain prices, particularly at the end of the year. This is when the pro's portfolio window-dressing is most obvious. (Some call this "burying the evidence.")

Focus during the last few weeks of the year on stocks that are at new 52-week lows. Assuming their fundamentals are still attractive, chances are good that these stocks will bounce back early in January once the end-of-year selling pressure is over.

Don't fall for the sales pitch that the pros know more than you do. The truth is that you could be better off doing the opposite of what they would do with your money. Detect the trends of large institutions, and trade at the same time. Usually, large volume surges accompanied by price appreciation are evidence that the big buyers are expanding their position in an issue. Institutional holdings are shown in many publications, such as *Value Line* and *Your Guide to Standard & Poor's Stock Reports.*

Magazines are probably the best indicator of the intermediate-term trend, say six months to two years. Paul Montgomery, an analyst, has looked through more than 3,000 issues of *Time* magazine, going back to 1924 when the magazine first began publication.

In four out of five cases, he found that whenever *Time* ran a cover story on an economic subject, the results within one year were exactly opposite of those predicted by the editors.

Any economic news that makes the cover of *Time, Newsweek,* or *BusinessWeek* is old news. The markets have already adjusted for it (discounted it, as Wall Street says). Thus, the next big price move is likely to be just the opposite of what the mass media is telling you to expect.

In the spring of 1984, *Time* and *BusinessWeek* regularly shouted for investors to buy utility stocks, particularly shares of companies engaged in constructing nuclear power plants. In February 1985, *Time* announced on its cover that nuclear power was "bombing out."

Three months later, in its May 21 issue, *BusinessWeek* took a swipe at the entire utility industry, asking, "Are Utilities Obsolete?"

Sure enough, the Dow Jones Utility Average made its low for the year only a week after the *BusinessWeek* article hit the newsstands. Utility stocks proved to be one of the best performing sectors of the market for the rest of the year.

The problems with nuclear power plants were (and are) real and serious. But when a controversy is splashed on the cover of a magazine like *BusinessWeek*, with a multimillion circulation, it's something that everyone knows.

There is an old contrarian saying, "What everyone knows isn't worth knowing." When everyone knows that utilities are in trouble, the stocks are probably bumping along near the bottom. Once all the bad news is out, the stocks have nowhere to go but higher.

Your daily financial Internet stations offer the most up-to-date insights into what the crowd is thinking. (For the short-term decisions, these broadcasts are especially valuable for discerning the day-to-day mood of the market.)

A market that has gone crazy is likely to turn around almost immediately. In fact, the peak for gold in 2008, when gold soared to over $1,000 an ounce, was not only a short-term turning point but an intermediate and finally a long-term turning point as well.

Unfortunately, another reliable contrary indicator is the advice provided by stock market advisers themselves. At major market turning points, most advisers lean the wrong way.

Most advisers, including newsletter writers, are crowd followers. In fact, many advisers make it their business to follow the trend. For that reason, they frequently become more bullish as prices go up, and often more bearish as prices go down.

Investors Intelligence, a newsletter and web site based in Larchmont, New York, tracks advisory opinion, tallying the number of advisers who are bullish, bearish or calling for a correction. (Bulls are expecting prices to rise, bears are looking for the market to go down, and correctionists are sitting undecided.) You'll see, when the stock market peaks, that more than 75 percent of advisers with a firm opinion are expecting the market to go higher.

Option buyers have about the worst record of investors in any market. They're a perfect foil for the contrarian, because they always buy calls heavily near the peak, and they buy puts heavily near the bottom. A call gives a chance to profit from a rise in the stock. A put gives a chance to profit from a decline in the stock. In short, the option speculators generally do the opposite of what they should be doing if they want to make money.

Finally, a word about television. Be sure to watch the TV investment programs if you're looking for a list of stocks to sell. Studies have tracked the performance of stocks recommended on these shows. The conclusions are startling. In good markets or bad, stocks recommended on them typically underperform the market by 5 to 10 percent within the next two months. Why?

Because most of the speakers work for brokerage firms or publish investment newsletters, their clients know what the speakers are going to recommend on the show. So they buy the stocks in advance. After the show has aired the recommendations, the crowd buys those stocks the following Monday, and the insiders gladly dump the merchandise into the public's hands. Be careful before you buy any stock that is recommended on these television programs.

> Don't try to buy at the bottom and sell at the top. It can't be done, except by liars.
>
> —Bernard Baruch

INSIDER INFORMATION

There is one guaranteed system that is universally successful: inside information. If you know that ABC Corporation is going to show a large and unexpected earnings increase, or that it will be a buyout candidate at a high price that will be made public three days from now, you can buy shares of ABC today and be confident of seeing them rise after the announcement.

Inside information is the very best stock advice. But there are two problems with it. First, it is illegal to use this information to make trades. Second, inside information is just that, inside, and is usually not available to an outsider.

When an individual investor gets to hear about it, it is no longer inside information. What masquerades as inside information is usually no more than a stock tip or, more appropriately, a stock rumor. Small investors love tips and rumors, mistaking them for true inside information.

This is a true story. A friend overheard an employee of a large Denver company in the cafeteria during lunch. He heard that the company was going to be bought out. The stock was sure to go for double what it was presently selling for. He wanted to pass this inside information on to a few close investor friends. The buyout proposal was true. Some investors did buy that stock immediately. When they had filled their orders on the stock, another item appeared on the local radio news. The purchaser had escaped from a mental hospital that day and was in no position financially or mentally to follow through on the buyout offer.

This type of inside information usually produces a loss instead of a gain. The important thing to remember is that people with true inside information do not broadcast it. First, it is illegal; and second, it will lose its value if widely known. Generally, it is safe to assume that any hot tips you hear are no more than gossip and rumors. Even worse, deliberately misleading information may be distributed by people who have already taken an opposite position on the stock. It is tempting to act on such tips; you will be happier sticking to sound investment principles.

How often in the trading room where I operated have I heard that the President has been shot? Or Armand Hammer slipped in the bathtub, and later it was revealed that it was his wife who slipped and not he. How these news items change the stock market, or one company, is amazing.

Everybody has a good story; brokers, financial advisers, bankers and your friends all have detailed and plausible-sounding explanations for their recommendations. If it didn't make sense to them, they wouldn't be interested in it in the first place. So how does the average investor go about deciding which story to believe? Where and when should you invest your money? Which is a winning stock? Which is a loser?

INSIDER TRADING IS NOT ALWAYS ILLEGAL

Insider trading can be defined as the buying and selling of a company's stock by its officers, directors, major shareholders, or other people with close ties to the company. These people may legally buy or sell stock of the company they are working for. The reasons for these insider transactions can be many and are not automatically considered illegal.

Insiders very often receive stock options as part of their regular compensation package. Having exercised their options, when they want cash, either to exercise more options or for personal reasons, they sell some of their stock. Thus, they tend to be net sellers most of the time. Insiders' sale of stock is not necessarily a negative indicator of the company's position. So do not cry foul the next time you see that a corporate insider has sold 500,000 shares of his holdings.

Instead, say, "thank you" when you discover the same person is buying an additional 500,000 shares for hard dollars. Such a purchase would be a reason to take a closer look at the company; insiders recognize low-risk value when they see it. It is an event that deserves further scrutiny when the person turns around and buys at the market price and not at artificial discounts.

Insiders generally buy under the following conditions:

- When an announced development will improve the company's profits.
- When the stock price has fallen so far below the intrinsic values that the shares are cheap.
- When stock buying is part of a regular investment program.

As an outsider, you can make money from any of these situations! However, insiders may be too optimistic about the company's future, so this is not a foolproof method.

Following insiders is much easier today than it was 25 years ago. Under SEC rules, insiders must report detailed information on their trades within certain time limits. This information is made available to the public in the financial press.

BUY, SELL, OR HOLD?

The heart of successful investing is determining *when* to buy, sell, or hold your stocks. Several factors are of extreme importance in arriving at a decision.

To buy a stock, you must research the following items. Needed information can be found in the financial press.

- *Low P/E*—Should be no higher than half of the market multiple.
- *Current price*—Should be less than the average of the 52-week high and low prices.
- *Increasing sales* and earnings trend over the last five years.
- *Dividend payout ratio*—Percentage of net earnings allocated to shareholders should not exceed 30 percent.
- *Annual report*—Analyze independent auditor's report; verify financial information and *study* all the footnotes; and read the CEO's report, which should state his opinion of the company's future outlook.

To sell a stock, you should research the same factors as above, using the quarterly and annual reports as your source material.

- *High P/E ratio*—If at market multiple or higher, consider selling.
- *Current price*—Should be higher than the average of the 52-week high and low prices.

- *Decreasing sales* and earnings trend.
- *Net dividends*—Should exceed net earnings.
- *Annual report* (see above)—Negative information should be an influence in your determination to sell.

To hold a stock, use the same procedure as for selling. Whether to sell or hold is based on judgments of the above factors. If two consecutive quarterly reports produce increasingly negative determinations, sell.

Upon the release of negative news about a company, many investors immediately dump their stock, causing the price to drop. Be patient and hold; in most cases, the price will rise, at which time the stock should be reevaluated. Sell if you wouldn't buy the stock. Base your decision to sell on the guidelines you established for your portfolio management. Do not sell based on emotions, because when the price of stock falls, you have already lost money.

Avoid this big mistake: Never wait to break even. Others are waiting also. Whenever the stock price moves up, the others will start selling, keeping the price of the stock from continuing up. When you decide to sell, don't make excuses for not selling. Make a decision and do it! Sell all or none of an issue; don't hold back. When selling stocks, have discipline and patience, and follow your rules.

> Don't gamble! Take all your savings and buy some good stock and hold it 'til it goes up, and then sell it. If it don't go up, don't buy it.
>
> —Will Rogers

Buying and selling stock is easy. The hard part is knowing what stock to buy and when to sell it. Remember that every transaction must have two parties—for every buyer, there must be a seller. Every time a trade takes place, there are two presumably well-informed individuals who have exactly opposite opinions of the future price of a stock. This is the heart of the stock market, where there is every reason to believe that if you are clever and diligent and lucky, you will consistently be able to do well.

Buy Low and Sell High

An efficient and personally rewarding investment plan uses a combination of all the strategies. Be contrary. Use fundamental analysis to select stock. Observe momentum and technical analysis on when to take action. Buy and hold the stock until fundamental analysis and contrarian opinion says to sell the stock. This, I believe, presents an opportunity . . . using all strategies to outperform the buy and hold method alone.

Any sensible investment strategy works well if you are patient. There is no single magic formula to do well in stock investing over the long term. There are several sensible investment strategies, and the key is to follow one of them consistently, with great discipline, because no particular investment approach always works well.

Where does all this leave you? How can you take advantage of contrarian investing, which I've described as the simplest, sanest, most powerful, and reliable investment tool ever devised? No one can do your thinking for you. If you'd like to take advantage of contrarian investing, you must make the time to apply all the techniques outlined for you.

A great mistake investors make is to try switching from one strategy to another to make sure they are always riding the fastest horse around the track.

Buying and Selling = Commission Costs

Wall Street brokerages make the bulk of their profits from transaction fees. Investors are aware that every transaction in the financial world is accompanied by a commission charge. Many investments that look profitable before taxes and commissions would show a loss if these were included. It is important to factor these expenses into any investment, because until transaction costs are figured in and paid, there can be no gain. Commissions can be had at all-time lows; check the discount brokerages.

However, commissions are only part of the costs. *Spreads* are hidden, and can be as high or higher than the commission charge. A spread is the same as a markup in the retail business. It is the difference between an investor's selling price and a buyer's bid price. The spread can be a major influence on the results for both the buyer and seller.

When you ask for a quotation on a security, you will be asked whether you are buying or selling. There are always two quotes. The *bid* is what you can sell the stock for, and the *ask* is what you would have to pay to buy it. The difference between the two is the spread. The spread divided by the ask price is the percentage that the spread contributes to your transaction costs. On the most popular stocks with high volumes of trading, this can be as low as .01 per share. On less-traded stocks, it can be as high as .25 per share.

For example, you wish to purchase ABC Corporation and the quotation is $4\frac{1}{2}$ bid, 5 asked; the spread is $\frac{1}{2}$. This contributes 10 percent to the cost of buying ABC stock. It means that ABC has to go up 10 percent before you cover the cost of the spread.

There are spreads on every security, even those traded on the stock exchanges. The stock quotation listed is the last trade price, generally in the middle of the spread. The spreads are necessary to have a market. A small spread, like those traded on the major exchanges, is a proper and necessary part of the business. Watch out for the large spread, the high-percentage spread that wipes out most of your potential profit before you even begin. Over the counter (OTC) stocks have the larger spreads. Low-priced stocks have higher spreads than high-priced stocks.

Penny stocks are the worst of all; the spread on some of these can be more than 100 percent. This is the one I alluded to at first in this book. "You don't have to pay a commission on this stock, it is included in the quoted price," says the friendly voice on the phone. Now you know how it is possible.

Remember, Bid Is to Buy, Ask Is to Sell, Last Is in the Middle

One of the best pieces of advice I can give you, when buying or selling, is to go in at the last price, which is the price of the last trade. Buy and sell at the last price. When you get quotes, ask for the last price. The last price is usually in the middle of the spread, unless the stock is moving up or down where the last price can be at the bid or ask. Trading at the last price minimizes the spread. Remember, if you buy with a half spread and sell with a half spread, that is one dollar in cost to you on a round trip, just for the spread. Remember whose money it is? Trade at a discount broker, minimize the spread, and make as few trades as possible.

PERFORMANCE RECORDS

Remember, "the little type taketh away," so read the fine print. The fine print I'm talking about is the seldom-noticed section at the bottom of the performance charts. It is used by mutual funds, stock brokerages, invest-ment advisers, and newsletters showing their performance record for the past years. "Commissions, management fees, and taxes are not always included in these calculations." The reason, of course, is that emerging growth can be turned to submerging growth if commissions, management fees, and taxes are taken into account.

INVESTING CONSIDERATIONS

Since I believe in managing my own investment account, I do have com-missions, the spread, and taxes to reckon with. This is what you have to consider when investing:

- Federal income tax on the gain
- State income tax on the gain
- The spread on the transactions
- Commissions on the transactions

You only pay taxes on profits. Yet expenses are incurred, whether you make a profit or not. Thus, a 10 percent loss on the market value of your securities could result in a greater loss when the trade costs are figured in while you hold the stock. If you sell the stock, you can figure in another loss.

If you can cut your transaction costs by only 1 percent for each trade that you make, you will save 2 percent from each round trip investment. If your performance would have averaged 10 percent per year, it will average 12 percent per year. Applying time value tables is very helpful in this regard. If you invest $10,000 over 30 years at 10 percent, it will grow to $175,000. At 12 percent, your $10,000 will grow to $300,000. So don't let anyone tell you that commissions and spreads don't matter.

The security industry doesn't like to talk about spreads. I'm amazed that even many seasoned investors don't know about them. The brokerage firm makes money every time you trade. They would like your trade to be profitable for you, of course, but that is not essential, since they get their money whether you win or lose. That is why your broker is so friendly and is willing to give you a break on commissions.

TRANSACTION COSTS COMPARED

The next step is to compare transaction costs:

- The highest in fees are the penny stocks: 20 to 300 percent (in and out).
- Limited partnerships fees: 6 to 20 percent (in and out).
- Secondary offerings fees: 5 to 10 percent (in and out).
- Full commission brokers: 6 percent, unless you are a good customer who haggles to get 3 to 4 percent (in and out).
- Discount brokers get between $5 and $10. There are management fees.
- Loaded mutual funds: 4 to 8.5 percent.

Most loaded mutual funds charge on only one end of the transaction, and competition from the no-load funds are forcing fees lower. Studies have shown that there is no correlation between a mutual fund's load and its performance. The only thing you get for the fee is a big smile from the salesman.

Finally, no-load mutual funds normally have no transaction fee costs.

We have to distinguish no-load from low-load. A true no-load has no sales or redemption charges. If you send in $1,000, you purchase $1,000 worth of shares at the current net asset value (NAV). All your money goes right to work for you. If you sell, you get all of the NAV back; there is no spread—the NAV is the same whether you are buying or selling.

Low-load funds have transaction costs. One little caveat to watch out for is that many former no-load funds are becoming low-load funds.

All mutual funds have advisory fees or management fees to cover their services and expenses. These ongoing fees range from 0.5 to 2.5 percent of the assets under management per year. You can multiply the assets by the charges and see that this is no charity business.

All costs have to be considered when comparing the different approaches to investing. If we have 100 shares of ABC selling for $20 and wish to switch to XYZ at $20, there are two transactions with two commissions. In addition there is a cost, due to the spread. The Bid-Ask Spread (bid is to buy and ask is to sell) will increase the cost of switching. The spread is the differences between the two prices' bid and ask, and constitutes a quotation. We may find in our example that the current spread on a $20 stock is 19.88 to 20.12: We would receive 19.88 for the stock sold, and pay 20.12 for the stock purchase, a difference of 25 cents.

TO MAKE MONEY IN THE STOCK MARKET, DON'T LOSE ANY

You pay commissions every time you switch holdings. Investment approaches that require portfolio turnover several times a year must outperform the market. You have to do this just to stay even, compared with a buy and hold approach.

Financial data reveals that common stocks provide high returns compared to "safer" investments, and the risk in a practical sense becomes unimportant as the holding period is extended. While there are stock market cycles, long-term investors can outlast the ups and downs of the roller-coaster ride they will experience.

If the stock market is not as risky as generally thought, why do we all know people who have lost money in the market? They have made every stupid blunder possible. The market is risky for the short-term investor. As we saw, playing the market or speculating costs more in transaction fees and taxes. The losers try to make large, short-term profits by trying to time and predict market swings. Many investors do not diversify; thus, they take on more risk and more loss than they would have had to . . . plus, they give up safety.

Common sense is the knack of seeing things as they are, and doing things as they ought to be done.

—C. E. Stowe

If fate throws a knife at you, there are two ways to catch it: by the blade or by the handle.

—Anonymous

CHAPTER 7

Dividend Reinvestment Plans

A company may take some of the cash it has available and pay it out to the shareholders of record. This is called a dividend. It is done on a per-share basis by dividing the cash amount by the number of shares outstanding. The dividend yield is determined by dividing the price of each share into the dividend paid.

Example: The stock price is $15, and $1 (annual dividend paid quarterly) is to be paid; that would be a 6.6 percent dividend yield.

Using the dividend yield to determine whether to buy a stock is informative, but by no means complete. Earlier, I did not reveal that the cash dividend was from profits or earnings. The dividend could be paid out of debt.

XYZ Corporation has paid dividends every quarter for 20 years, and every dividend is slightly more than the previous year. You may think by this action that all is well. Lately, however, the market share of the company's products has been declining. The board of directors meet. They have seen their stock value rise. They want the shareholders to see the dividend and see it increasing. Profits are down and the cash flow is drying up. The directors borrow funds for operations and to pay an increased dividend.

The dividend is paid continually for the ensuing year. The board feels, at first, that they can turn things around. But the problems cannot be solved.

The quarterly dividend is paid for the year as the company drops into complete insolvency and possible bankruptcy. Finally, the dividend is stopped and the stock falls.

Remember, dividend yield is important, but you have to:

- Keep it in perspective.
- Study other information, such as the company's balance sheet.
- Do not rely on yields for buying or selling stocks.

Now let's look at the other extreme. A company is doing well. Debt is decreasing, earnings are up and increasing, but the dividend is small. Yes, the company could pay out more, but the board of directors has decided to use the funds to grow the company, by modernizing the factories or perhaps to buy out a competitor. Another concern could be taxation.

In the current tax code, dividends are not deductible. The company has to pay taxes on the money it makes to give out in dividends. The company may be in the 15, 25, 31, or 35 percent tax rate. Now when you, the shareholder, receive the dividend, you have to claim and pay tax on the dividend and do so in your tax bracket. This is double taxation. I hesitate to say what the new tax rates will be with a new administration taking over the government. They have said taxes will have to go up.

At a meeting of the board of directors they realize that if they pay out the dividends, they know you will be taxed. The company will be taxed no matter whether they pay, but they can stop the second level of taxation simply by not paying it. They could use this money to increase the value of the company; would you be better off?

If we are investing for income, then we would look for companies with a high dividend payout and take the growth part of the earnings as a bonus.

I like to share in the profits of the corporation. I take all the dividends I can take, but for the most part I would rather the company keep the profits and expand the business. These dividends include regular dividends (which I look for all the time).

> Money is of no value; it cannot spend itself. All depends on the skill of the spender.
>
> —Ralph Waldo Emerson

Many companies distribute a share of their net profits to shareholders in the form of dividends. The dividends are paid in a fixed amount for each share of stock held. Although most companies make quarterly payments in cash (checks), dividends may also be in property, script, or stock. Dividends must be voted on by the company's board of directors before each payment.

A dividend reinvestment plan (DRP, pronounced "drip"), also called automatic dividend reinvestment, is a plan whereby stockholders may automatically reinvest dividend payments in additional shares of the company's stock. Instead of receiving the normal dividend checks, participating stockholders will receive quarterly notification of shares purchased and shares held in their accounts. DRPs are normally an inexpensive way of purchasing additional shares of stock, since the fees are low or are completely absorbed by the company.

DIVIDEND REINVESTING PLANS AND DOLLAR COST AVERAGING

When asked what the market was going to do, J. P. Morgan reportedly said, "It will fluctuate." Morgan was right!

Why pay top dollar for shares when you can average out your costs with dollar cost averaging? In fact, whenever the stock price is below your average cost, invest more money for more shares and average your cost down.

Dollar cost averaging takes the ups and downs in the market and turns them to your advantage. Instead of trying to time the highs and lows, you should invest the same amount of money at regular intervals over a long period in your DRP portfolio. Since the plan is to ride out the ups and downs, it makes little or no difference in your results what the mood of the market is when you begin. During the holding period, one's average price per share is lower than the mean average price. This is basic: $100 buys 10 shares of stock at $10, only 5 shares at $20 when the market is higher. The mean average price was $15. But the investor owns 15 shares and paid just $200 for an average price per share of just $13.33. In a DRP monies are added continually. When funds are available, you should periodically purchase additional shares, to enhance the value of dollar cost averaging.

There are approximately 1,000 high-quality companies, from Abbott Labs to Zurn Industries, who offer their shareholders the opportunity to buy shares directly through the company's transfer agent, completely bypassing brokers and brokerage commissions. DRPs permit plan members to make optional cash investments from as little as $10 to as much as $10,000 a month.

Discipline is all-important. You can't chicken out when you see the market dropping. You have to be consistent and persistent and follow the dollar cost averaging system. Long term is the only way dollar cost averaging works. The average person wouldn't invest this way. Many filled with fear would panic and want to get out of the market when it was low but rush in when it was high.

Dollar cost averaging doesn't guarantee a profit. If you have to sell at the bottom of the market, no system is going to give you a gain. You've got to have the mental and financial resources to ride out the roller coaster.

THE COMPOUNDING EFFECT

Dividend reinvestment plans represent a truly "win-win" situation for shareholders and corporations. On the one hand, they offer a low-cost (often no-cost) way for stockholders to accumulate shares. For the sponsoring corporations, they provide a way to raise equity capital inexpensively and also increase shareholder loyalty.

When you participate in a DRP, the dividends increase your number of shares; thus the next dividend is computed on an increased ownership. This compounding effect will make a dramatic impact on your investment results.

DRPs: ADVANTAGES FOR THE INVESTOR

For purchasing stock, there is no commission charge, or just a small charge, depending on the company policy. More than 100 firms have DRPs that permit participants to buy shares at discounts from market prices. These discounts usually range from 3 percent to 10 percent.

Most plans permit optional cash payments directly to the DRPs to purchase additional shares, usually at market prices. The minimum purchase in many plans is as low as $10. When the cash available for a purchase will not buy a full share, fractions of a share are purchased. These are figured to four decimal places, and these fractions have dividends paid to them as well.

A few plans permit new stockholders to buy directly from the company, bypassing a broker completely.

When you want to sell, many firms will let you sell through the DRPs. Usually, you pay a small fee, less than a discount broker's fee. A few DRPs allow you to redeem your shares at no charge. Most companies will send you stock certificates, which you then have to sell through a broker. If your holdings include any fractional shares, the company normally will buy these back, as fractional shares are not issued. Regular statements are mailed for recordkeeping.

There are some disadvantages. The purchases are done automatically on the purchase date set by the company, usually once a month or quarterly. You cannot enter a limit order, or specify a price upon which you want to purchase. There will be a time lag between your decision to buy and when the transaction is made.

DRPs: ADVANTAGES FOR THE COMPANIES

DRPs improve shareholder loyalty and goodwill. Investor shareholders will favor their companies when it comes to buying goods or services.

Corporations like wide ownership of their shares. A corporate raider or unfriendly suitor would have difficulty accumulating votes for a proxy battle or hostile takeover.

Individual investors generally invest for the long term, which keeps the volatility of a stock low. Wide ownership and continuous purchases through a reinvestment plan give market support for the share price.

DRPs reduce the number of dividend checks and stock certificates that must be prepared and mailed. These savings offset some operating costs of a reinvestment plan.

The investor relations office of a company will supply information about the company's DRP program, its availability, and what offers are obtainable through it.

Most DRPs limit participation to shareholders of record and require that the stock be registered in the participants' name, not a *street name*. (Street name describes stocks held in the broker's name on behalf of their customers).

Some plans provide a discount, not only on the shares bought with reinvested dividends, but also on shares purchased with optional cash payments.

> When prices are high, they run to buy. When prices are low, they let them go.
>
> —Ian Notley

USING DRPs TO SELECT STOCKS

First, you need to decide which of the thousands of stocks you wish to study and eventually add to your portfolio. To cut down the list of potential investments, consider companies with dividend reinvestment plans, as the use of these plans will develop a sizeable portfolio more quickly.

Some thoughts on money management: Saving is done a little at a time. Few people can save money by saving only the big chunks, such as the sale of a house or receiving an inheritance. True savings comes from the few dollars that are put aside out of every paycheck. This money should be put into a separate savings account and used only for stock purchases when they are a "buy." DRPs are an excellent way to enhance your investment savings account.

SAFETY WITH A SMALL INVESTMENT

You can be in the stock market with a small investment. With only $500, you can diversify your portfolio to include up to 10 different stocks by the use of DRPs.

Dividends are automatically reinvested. You will receive a computer-generated confirmation of each transaction (including dividends) and a quarterly statement of the activity in your account.

Once the money goes in, it must stay in. To reach your goal requires a long-term commitment.

Remember: Money × Return × Time = Your Goal

DIVIDEND REINVESTMENT PLANS AND THE COMPOUNDING EFFECT

The money your investments earn in the plan—the dividends—are reinvested in the plan instead of being paid to you. Over time, your returns also produce earnings. This *compounding* effect can make a dramatic impact on your investment results. The sooner you begin investing, the greater the effect. Look at the stock and reinvested dividend performance below to see just how big a difference starting now, rather than later, can make. Remember, investing takes time and money.

THE DIVIDEND DEBATE

"Dividend increases are always good, they make the price of the stock go up."

"Dividend cuts are always bad, they make the price of the stock go down."

Both of these statements are false.

"Dividends are always welcomed and expected by most shareholders, without regard from where the money is actually coming." This is true.

A dividend increase is not always perceived as a positive by the market, although executives want it to be viewed that way. If management is signaling its own expectations of increased future cash flow, that is a positive signal. A dividend increase also can mean that the firm is not investing in the future, resulting in a lack of growth potential, which is a bad signal.

> Because change is inevitable, vision is essential.
>
> —Anonymous

One should not assume a dividend cut will send investors rushing to the exits. If the dividend is reduced for all the right reasons, and if the news is not a total surprise, the market reaction may indeed be confident. In a tough business climate, with many companies desperately trying to maintain their dividend payout, a dividend cut may appear to be smart. The trick, of course, is to send a clear message that the company is serious about a successful and profitable future operation.

A dividend cut will not always lead to a decline in the price of the stock. There are many noteworthy cases where cutting the dividend was a good thing and was recognized as such.

For example, in 1993, because of a hint three months earlier about a long-overdue shakeup at a multibillion-dollar conglomerate, Wall Street was not caught by surprise. The dividend cut was much less significant than the pluses of the restructuring program implemented by the company.

The turnaround plan called for cuts in staff and capital spending, consolidations, and asset sales. The company hoped to reverse the direction of its cash flow, which was a negative $300 million in 1992. The dividend cut alone was predicted to save about $400 million annually. The company hoped to boost return on equity to 18 percent in 1994, up from 10 percent the prior year.

Generally speaking, U.S. corporations go to great lengths to keep from cutting their dividends. Boardroom logic holds that steady dividends keep shareholders happy and maintain the stock's price. Most corporations have a policy of paying consistent dividend increases. The companies keep raising their payout, even when they are sustaining losses. They believe that above all else, their investors value consistency.

In difficult times, dividends don't decline as much as earnings, because companies absorb some reduction of profit with their retained earnings account. If more cuts and omissions of dividends become unavoidable, it's not so much what companies do as how they do it. A firm that suddenly omits its dividend without explanation or warning is probably going to have the price of its stock collapse.

On the other hand, some companies prefer to increase their dividends, even if it means stretching themselves thin. They believe that this will make them appear stronger than other companies in their industry. Investors should look at the payout ratios of other companies in that industry group. If a couple of widely tracked companies have cut their dividends, and yours did not, current research is necessary.

Once a dividend is raised, it's hard, if not impossible, to backtrack unless there is a crisis. CFOs (chief financial officers) have an obligation to consider all possible uses of the earnings, including keeping the money in-house and building up retained earnings. Raising the dividend is the easy and popular thing to do, and stockholders welcome increases. Increasing the dividend might not be best for the company.

DRPs depend on dividends. Do some research to find out whether your company's dividend is secure; check the *dividend payout ratio* (the percentage of net earning allocated to stockholders, which should not exceed 30 percent). For example, a company earning $5 per share and paying a dividend of $4.75 per share has very weak dividend coverage. Poor coverage means the company has less leeway to raise dividends or keep them at the same level, in the event that earnings decline. Companies paying most of their earnings in dividends have little left for investment to provide for future earnings growth. Stocks of firms with high payout ratios appeal primarily to investors seeking high current income.

Should investors seek companies with high payout ratios? Most firms pay out a reasonably constant percentage of their earnings. Earnings not paid out are reinvested in the business. Therefore, a company with a low or nonexistent payout ratio has high need for capital, either because of high debt or high growth or both. Investors should choose the combination of yield and growth that best meets their objectives. Typically, one must be traded for the other.

For those interested in the long pull, $1,000 at 8 percent will grow to over 42 quadrillion dollars in four hundred years. Evidently the first hundred years are the hardest.

—Sidney Homer

Thrift is a wonderful virtue ... especially in an ancestor.

—Anonymous

CHAPTER 8

Picking and Dealing with a Stockbroker

Wall Street is the only place that people ride to work in a Rolls Royce to get advice from those who take the subway.

—Warren E. Buffett

The classic warning "buyer beware" has never been more timely.

Investors who believe in financial planning, who think that the future can be secured through the valued advice of their trusted brokers, are in for a rude awakening. Most brokers are not investment experts; they are super sales people.

Stockbrokers these days are particularly anxious to build up their client rosters. For example, during the past week I received an engraved invitation from a stockbroker with a major house, offering to put me on his mailing list for special investment opportunities. I also received a personal letter from a lawyer friend recommending a particular broker, and a hard-sell phone call, from a total stranger, urging me to invest immediately in what he described as a hot new stock issue.

Present or potential investors across the country are receiving similar recommendations and solicitations. Cold calls have always been part of the brokerage business. Brokers are now under pressure from their firms to produce high levels of commission business to cover such steadily rising costs as electronic devices, office rents, transaction charges, printing, mailing, postage, and other overhead costs.

Any broker worth his salt these days functions more as a financial planner than as an old-fashioned customer's representative.

In one respect, very little has changed: Brokers' compensation still depends on commission income. (It's not hard to understand, therefore, why some brokers may encourage heavy turnover in their customer's accounts.)

Naturally, the more money you have, the more appealing you are to brokers. Even if you're not a big hitter, many are still interested in handling your investments. The problem is finding the one who's right for you.

WE INVEST TO MAKE MONEY

What is the reason you invest? Do you want to own securities that increase in value, sell securities at a profit, or receive cash dividends?

If these are the reasons you are investing, then in seeking advice from others you are asking them how to make money. Previously in this book, you learned that to succeed in the stock market you had to think and act like a smart businessperson. Business people seek professional advice on various aspects of their business. They do not expect to be told how to operate to make a profit. Decision making, research, and actions result from your required time commitment for successful investing. When you rely on others to make investment profits for you, you are expecting a service for which there is no equal in any other business.

> We are all manufacturers; some make good, and others make excuses.

Investors often seek the advice of experts: When they are sick, they visit a physician; if they have legal matters, they consult an attorney. Because they know little or nothing about medicine or law, they must place their trust and faith in professionals.

Investors seek investment advice from experts and trust them with their most precious possession, their money. They expect these experts to help them stay ahead of inflation while at the same time reaching their financial goals.

This concept of trust in these matters is so important that the law gives a special requirement to anyone who handles other people's finances. These people are known as fiduciaries. Bankers are fiduciaries, and so are attorneys and of course, investment advisers. A fiduciary has a duty to always act in a positive manner toward his client. The investment adviser must avoid any conduct that would harm the investor.

Stockbrokers are not fiduciaries. They are salespeople.

THE BUCK STARTS HERE

The buck, as in a dollar bill, starts with you . . . to make it or lose it.

Investment advice can be obtained from a variety of sources. You can use darts, astrology, your brother-in-law, friends, barber, hearsay, and yes, stockbrokers. Some of the above-mentioned investment sources work some of the time—but not always, as we now know.

Why do you need a stockbroker? Only a broker can execute an order to buy or to sell stocks. Only a broker whose brokerage firm is a member of a stock exchange can trade stocks on that exchange. Stockbrokers are called registered representatives. This means that they have passed a Series 7 exam and are registered with the Securities and Exchange Commission (SEC) to represent their brokerage firms.

Stockbrokers electronically send their customer's orders to the floor brokers. They are employees of a member firm, and execute orders, as agents, on the floor of the exchange. The floor broker joins other brokers and the specialist dealing in the security being bought or sold. They execute the trade at the best competitive price available. A specialist, a member of a stock exchange, is given an exclusive right to conduct transactions in certain stocks. In return, they maintain an orderly market. All orders to buy or sell a specific stock go to the specialist in that stock. The specialist matches the buy and sells orders and completes the transactions.

The specialist has the responsibility to see that there is an orderly market with no gross imbalances of buyers and sellers. If, for a brief period, there is a shortage of buys or sells, the specialist either buys or sells shares from his personal account to keep the trading going. If there is a large difference in the bid and ask price of the stock, the specialist may temporarily suspend trading until the imbalance corrects, either by the appearance of buyers and sellers or by a change in the price of the stock. The system of specialists operating on the stock exchanges serves to maintain a very liquid and orderly market. That is why it is possible to buy or sell stock at any time.

On completion of the transaction, the stockbroker back at the firm notifies the customer. The trade is printed on the ticker tape and is displayed electronically around the country. All this can be done in 10 seconds on an actively traded stock. If you are monitoring the tape you can see your trade completed.

Stocks are identified by *stock symbols*, which are the letter or sequence of letters used to identify a security. For example, on the consolidated tape, F is for Ford, T is for AT&T, EK is for Eastman Kodak, and SGP is for Schering Plough. Some symbols of other well-known stocks include KO for Coca-Cola, PEP for Pepsi Cola, XON for Exxon, MOT for Motorola, MSFT for Microsoft, and HPQ for Hewlett-Packard.

Stock symbols are different from the abbreviations used to identify the same companies in the stock tables of newspapers. The *Wall Street Journal* displays the symbols for stocks every day. You can request a stock symbols guide from your broker. You will need to know the symbols for all your stocks. This enables you to watch them on the ticker or when using video display terminals.

Seats are bought and sold on the exchanges, though there are actually no seats (chairs) on the trading floor. Trades are made while everybody stands, jumps, yells, and writes. The trend is to go to all-electronic trading, and soon this scene will become a thing of the past.

Each time you buy or sell stock, you pay a commission. A portion of that commission goes to your broker. The rest goes to the firm to cover costs and provide a profit.

Brokers will quote you their commissions; all commissions are open for negotiation. Usually, only investors who trade frequently or in large blocks of stock receive lower commission rates. This applies as well to the discount brokers. Remember, commissions are negotiable; it pays to ask for a better rate.

The ideal stockbroker is highly experienced, ethical, brilliant, cordial, patient, wise, levelheaded, and spends all day at it. In 38 years of dealing with registered representatives (also known as vice presidents, first vice presidents, senior vice presidents, account executives, investment representatives, financial planners, account executives, agents, money managers, dealers, customer's men, principal, brokers, broker dealers, sales representatives... but generally called stockbrokers by the investing public), I love the title "broker" the best—because, for most of the unaware, he will keep you that way (broker). Mostly, I have been disappointed, disillusioned, discouraged, and de-moneyed with brokers and brokerage firms.

In recent years, "stockbroker" has become something of a dirty word, even at brokerage houses! Every major firm now avoids the term, using any of the above titles ... anything but stockbrokers. Why? Because these firms try to hide what their brokers really are ... salespeople. Their first goal is to make commissions, not give you objective advice. Success in the brokerage business is measured totally in terms of commissions generated, not in financial benefits for the investor.

SHOCKING FACTS: IS RESEARCH FROM WALL STREET USELESS, OR WORSE?

Most brokers have very little background in security analysis. Many salespeople are recruited from other fields.

Research produced by brokerage houses is almost worthless. My study of stock recommendations by 147 investment professionals and brokerage firms found that no brokerage firm placed in the top 50.

Nearly all major brokerage firms were officially bullish on the eve of the October 1987 market crash ... and again before the October 13, 1989 plunge of 190 points ... and now, right before the 2008 market plunges.

It is rare for Wall Street to badmouth any stock. Sometimes the worst stocks are recommended for purchase with the caveat "high risk."

One Wall Street analyst was saying unflattering things about the stock market. The employer, a large brokerage firm, requested that he resign. The analyst says that the firm said talk like that was bad for business.

Often, analysts get around the scorn for sell recommendations through use of semantics. Instead of urging customers to unload the stocks of dangerous companies, analysts will issue a weak hold. The recommendation I like the most is "accumulate for aggressive accounts." Interpreted, this is Wall Street's suggestion that a particular stock isn't the best. Accumulate for aggressive accounts is the equivalent of a bet at the racetrack. The statement is telling investors that they are gambling, although the wording doesn't convey the risk.

Frequently, an investor has to ask: Is Wall Street's research useless, and maybe even dangerous? The research department or research analyst is a sales tool, selling ideas to the sales force of a given firm and to individual clients. They do have a bias. Analysts are not allowed to hedge their bets when issuing reports at some firms. Recommendations have to either be for a buy or a sell, nothing else. These firms deal mostly with individual investors.

I see other reasons why Wall Street is so optimistic. Analysts "marry their stocks" ... they are too close to the companies they are following. Most brokerage firms do not restrict their analysts from owning shares in the companies they follow, so they love the companies even more. Also, they are reluctant to say *sell* about a previous *buy* recommendation.

Wall Street salespeople are in love with selling stock, any stock, and any time. They are no different than any other salesperson; the broker does not make the time or have the talent or expertise to select stocks, manage portfolios, time the market, and watch the news on your stocks.

A stockbroker spends all day selling. They are salespeople, dialing for dollars all day. The only way they can make any money is by commissions. The only way they get commissions is to have you buy or sell something. They can be right 50 percent of the time by flipping a coin. They can tell one customer to buy ABC stock and can tell the next to sell it. If they told you to buy and the price goes up, they can later tell you to sell. Since they made you money, now when they tell you to buy XYZ stock because "it is going to move," you follow their advice.

If their 50-percent guess is wrong frequently enough, they will trade your name with another broker for their bad-call customers. Often the new broker will tell you that the other broker is no longer with the firm and your account has been transferred to him.

The stockbrokers receive a telephone directory and a canned speech, sometimes based on meager research that may be out of date, and may be inappropriate for a client's investments. The broker rarely has the time, experience, or documentation to form his own conclusions about the brokerage's sponsored products. The brokers are told to sell new issues and secondary offerings with the ploy, "No commission when you buy this stock." What they conveniently forget to tell you is that the commission was factored into the price of the security, usually at a higher amount than on the listed commission schedule.

Think about your business. Can you afford to spend a lot of time on a small customer, one just starting out, who does not generate any real money for you? Brokerage ads try to insinuate lots of handholding to help the small investor become a large investor. What makes a true bargain? The stock price is low in relation to the earnings, the book value, and the cash flow per share.

It is important to understand that low-priced issues are riskier than higher-priced ones. The risk of 100 percent loss is present with any investment, and that happens more often with low-priced stocks than with high-priced stocks. Of all the stocks listed on the New York Stock Exchange (NYSE) in the past 30 years, only 5 companies have been a total loss to their investors.

Does that mean low-priced stocks should be avoided? No. Individual issues may have fantastic performances. You should regard cheap stocks with suspicion. If you can't resist the temptation of cheap stocks, be mindful of the fundamental rules for stock selection.

So often we rob tomorrow's memories by today's economies.
—John Mason Brown

THE STOCKS IN THE DOW JONES AVERAGES

The Dow Jones Industrial Averages (DJIA) are by far the most popular indicators of general, day-to-day-stock market direction. The top news editors of the *Wall Street Journal* are solely responsible for selecting the stocks that comprise the Dow. Currently, it is simply an average of these 30 stocks:

Alcoa (AA)
American Express (AXP)
AT&T (T)
Boeing Company (BA)
Caterpillar (CAT)
Citigroup (C)
Coca-Cola Company (KO)
Disney (DIS)
E.I. DuPont de Nemours (DD)
Eastman Kodak Co. (EK)
ExxonMobil (XOM)
General Electric (GE)
General Motors (GM)
Hewlett-Packard (HPQ)
Home Depot (HD)
Honeywell International, Inc. (HON)
Intel (INTC)
International Business Machines (IBM)
Johnson & Johnson (JNJ)
JPMorgan Chase (JPM)
Kraft Foods (KFT)
McDonald's (MCD)
Merck (MRK)
Microsoft (MSFT)
Minnesota Mining & Mfg. Co. (MMM)
Philip Morris Companies, Inc. (MO)
Procter & Gamble (PG)
SBC Communications Inc. (SBC)
United Technologies (UTX)
Wal-Mart (WMT)

The DJIA is calculated with a complicated formula, and results are expressed in points rather than dollars. When a financial reporter announces that the market was up 20 points today, it means the Dow Jones 30 Industrial stocks were, overall, up today from the close of the stock market yesterday.

As the status of individual companies changes, so does the list of companies represented in the Dow. Congratulations, Mickey Mouse; you are now a more important measure of America's economic success or failure than U.S. Steel. Now I have nothing against Mickey Mouse; In fact, the Walt

Disney Company is an absolutely terrific company. Other businesses might learn a lot from them.

The DJIA is important to investors, as it shows broad market direction. Another average used is the Standard & Poor's 500 index. The S&P 500 index accounts for about 85 percent of the market value of all the stocks listed on the NYSE. The S&P 500 index is a guide to relative values of the averages of the earnings and dividends of the component companies. This information is readily available and used by investors as a basis for comparison of individual stocks.

There are two other Dow Jones indexes that gauge selected stocks. They are the transportation and utilities indexes. Some market analysts watch for an upturn in two of the three indexes before making any stock market decisions.

In trying to beat the averages, a few money managers have invested in index funds ... funds that mirror the stock market averages. Those managers give up their responsibility to look for the best values. They ignore the thousands of publicly traded stocks that are not among the DJIA or S&P 500. They have guaranteed themselves that they will not do worse than, nor better than the averages. In essence, they ignore stock selection and buy into all the stocks as represented by the particular index.

This shows how difficult it is to come up with a winning portfolio. It proves how the professionals will concentrate on the stocks in the averages, no matter whether the thousands of other stocks are a good value or a bargain.

TODAY'S BARGAINS CAN BE TOMORROW'S WINNERS, AND TODAY'S WINNERS CAN BE TOMORROW'S LOSERS

The *Wall Street Journal* periodically publishes the results of the large investors, mutual funds, insurance companies, and banks. More than 75 percent of the professional managers didn't beat the market averages. The market averages do not have to pay transaction costs or advisory fees, so they usually can outperform institutions that do. If the professionals do no better than you, you are probably better off cutting your costs and paying as little as possible for brokerage and advisory fees.

You know about the editors at *Forbes* magazine and the dart theory of investing, and how they did better than the managed portfolios. The stock market is not all luck. However, it is enough of a horse race that luck does figure into the results more than some professional money managers are willing to admit.

The stock market isn't a gamble, because the race never ends. If your stock (like the horse) falters, you can pick another and keep on going. With stocks you own something. If you pick a good value, you will share in future growth and receive dividends. With the long-term investment strategy you will win.

You should manage your money. No one will care about you and your money as much as you do. This runs contrary to popular belief. "My money is too important to me to manage in my spare time, so I will let a full-time professional manage it for me, even if it costs me to do so."

There are only 37,000 RIAs (registered investment advisers) in the United States. They provide investment advice for a fee. Their actions are controlled by the provisions of the 1940 Investment Advisers Act, which is designed to protect the public from fraud or misrepresentation and requires disclosure of all conflicts of interest. Many specialize in a particular kind of investment. Some registered investment advisers will manage the investor's portfolio.

RIAs do study and analyze the necessary factors that determine *when* to buy, sell, or hold stocks.

If advice is needed, do not seek it from a commissioned salesperson; pay the fee for the unbiased opinion of an RIA, rather than a salesperson who only makes money when you trade.

If information is readily available for you to study, and brokers are wrong as often as they are right, why do you even need a broker? You need him to execute your trades; to give you stock quotes; to hold your certificates; to credit and debit your sales, purchases, and dividends; and to send you accurate monthly statements and annual reports.

These services are available from discount brokers at discounts of up to 76 percent. What they won't do is give you any advice, hold your hand, or try to sell you into or out of investments. If you are wondering why your stockbroker is driving a Porsche and you are driving a Volkswagen Beetle, it is time to look for a discount brokerage house.

WHY USE A DISCOUNT BROKER?

Trades are easy and fast. Substantial commission discounts can make the difference between profit and loss on your securities transactions. How do they do it?

First, there is no expensive research department. You make your decisions, so you don't pay for advice you don't need.

Second, you realize savings of 30 to 45 percent of the fees charged by full-commission firms used to pay their broker's sales commissions. At discount brokers, all account executives are salaried employees. This not only saves you commission dollars, it also ensures you will never get a sales talk to buy or sell a stock.

Most large discount brokers are highly automated and use the latest in telecommunication technology. The efficiency of these methods generates additional savings that are passed along to you.

Discount brokers offer several services that full-commission brokers do not. You'll find 24-hour order entry and low-cost margin loans.

Assets held by most discount brokers, the accounts are protected by private insurance up to $2,500,000 and additional SIPC insurance is $500,000 (Securities Investor Protection Corporation).

When a discount broker holds your securities, you eliminate the risk and inconvenience of sending the securities by mail. You will still be notified of rights offerings, advised of matters requiring stockholder action, and receive proxies and financial reports.

Every month that there is activity in your account, you will receive a comprehensive monthly statement. You will have clear and accurate financial records.

And you won't spend time waiting on the telephone for a particular person—the trading specialist who answers can place your order, give a quotation, or check to see if a previous order was filled, giving you prompt, accurate, and courteous service.

UNDERSTANDING PROCEDURES

Understanding procedures will enable you to get the best execution service possible at the lowest commission cost. To achieve this goal, you must know what to do and how to accomplish it with your broker.

Help the person answering your request for quotes by knowing and supplying him with the symbol needed to get the quotation. This eliminates errors and wasted time for both of you and improves the level of service you receive.

Stock symbols are listed in the financial press or in directories supplied by your broker. When using a directory, the listing for the U.S. Exchanges is a composite of the issues traded on the New York, American, Pacific, Midwest, and NASDAQ system.

United States Stock Exchanges	
New York Stock Exchange	N
American Stock Exchange	A
Pacific Stock Exchange	P
Midwest Stock Exchange	MW
Over the Counter	OTC
Boston Stock Exchange	B
Cincinnati Stock Exchange	C
Canadian Exchange Listed	+

Entering Buy and Sell Orders

Initiate your order by saying you wish to *buy* or *sell*. The trading specialist will need your *name* and your *account number*, with the *security name*, *symbol*, and the *quantity you wish to buy or sell.*

Orders before the Market Opens

To ensure that your order is executed at the opening price, you must enter your order a minimum of one-half hour before the market opens. The trading day opens at 9:30 A.M. and closes at 4:00 P.M. Eastern time (New York hours).

Completed Trade Reports

When you enter your order, you will be asked for your area code and telephone number, which will be written on the order ticket. This information enables a prompt call back to report the execution price of your transaction. Many investors prefer to call the brokerage back to receive their reports, as they know they will not be at a location where they can be reached. If you prefer to call back yourself, tell them when you place the order. Today, many brokerages have a sophisticated telecommunications system installed so you can call a computerized system to get these messages.

Limit Orders

Limit orders may be entered for the day only, or can be placed as *GTC* (good till canceled). If you enter your order as a *day order*, it will automatically be canceled after the trading day if it did not fill. GTC orders remain in effect until you cancel the order or the order is filled. If the price of the security you wish to buy or sell moves dramatically away from the *limit price* on your GTC order, your order remains in effect and continues to be good until you cancel. You are responsible for GTC orders. It is recommended that investors keep a record of them. Remember, you can cancel your limit order at anytime.

All or None Orders

If you do not wish to accept an execution for part of your order at your limit price, you must specify *All or None* at the time you place your order. All limit orders placed All or None, or with a minimum number of shares acceptable to the investor, *lose priority* to market and limit orders placed without these restrictions on the applicable exchange floors. Securities that you wish to purchase or sell can *trade through your limit,* and you are not entitled to an execution because of the All or None or minimum amount restrictions placed on your order. By instructing All or None, you are avoiding the possibility of multiple fills and commissions.

The Composite Tape

The securities industry has consolidated, for reporting purposes, all transactions that occur in securities. Various financial periodicals incorporate the trading ranges for all trading that occurs in all markets for each individual security on any given day. Be aware that some limit orders placed may not be executed, though the price range of the composite market printed in your newspaper reflects that the security has traded at or through your limit price. This can occur because your security has not traded through your limit price on the exchanges where your order was placed. The brokerage reserves the right to choose the exchange when listed securities trade on more than one exchange.

Odd-Lot Orders

All NYSE-listed odd-lot orders for fewer than 100 shares (round lot) received for common stocks one-half hour or more before the market opens will be executed at the opening price without an odd-lot charge added or subtracted.

All other odd-lot orders in NYSE-listed common stocks can be charged an odd-lot execution charge by the odd-lot specialists who executed the order. Preferred stock odd-lot charges are variable.

All odd-lot orders in stocks on the AMEX that trade below $40 a share can be charged an execution charge. All odd-lot orders in stocks that trade above $40 a share can be charged an execution charge.

Charges for Odd-Lots Attached to Round-Lots

Orders placed on the NYSE are left to the discretion of the specialist who executes the order. Round-lot orders with odd lots attached that are entered as a market order will generally be executed at the same round-lot price.

Round-lot orders with odd lots attached should be entered *odd lot on sale*, as often the round lot will be executed, but the odd lot will not. This is because the stock did not trade through your limit to effect the execution of the odd lot. When the odd lot does not execute on the same day as the round lot shares, you must pay a full commission. Since brokerage fees combine for commission purposes, the round and odd lots together, odd-lot orders entered *odd lot on sale* will be executed on the same day as the round lots, and the commission charge will be based on the total shares executed that day.

The Broker's Computer and You

We are living in a computer era. The instructions you provide will be entered on the computer, and the broker's computer will decide how your account is handled—for example, what will be done with your stock certificates, proceeds from sell transactions, and dividends and interest income earned in your account.

Take Advantage of the Free Safekeeping Services

If you are an investor, you may avoid delays in receiving payment and unnecessary handling of certificates by having the brokerage hold your securities in street name as well as your funds for safekeeping. Street name describes securities held in the name of a broker for a customer. As a member of the SIPC (Securities Investor Protection Corporation), your account is protected. Ask for the official brochure, which explains the purposes of the corporation and the amounts of protection it affords. Funds left on deposit will earn market-rate interest.

Many investors leave the proceeds from sales transactions in their account. While waiting for reinvestment, they earn interest. You can call your brokerage at any time to request a check to be sent to you for all or part of your funds left on deposit.

Investors Wishing to Receive Payment

You can receive payment for securities sold and can expect a check to be issued on *settlement day* or the day following receipt of securities sold (whichever is later). Settlement day is three trading days after the transaction.

Investors Wishing to Receive Securities

You can receive securities (certificates) registered in your name(s), and can expect to receive them approximately four weeks after the settlement date. Securities you purchase do not go to the transfer process until your payment is received.

Dividends and Interest

These can be credited automatically to your account during the month and held for reinvestment or can be paid to you by check monthly.

Endorsing Stock Certificates (for Mailing)

1. Do not sign in spaces indicated as blank.
2. Appoint your brokerage firm as *power of attorney* in the space on the back of the certificate. This renders your endorsed certificate nonnegotiable until they release this power with a stamp and a signature. You may now safely mail your certificate(s) via first-class mail.
3. Date the certificates.
4. On the bottom of the certificates' reverse sides, sign your name exactly as it appears on the face. If your certificate(s) are in the name of two or more parties, all must sign.
5. When you mail securities or checks to your brokerage firm, include a copy of your trade confirmation or write your account number on the check or stock certificate(s) being mailed. This will ensure that your deposit or payment will be credited to the proper account.

Pay by Settlement Date

You must pay for your securities purchased and deliver securities sold by the settlement date of your transactions. If your funds or securities are not received on time, the brokerage may be forced, pursuant to Regulation T of The Board of Governors of the Federal Reserve System, to sell out securities purchased or buy back securities sold to cover any unsettled portion of your account deficiency. You are liable for any deficit incurred by the broker on your behalf, as well as the commission for both transactions. If, for any reason, you are unable to meet the settlement date, call your broker and ask for a possible extension of time to settle your transaction.

Solving Account Problems

When you have a problem to resolve, you should call after the market closes. After you have made your request, feel free to ask that you be informed by a return call regarding the status of your problem and the proposed action for its resolution. Remember the name of the person to whom you made your request. You may check back with that individual to be assured that your problem is receiving proper attention. Remembering the name of the individual from whom you requested help will eliminate duplicating the workload and avoid unnecessary confusion.

Transacting a Phone Order

Let us listen in on a typical phone call to a discount broker.

Broker: Discount broker. Good morning. This is Mary Swift and we are on a recorded line. Your account number please.

Investor: My number is 24659713. I am Dick Thomas.

Broker: Thank you. What can I do for you today, Mr. Thomas?

Investor: I'd like price quotes on a couple of stocks.

Broker: Of course, Mr. Thomas. Which stocks?

Investor: XYZ Corp. and ABC Co. XYZ's ticker symbol is XYZ. I'm sorry, I don't know the symbol for ABC Co.

Broker: XYZ Corp. is at $16^3/_4$, up $^1/_4$. ABC Co.'s stock symbol is ABC. It is at $22^1/_2$, no change.

Investor: I'd like to buy 100 shares of XYZ at $16^3/_4$.

Broker: Please listen closely as this is the order that you will be responsible for. I'm entering an order into your cash account to buy 100 shares of XYZ Corp. at a limit price of $16^3/_4$. Is this correct? It's currently offered at $16^3/_4$.

Investor: That is correct.

Broker: Mr. Thomas, is there any other way I can help you today?

Investor: Can you tell me how many shares of DEF Corp. I have in my account, and the current price?

Broker: You have 300 shares that are presently trading at $5^1/_4$ bid, $5^1/_2$ ask.

Investor: Thank you. That's all for now.

Broker: Mr. Thomas, you just bought 100 shares of XYZ at $16^3/_4$. Your written confirmation will go out tomorrow. Is there any other way I can help you today?

Investor: No thank you.

Broker: Thank you.

Transacting an Internet Order

All the details entered into during the phone order apply. You go to the broker's web site and enter your identification (ID) and your password, and fill in all the order form information. This process is completely do-it-yourself. You have the opportunity to watch the quotes change on your order, which is nice, and makes it more profitable for the trade. The other advantage is that Internet trades can cost less than broker-assisted trades.

Discounted Investment Information

As a customer of a discount broker, you will receive from time to time a special reduced-rate offer to buy a variety of financial magazines, books, and newspapers. They make these special offers so that you will have helpful information on investing. Most importantly, they will help you keep up with the ever-changing investment scene.

> Great opportunities come to those who make the most of the small ones.
> —Anonymous

At the full commission brokerage house, one personal broker is assigned to your account. At the discount brokerage house, all members can act on your behalf. Since I started investing in the stock market, I have had 12 personal brokers at 5 different brokerage firms. I now have no personal broker and use Scottrade Advisor Services. What I do have is a helpful team of representatives. I can count on them for helpful, objective investment information and expertise in handling all my trading needs at the right price. At Scottrade, discount brokerage means efficient, accurate handling of my orders.

Since I make all my investment decisions, why should I pay for questionable advice I don't trust or need? Scottrade lets me save up to 30 percent in commissions, compared to what I would pay at a full-commission broker. I receive the easiest-to-read confirmation slips and monthly statements. If I need to, I can call at any time, 24 hours a day, for account service and order placement. And the best is last; they can confirm most trades through their order system while you are still on the phone. They mail confirmations the next business day.

This is an unsolicited testimonial for Scottrade Investments Brokerage Services. Call 800-619-SAVE(7283) and ask for their free fact kit and compare for yourself.

You can also use their web site: www.scottrade.com.

Many of my clients already have accounts when they go with my investing service. Because of this, I am trading at Fidelity Brokerage, Charles Schwab, and many other investment houses, so I have seen the competition.

Remember—if you don't ask, you don't get.

> There are two times in a man's life when he should not speculate: when he can't afford it, and when he can.
>
> —Mark Twain

CHAPTER 9

Advanced Investing and Goal Setting

The will to win is worthless if you do not have the will to prepare.

—Thane Yost

Optimism is a tonic. Pessimism is poison.

—*Forbes* magazine

Your main reason for investing is to make money. A main reason many investors fail is that they never set a financial goal. If you aim at nothing, your chances of hitting a target are very poor. Most investors' financial goals are vague, such as "making a million dollars" or "having a net worth of $500,000" or "earning $100,000 a year" or "retiring at 50." These are not very satisfactory goals, because they are not specific. They express only a general desire to do well. You must specify in your plan how and when in order to have a well-defined estimate of what you wish to obtain. Without a clear idea of where you are going, it is hard to know whether you are getting there in a timely manner.

Your financial strategy must be different if your target is 5 years or 25 years. Retirement can be one goal. Other goals could include providing for your children's education, travel, purchasing a vacation home, or purchasing a new car every year. Everyone's goals will be different and will change as time passes. It is important to start now.

A goal should not be too conservative; it should represent what you hope to attain at certain points in the future. You may only be partially successful, but you will have nothing if you do not try. However, the goal must also be realistic, or you will be forced to take unnecessary risks and will tend to make bad investment decisions. The most important thing is to start today.

It is important to identify how much you can realistically commit to your program. The more you commit now, the less risk you will need to assume to reach your goal. Most individuals seriously underestimate the number of dollars they have available for investing.

We shall discuss ways to maximize the dollars available for investment later. It is important to realize that the more resources you have working for you, the more likely you are to achieve your goals on time.

Another reason most investors fail to accomplish financial goals is a lack of discipline. The carefully planned financial goals and well-thought-out financial plans are worthless if they are never implemented. Delay is probably the greatest single reason financial goals are not achieved.

Lack of investment discipline is a severe problem for many investors. The reason may be that before their good earning years, most investors live lives of deferred gratification. Many debts are incurred in obtaining an education, in gaining marketable skills, in the early years of marriage, in buying a house, in raising children, and so on. Finally, when they can afford it, their first investment is more likely to be a sports car or an expensive vacation than a mutual fund.

Whatever the reason, those who do not develop the discipline to commit funds today to obtain financial goals in the future will end up with considerable disappointment. The investor who is always waiting for the right time to start an investment program will never get anywhere. The right time was yesterday. You will never have extra unallocated funds. Your expenditures will always rise to consume available dollars.

> Some people dream of worthy accomplishments, while others stay awake and do them.
>
> —Anonymous

FINANCIAL FAILURE

I have noticed over the years that unsuccessful investors are either not true to themselves or are too rigid in their thinking. These qualities do not have to become permanent traits fated to destroy investing success. They can be easily overcome by honestly defining and evaluating your personal style and trading beliefs. You will have to develop your own personal investing philosophy, based on what works best for you.

The three major causes of financial failure are having no goal, no plan, and no discipline, and these deficiencies can apply to many investors. Many investors tend to be overconservative. They put their money in low-yield, "safe" investment vehicles (a mistake), such as bonds, certificates of deposit, and low-yield mutual funds.

A smaller group of investors takes the opposite position. They throw handfuls of money after wild speculative gambles with little chance of success. These individuals make enormously risky investments with the hope of potentially enormous returns. They get their advice from relatives, friends, or high-pressure salesmen. The vast majority of these investments end in failure. So what? They can always start over after re-earning the money and try again.

The most common maneuver is to blend the above extremes. A major share of the funds is committed to low-yield, "safe" investments and the remainder is used for speculation. This investment attitude makes it difficult to formulate a workable investment plan.

Investors get more than their share of poor investment advice. Much of this results from delegating financial decisions to unqualified persons. Another source of difficulty is the vast variety of potential investment vehicles, each promoted by an aggressive, commission-oriented salesperson. The salesperson with the best pitch often wins the day, even if his product is not appropriate for the individual's goals.

Most investors fail to appreciate the subtle difference between an investment adviser and a salesperson. A salesperson is not necessarily dishonest. The problem is that salespeople have an inherent conflict of interest; they want to sell a product whether it is or is not the most appropriate one for a particular individual's financial plans.

Sometimes the distinction between a salesperson and an investment adviser is difficult to perceive. The life insurance agent, a salesperson, advises the purchase of ordinary or whole life insurance as an investment vehicle, in spite of its low return. Easier to identify is the high-pressure real estate agent trying to sell you a condo, promising to double your money while providing you a vacation paradise. Stockbrokers are not so obvious. They and their firms make money on commissions and therefore are interested in convincing you to make transactions. Most of the time, they will not deliberately steer you toward a bad investment, but their prime goal is to complete the sale.

The bank trust officer who pushes certificates of deposit is also a salesperson. Your accountant who sees only your tax liability and stresses tax shelters may be an unwitting salesperson, since he or she emphasizes the need for tax shelters without regard to your total investment plan. Failure to distinguish between an investment adviser and a salesperson can lead you into many poor investments.

Small investors have a terrible sense of investment timing. Contrary to the established principle of successful investing, they tend to buy high and sell low. This is directly traceable to a lack of investment knowledge and discipline. Lacking a satisfactory investment plan and the resolve to use it, they are unduly swayed by the morning's investment news and tips. When the Dow Jones Industrial Average (DJIA) is down, they wait until it has risen 200 points. They finally conclude that a bull market is on, and buy at or near the top. As the market starts downward, they quickly try to correct their mistakes by selling out before their investments get any lower.

Investors tend to lack investment flexibility. In the financial and economic world, everything cycles: stocks, bonds, real estate, interest rates, inflation, the economy, and the weather (wheat futures). The successful investor knows all this and commits his funds before the moves have run their course. He makes regular investments despite market action.

> The differences between persistence and obstinacy are that one often comes from a strong will, and the other from a strong won't.
>
> —Henry Ward Beecher

MONEY × RETURN × TIME = YOUR GOAL

The first requirement for investing is money. You must be willing to commit an adequate portion of your current assets to arrive at your goal. By looking at the above equation, we can see that by increasing either the time or the return, one can decrease the size of the money factor. Even with all the time in the world, it is impossible to reach your goal without having some money working for you.

> The Use of Money is all the Advantage there is in having Money.
>
> —Benjamin Franklin

Successful investors must have partners working with them. The efforts of one person are not enough. Ray Kroc was a hard worker with a brilliant idea and a taste for hamburgers. He did not make a fortune by cooking and selling McDonald's hamburgers himself, however. He made it by having 3,500 other McDonald restaurants cooking and selling the hamburgers and giving him a fraction of a penny on each one sold. The

Vanderbilts did not get their wealth by loading and driving the family trains. They paid their employees to do this work and made a small percentage on each transaction.

Dollars in wise investments can be as effective a worker for you as a teenager cooking at McDonald's or a train engineer. It helps to start thinking of every dollar you invest in stocks as buying you a partnership in a going company. Make certain that every dollar you own is busy earning its keep, rather than getting a free ride in your wallet or loafing in your bank account.

YOUR MONEY

It is dangerous for investors to deceive themselves into thinking they possess the capital to carry stock positions which they know, in their heart of hearts, would wipe them out should the market turn against them. Intellectual honesty enables an investor to be aware of personal financial limitations and avoid falling victim to wishing, hoping, or praying.

Do not wish, hope, or pray while investing. It will not help you.

Money falls into one of three categories: active, loafing, or dead.

Active money is that which is invested and produces an after-tax rate of return greater than the current inflation rate. Active dollars are producing yet more dollars that also can be put to work. Active money makes use of the compounding principle and is the foundation of a successful investment program.

Dead money is exactly the opposite. Dead dollars just sit around, not invested in anything and not producing any return. Whether they are in a coffee can or in wallets, they might as well stuff a mattress. Some dead dollars are providing real services by paying the grocery bill and the home mortgage. To this extent, these dead dollars provide for the necessities and comforts of life. The problem is that most investors have dead dollars—money not working and not being used for enriching their lifestyle.

Those traveler's checks you have been saving for an emergency are dead money. "Don't leave home without them, and (in a low voice) don't bring them back either." American Express tells you to keep one in your wallet for an emergency. Every time you pay cash for purchases, instead of charging them on your Visa or MasterCard and paying for them in 30 days, you have created more dead money. These were active dollars you could have used for the 30 days.

Loafing money is working and earning some return, but after taxes, the gains are not keeping up with inflation. Money in a conventional savings or checking account is a prime example of loafing money. Most investors have more loafing money than they realize. This is another reason most investors don't meet their goals. Loafing money loses buying power because of taxes and inflation. Time is working against loafing money, eating it away and decreasing its value.

The first step on the road to successful investing is to examine every dollar under your control and decide whether it is active, loafing, or dead. Most investors have enough total dollars available to attain their financial goals. The problem arises because too many of these dollars are loafing or dead rather than active. A basic principle of successful investing is to convert the loafing and dead money into active money.

YOUR RETURN

It is tempting to look at a high rate of return as a means of attaining your goal. It is easy to fantasize that money will earn 30 percent or more, so that one could skimp on the amount of money invested. High return is almost always associated with high risk of loss. In a financial investment program, there are no free lunches; you have to try to make only prudent investments rather than aiming for pie in the sky.

The need for sensible investment seems obvious. After all, who would want an irrational investment? Nevertheless, most investors own some of these types of investments. One of the poorest investments is the low-yield, safe, federally insured bank account. If you have money sitting in a 2 percent passbook account and the inflation rate is 5 percent, you are losing money. If you are making large annual payments on a whole life insurance policy that is yielding 4 percent, that is an unreasonable investment! If you buy a triple-A rated bond when interest rates are low, you will find that the value of the bond is drastically reduced as interest rates rise . . . making it another ill-considered investment.

YOUR TIME

Time is the one great difference between the successful and unsuccessful investor. The successful investor realizes that patience pays! Every successful investor has a special talent for watching and waiting, and waits until trading behavior has dictated when to enter the market.

Lost wealth may be replaced by industry, lost knowledge by study, lost health by temperance or medicine, but lost time is gone forever.
—Samuel Smiles

Time is the final factor for investment success, and the least appreciated. In many ways, it is the most important element, because through time we realize the compounding effect on money and return.

Bernard Baruch, a legendary investor and my hero, described compound interest as "the eighth wonder of the world." Compounding means that you earn interest on the principal and also earn interest on the interest.

As the rate of return increases, the growth becomes impressive. As an example, consider a principal of $100 that produces an annual compound rate of 6 percent. After five years, the future amount would be $134. After 10 years the future amount would be $179. At 15 and 20 years the amounts are $240 and $321. Notice that the annual return gets larger the longer the compounding runs. In the first five-year period earnings were $34, in the second five-year period, $45, in the third, $61, and in the fourth, $81, more than twice the return for the first time period!

Receiving 6 percent isn't much of a return. Suppose the rate of return is 10 percent, still modest and attainable at little risk. Now the future amounts after 5, 10, 15, and 20 years are $161, $259, $418, and $673. The earnings in the first period are $61, and in the fourth period $255! Thus a small increase in rate of return greatly increases the effect of compounding.

As the rate of return increases, the growth becomes impressive. At a 15-percent rate, the fourth period would earn eight times more than the first period. At 25 percent, the fourth period outstrips the first by a factor of 47; the $100 would earn $5,832 during the fourth period alone! Now, you should not expect to get a compound annual return of 25 percent. But 15 percent is not unreasonable with modest risk, and 10 percent is possible with almost no risk!

The point is not rate of return but compounding. Despite the rate, compounding greatly increases the final return. Compounding takes time to work. You can't reap the benefits of a fourth period unless you have gone through the first, second, and third periods. This is why the time component of investing is so important. Remember, wasted time comes off the compounding period. If you waste time getting started on your investing program today, it comes out of the fourth period, the high-return time, not out of the first period, the low-return time.

Most investors delay because of their fear of the uncertainties and risk in investing, little realizing that their delay is simply increasing their risk of failure. Money that you earn today can immediately go to work, making the maximum use of time.

INVESTMENT RISKS

An investment's risk is simply the probability that your return will be different; not specifically higher or lower, just different from what you expect it to be. Increasing risk means a chance of not only losing money but also making more than you expected. For practical purposes, everyone automatically feels that risk means a negative outcome—a loss. In our discussions, we will use the term *risk* to mean the chance that an investment won't produce its hoped-for return. Remember, no hoping.

> By gaming we lose both our time and treasure—two things most precious to the life of man.
>
> —Owen Felltham

There are several factors that can influence the risk of an investment; we'll discuss each in turn.

First, *inflation risk* has different effects on different types of investments. In times of increasing inflation, the value of so-called hard assets, such as real estate, gold, and physical properties, will increase dramatically. Anyone who purchased a home in the 1970s was the beneficiary of a rapid inflationary increase in value.

Inflation has the opposite effect on cash. During inflationary periods, cash loses value. Remember when a McDonald's hamburger cost 15 cents, a bag of fries was 10 cents, and a shake was 20 cents? The sales tax alone at today's prices costs more than that meal once did. In formulating any investment program, it is vital to project the rate of inflation for the next five years so that you can periodically adjust your strategy to minimize the risk.

Interest risk in the short -term rates tends to respond to the supply and demand of money, crowd psychology, and government manipulation. Long-term interest rates tend to be governed by the prevailing inflation rate. A change of interest rates can have a profound effect on the value of investments that are designed primarily to yield income.

Business risk is measured by the net earnings of a company. When these begin to have a negative trend, the dividend, as well as the stock's price, may decrease. This is simple. If the company in which you own stock does well, your stock will do well. If the company is a "dog," it will be reflected in the value of the stock.

Market risk figures into the price of any investment. It is determined by competitive bidding, and in this situation, prices follow the law of supply and demand. Investor's choices affect supply and demand. Changes in these choices can drastically alter an asset's price, which also alters the market risk. An unreasonable price in the marketplace, either too high or too low, will determine the risks of an equity. Crowd psychology and the news media often influence investor choices. This combination can result in an over- or undervaluation of investments for considerable periods of time.

Economic risk can adversely affect valuations by a sudden change in the economy of a country. For example, the increased number of bankruptcies in 2008 and 2009 were caused by a general economic recession, rather than a specific failing of the company.

And finally, *political risk.* Consider the nuclear power industry. Despite a flawless safety record, the political forces at work have destroyed the industry by requiring so many excessive safety features that the cost became prohibitive, and where that was inadequate, by denying operating permits to the facilities. Political forces are frequently irrational and can cause economic and financial chaos to companies or industries.

RISK-REWARD RELATIONSHIP

In school the three Rs were "readin', 'ritin', and 'rithmetic." In the financial world, the three Rs, risk, reward, and relationship, stand for a fundamental principle of investing. Risk is directly related to reward; in other words, a larger reward can only be obtained by increasing the exposure to risk. If you undertake a more risky investment, you will be entitled to a higher rate of reward.

It has always been better to be lucky rather than smart. You can't rely on luck, so most of us must make do with smart. It is the best policy to assume that the reward on an investment will bear a direct relationship to its risk. It is necessary, before making any investment, that you make some assessment of the risk involved. Then decide whether the potential reward justifies that risk.

To assess risk, you must have some standard by which to compare the rewards versus risk on any given investment. The place to start is with the truly risk-free investment. In this country, the closest you can get to a risk-free investment is the 91-day U.S. Treasury bill. The U.S. Treasury has never defaulted, and unless the country completely collapses, will never default on paying the interest and principal on its obligations.

Three Risk Ideas and Principles:

1. Any investment you make should give you a higher return than the current U.S. Treasury bill (T-bill).
2. If two investments have the same rate of return, always select the safer one for less risk.
3. If two investments have equal risk, always select the investment with the higher return.

Wasted time is the ultimate risk in any investment. Every day that an investment dollar is not at work is a lost and wasted day. This means that any subsequent investments must provide a higher rate of return, so you have to assume more risk to reach your goal.

Make maximum utilization of the time value of money.

> *If time be of all things the most precious, wasting time must be*, as Poor Richard says, the greatest prodigality; since, as he elsewhere tells us, *lost time is never found again; and what we call time enough always proves little enough.* Let us then up and be doing, and doing to the purpose; so by diligence shall we do more with less perplexity.
>
> —Benjamin Franklin
>
> Money lost can be replaced, but time lost is gone forever.
>
> —Anonymous

CHAPTER 10

Building Your Portfolio

Our perceptions of the world are corrected by our knowledge.

—Arthur Koestler

From August 1982 through August 1987, the stock market had a 250 percent gain. One day in October 1987, the stock market lost 24 percent in value. Sanity and reality had returned. I dedicate this chapter to building a strong portfolio for the long term, five years or more.

Build a portfolio to be proud of, an investment club–style portfolio. I am no different than most prudent investors. I look at my portfolio and I see huge, brand-name stocks like AT&T, General Electric, Pfizer, 3M, Bank of America, Microsoft, Dow Chemical, and Hewlett-Packard.

I want to own stock in companies that will let me eat, shop, and sleep peacefully. I like great companies with quality products and services. I want to own companies with good earnings, growth, trademarks, and earnings; strong patents and products; and sheer strength of size. I want to own all the good ones with dividends too.

There is more risk and reward in common stocks than in any other form of investing. For a stock, there are times when the risks outweigh the rewards and other times when the rewards outweigh the risks. Investment in the larger companies on the New York Stock Exchange (NYSE) has averaged greater than 12 percent annual yield over many years (dividends and market appreciation). The price of any stock is set by a competitive bidding market. A stock is worth only what someone is willing to pay for it. The price of a stock may bear little or no relationship to its long-term worth.

Stock investing can be as simple or complex as you make it. Some individuals buy stock just because they like the company from a customer's point of view. Many individual investors have good common-sense opinions about the prospects for some publicly traded companies. For example, people who shop at Sears or Target may sense that management is not as innovative as its competitors, such as Wal-Mart or Home Depot. Individuals sense that the new car models at Chrysler showrooms will not become overnight sensations. Instead of putting up with substandard service at the post office, some consumers quickly discover the advantage and convenience of using FedEx for their mail boxes. These well-run companies tend to increase sales rapidly, benefiting the value of the shares of their traded stock.

This gut feeling may be worlds apart from the lengthy analyses written in obscure terms by the industry analysts employed by the brokerage firms. Apparently, there is no monopoly on sound judgments by well-known brokerage firms. If you have a good feeling about a company, you then must do the research before making a final determination about buying.

> There are few ways in which a man can be more innocently employed than in getting money.
>
> —Samuel Johnson

HOW THE PROS CHOOSE STOCKS

If there was a way to make the selection of a stock and building a portfolio of solid stocks a nonlengthy process, I would appreciate it. A few assumptions: (1) we want to find stocks at bargain prices, and (2) we surely do not want to overpay for the stocks. This is where the use of a computer and the financial sites is of immense assistance.

Is this not the essence of it all? The task is to find great stocks at bargain prices, to buy stocks with the highest likelihood of increase in value and the lowest likelihood of losing value. We should look at the most successful investors of our time.

No investor is more revered on Wall Street than Warren E. Buffett. He is the second-richest man in the United States and the premier investor of the past 25 years. If you had invested $10,000 in 1956 in Mr. Buffett's Berkshire Hathaway holding company, you would now have more than $40 million. He doesn't use fancy trading strategies. He just buys and holds.

He doesn't chase hot industries. He prefers cold ones. He doesn't use insider tips. He just waits and ignores market swings and economic cycles.

Mr. Buffett is the world's most successful practitioner of *value investing*, the investment approach developed by his one-time employer and mentor, Benjamin Graham. First, Mr. Buffett carefully searches for safe, established companies whose stocks are selling cheaply. He makes sure he likes the management and understands how the company works and how it plans to prosper in coming years. He buys shares and waits for the market to value them highly.

> Rule No. 1: Never lose money. Rule No. 2: Never forget Rule No. 1.
> —Warren E. Buffett

BENJAMIN GRAHAM, THE VALUE INVESTOR

Graham is one of America's most respected investors, whose sound principles have been proven by the success of hundreds of his followers for more than 40 years. The main objectives of his philosophy of value investing are to protect the investor against possible substantial error and to develop rational policies with which the investor will be comfortable.

Benjamin Graham has done much for my investing knowledge. I encourage you to read his books, which are listed in the Resources section at the end of this book. After many years of using his ideas and teachings, I found a small trail leaving his main well-traveled road. Perhaps if he had not died in 1976, some of his criteria would also have changed. I humbly offer his ideas, with mine.

As a student of Benjamin Graham, I use many of his investment criteria. Due to the changed economy, new government regulations, the unreliability of government's economic reports, and frequent actions of the Federal Reserve, I have modified some of Graham's policies and principles, as outlined below:

Unmodified Policies:
1. Use mostly fundamental rather than technical data.
2. Use a low P/E ratio as the primary investment criterion to rate the performance of companies.
3. Maintain high diversity (not less than 30 stocks).

4. Be patient.

5. Wait for at least 50 percent advancement in the stock's price for most investments before selling.

6. Do not consider gold, silver, or other precious metals.

7. Do not consider real estate or collectibles.

8. Do not believe in the *Efficient Market* or *Random Walk* theories.

9. Do not use *Indexing* methods.

10. Do not invest in *penny stocks* or *new issues*.

11. Do not invest in foreign stocks, because reliable fundamental data is not usually available.

Modified Policies:

1. Graham's criteria for earnings yield and dividend yield varies directly with the average rate for industrial bonds. I do not tie my criteria to the industrial bond rate.

2. Graham's criteria are more easily subject to computer analysis, whereas my criteria are based on news of nonrecurring events and therefore are not subject to computer analysis.

3. Graham would only invest in companies with low debt-to-equity ratios. I will accept higher debt-to-equity ratios, especially under conditions of high inflation rates.

4. Graham's latest research showed that past earnings growth was partially important, whereas I consider it important.

5. Graham's latest research showed that past stability in earnings growth was partially important, whereas I consider it important.

6. Graham's impatience time in holding a stock was 2 to 3 years, whereas I wait 4 to 5 years.

7. Graham did not try to predict a company's future growth in earnings. He felt that high diversity was of more value than the in-depth research required to predict the future growth in earnings. I consider estimates of future growth as very important, and so I require in-depth research to estimate a company's future growth in earnings.

8. The proportion of Graham's portfolio invested in common stocks usually varied between 25 percent and 75 percent. It varied directly with the number of stocks that met his criteria. I am nearly always fully invested in common stocks.

9. Graham preferred to invest in companies with no loss years in the last 10, but agreed to none in the last 5, if there were no more than 1 in the

last 10. I am willing to invest in turnaround companies if my in-depth research shows that future earnings justify this.

10. Graham would not pay more than book value for a stock. I buy over book value if the other criteria justify it.

11. For a small investment, Graham's original investment criteria is based on a bargain in the balance sheet (price equal or less than net-current-asset value), but only for profitable companies. I am a contrarian investor, so I cannot use these criteria for my investments.

HOW OTHER PROFESSIONALS INVEST

In contrast to Buffett and Graham, other pros search the corporate scene for growth stocks and are bearish on cyclical companies. How do you know when a stock has hit its bottom or top? Price follows earnings. If a cyclical company's stock is rising while its profits are barely keeping up or even shrinking, then you've got a short-lived market occurrence. The stock is very hot for very poor reasons and is therefore not a good long-term investment.

These pros search for solid, established companies that can grow despite the economic trends. They look for a company that has a few products today, one that can increase its current product line by introducing new products or expand geographically. They might buy the stock of a successful store or restaurant chain that is planning to open new locations.

They do not rule out a promising company that is experiencing a few problems. However, they need evidence that the problems will be fixed. If a company has a great product, but has been selling it the wrong way, that can be corrected.

After identifying a prospective investment, examining its sales volume growth is of extreme importance. It is essential that an increase in revenues depends on sales growth (which is more sustainable) and not simply on price hikes. These pros would have concern if a company's sales had slowed over the last few quarters, and if there were no new products in the pipeline, or if a competitor had just introduced a new product.

Their focus is on how a company is handling its internal affairs and, despite the economy, whether its products will sell. They look at how sales growth was achieved over the last year. History has shown the economy matters less to companies that have a strong product line.

Other pros search for trends and companies that stand to benefit from specific economic developments. One of their favorite leads is new government regulations. Recently, increased government regulations have forced many S&Ls (savings and loans) to restrict mortgage lending. People still need to buy homes, and mortgage financing companies have stepped in to fill the need. They are gaining market share and are increasing earnings even in a soft real estate market.

The United States is experiencing a serious recession. Some solid companies are going to emerge stronger, but weaker companies will fail.

When investing, most pros prefer companies that already have been recognized as leaders in their industries, rather than "up-and-comers." Companies with a track record of good performance, strong management, and a powerful position within an industry are best able to capitalize on business trends. The best strategy these pros know for long-term successes in the stock market is to invest in companies with well-established histories.

VALUE VERSUS STOCK PRICE

The stock market is irrational, unpredictable, and volatile. A company's earnings may be lower than anticipated. The earnings may still be good; they just aren't as high as everyone thought they would be. This announcement causes the price of the stock to drop one-half in price. This sudden fall from grace was obviously not due to any fundamental change in the company, but to a sudden change in many investors' perspective of the company.

Volatility can work both ways. A new company offered its common stock for public sale. The company lacked a product, lacked sales, and had no earnings. Investor enthusiasm for the few shares that were available was so high that within a week the stock's price doubled.

There are no fixed prices for stocks; they trade in an open bidding market. The price of a stock is simply the price at which someone who wants to buy the stock can purchase it from someone who wants to sell it. When there are more buyers than sellers, the price of a stock will rise; when there are more sellers than buyers, it will fall, despite any change in the fortunes of the company. The balance between the supply and demand for a stock is what determines its price.

There is a lesson here. Over several years it is the underlying value of a company, as reflected in its earnings and dividends, that controls the price of its common stock. Between tomorrow and the long term, the price of the common stock can and will vary widely and often, seemingly in no relation to the company's true worth. These fluctuations make up the "market game." If you can understand this, you will have no trouble doing well investing in stocks.

BUYING AND SELLING STOCKS

Buying and selling stocks can be done in several different ways.

- The *market order* is an order to buy or sell a security at the best available price. With market orders, you are saying, "I must do this, no matter what the price."
- A *limit order* is an order to buy or sell a security at a set price or better.
- A *stop loss order* is an order that sets the sell price of a stock below the current market price.

Market Orders: Use Only When You Absolutely Want a Transaction Completed

The most popular is the market order. After overhearing some favorable comments on ABC Corporation in the club's locker room, an investor decides to buy 100 shares. He calls his broker and asks him to purchase 100 shares of ABC for him *at the market*. This phrase means that the broker has authority to go to the specialist and purchase 100 shares at the best price available, no matter what that price might be. If the broker arrives at the specialist's station and is lucky, there will be more sellers than buyers, and he will get a lower price. If the broker is unlucky, there will be more buyers than sellers, and he must pay more for the stock. Despite the price, the broker must close the deal, when possible. On the large exchanges, usually the price will be very close to the recent price at which the stock had been trading. But there can be exceptions.

ABC Corporation had been selling at 20 for several weeks. It just announced that it had received a major government contract that would double its earnings in the next two years (this had been the source of the excitement in the locker room). When the broker received the call, the stock exchange had closed. The broker informed him that ABC Corporation had risen two points that day based on the good news. Delighted, the investor, with a big smile on his face, placed his market order for 100 shares. The evening news on television carried the story about ABC and its government contract, and as a result, many investors around the country became interested in ABC stock. By 9:00 the next morning, other investors, having read the business page of their morning papers, became interested in the stock of ABC Corporation; orders for thousands of shares were placed with brokers around the country.

The specialist in ABC was having a real difficulty; there were 10 buyers for every seller. The only way he could fill the orders was to let the price rise rapidly. The stock had closed at 22 the previous day. The next morning, trading was halted. ABC finally opened around noon and was trading at 28. The order filled about 1:00 P.M., at a price of 29.

When the broker called to tell the news, our investor was shocked; he had thought that the price would be around 22 but instead had paid 29. Later that day, the company announced a correction in the previous day's story. Instead of doubling the company's earnings, the new contract probably would only increase earnings by 2 percent. Within two days, the price of ABC had fallen back to 23. Our investor had an instant loss, which showed on his frowning face.

This is a dramatic example that illustrates the dangers of market orders. Although the use of market orders guarantees that the stock will be purchased or sold, an investor who places market orders may find that the trade is executing at a price that is considerably different from the one he or she anticipated.

Using market orders to sell stock is the same as buying. The only difference is that the broker has to sell the stock for whatever price he or she can get.

Our investor kept his $29 ABC stock, and during the year the price rose to 32. One evening, in the locker room, a friend asked him if he had heard about "the big investigation at ABC Corporation." It seems that on the evening news there had been a report that the government was suspending all payments to ABC, pending the investigation of alleged faulty design and manufacturing defects in their products.

Our investor decided to take his profits in ABC Corporation and called the broker to sell the stock. The broker informed the investor that despite the bad news, ABC had dropped only one point to 31 and might still do well. After hesitating a few days, the investor decided to sell when the stock reached 32, assuming the price was still available. The broker found that no one was willing to pay 30 for the stock that day and, unfortunately the news continued to get worse. Two days later the stock was down to 15. The investor still owned all the shares, but now instead of having a $3 profit, there was a $14 loss per share.

When you decide to sell a stock because of *real* bad news, sell it at the market to make sure you sell. Buying is another matter, if you miss your price in one stock, there are hundreds of other stocks from which to choose. The only way to decide when to sell is ask, "at today's price would I still buy it?" If the answer is yes; keep the stock, but if you would not buy it, *Sell! Sell! Sell!*

Limit Orders: Keeping Control

Limit orders are similar to market orders, except that the broker has to make the trade at a previously specified price or better. If an investor wanted to place a limit order when buying ABC Corporation, the broker should have been told to "Buy 100 shares of ABC at 22 or better." This means that the broker would enter the trade at the exchange. It would be executed whenever the stock could be purchased for 22 or less. Since the price was above 22, the order would remain on the books and would not be filled.

I believe that it is wise to use limit orders for stock purchases, since there is a price at which any stock is no longer a good buy. When you decide to buy a stock, you should set a price that the stock is worth. Use a limit order to make sure you do not pay more. When you place a limit order, you will be asked, "How long is the order good? "You may wish the order to be in effect for one day or good till canceled (GTC). Since I have patience when trading stocks, my orders are typically GTC. GTC indicates that the order will be open on the books for 90 days or more. Of course, during this time you can cancel the order or change the execution price.

Stop Loss Orders: Insurance for the Investor

Stop loss orders are limit orders to sell a stock to protect the investor against a sudden decline in price. Had the investor placed a stop loss order at 27, when the bad news about ABC Corporation came out, he would have been protected against a big loss.

Stop loss orders are like insurance. You do not place a stop loss order because you really want to sell, but because you want to protect yourself if the stock drops in price rapidly. Many successful investors use stop loss orders routinely, placing them 5 to 20 percent below the current stock price. As the stock rises in value, new stops are entered 5 to 20 percent below the new current stock price. Using stop loss orders is a wise investment strategy, as it eliminates the possibility of taking big losses.

I do not use stop loss orders. They look good on paper, but have some serious problems. You must realize that normally, stock prices fluctuate. You do not want to be in the position of selling your stock simply because it temporarily dipped in price. The reason for the stock's dip is of utmost importance in your determining whether to buy, hold, or sell. Another reason not to use them is the occurrence of large down days as in the 1987 crash. Stocks fell so rapidly that the price was below the stop loss limit before a sale could be made. A stop loss order in this situation is like a limit order. When they got to your order the price was already lower, so you did not get an execution.

Therefore, I believe that when you want to use stop loss orders, you should keep them as mental orders, not on file with your broker. This will keep your commissions down by not trading out of a stock that is merely experiencing a temporary price decline.

Investments in common stocks over the course of years have been a very profitable endeavor. The general trends of a stock price and dividend payments have been upward. It has not been a smooth road; there have been many dips and peaks in performance. Despite some bumpy downward slides, the overall course of the stock market has been up. I believe this trend will continue.

PORTFOLIO MANAGEMENT GUIDELINES

The industry is filled with limitless philosophies toward opportunity in the markets. After all my years in the industry, I cannot teach you how to trade. What I can do, however, is introduce you to the most well-known investing rules and comment on which ones my experience has taught me to either respect or disregard.

I have been managing portfolios for more than 30 years. Over that time, I have found that while stock selection is important to general success in investing, portfolio construction and management are of almost equal importance.

Most investors tend to make two crucial mistakes: having too many stocks and selling them too soon. Getting better performance out of a portfolio would include the following guidelines: diversify by industry, limit total stock offerings, buy quality stocks, limit trading, sell losers, and use dollar-cost averaging.

Diversify by Industry

Assets should not be concentrated in too few or too many industries. A maximum of 10 percent for each industry is about right. Note the emphasis on *industries*, rather than stocks.

A list of the basic industry groups, and some major subindustries, as well as some representative companies, appears at the end of this chapter. The entire list of industries and subindustries is published periodically in the *Wall Street Journal* and/or in *Barron's*. Financial web sites are excellent for this research also.

The Dow Jones Industry Group Components   This is a partial list of the securities that are available for you to study and buy into:

- Aerospace
  - Boeing Company
  - United Technologies

- Air delivery and freight services
  - C.H. Robinson Worldwide
  - Expeditors International
  - FedEx Corporation
  - United Parcel Service
- Airlines, major and regional
  - AMR Corporation
  - Continental Airlines, Inc.
  - JetBlue Airways Corp.
  - Southwest Airlines, Inc.
- Aluminum
  - Alcoa
- Automobiles
  - General Motors
- Banks
  - Bank of America
  - Citigroup
  - JPMorgan Chase
- Broadcasting and entertainment
  - Walt Disney Company
- Broadline retailers
  - Wal-Mart Stores
- Commercial vehicles and trucks
  - Caterpillar Inc.
- Commodity chemicals
  - E.I. DuPont de Nemours & Co.
- Computer hardware
  - Hewlett-Packard
- Computer services
  - International Business Machines
- Consumer finance
  - American Express
- Diversified industrials
  - 3M
  - General Electric
- Diversified utilities
  - CenterPoint Energy
  - Consolidated Edison
  - Exelon
  - NiSource, Inc.
  - PG&E Corp.
  - Public Service Enterprise Group

- Electric utilities
  - The AES Corp.
  - American Electric Power
  - Dominion Resources
  - Duke Energy
  - Edison International
  - FirstEnergy
  - FPL Group
  - Southern Company
- Fixed line telecommunications
  - AT&T
  - Verizon Communications
- Food products
  - Kraft Foods
- Home improvement retailers
  - Home Depot
- Integrated oil and gas
  - Chevron
  - ExxonMobil
- Nondurable household products
  - Procter & Gamble
- Oil and gas pipelines
  - Williams Companies
- Pharmaceuticals
  - Johnson & Johnson
  - Merck & Company
  - Pfizer Inc.
- Railroads
  - Burlington Northern Santa Fe Corp.
  - CSX Corp.
  - Norfolk Southern Corp.
  - Union Pacific Corp.
- Rental and leasing services
  - GATX Corp.
  - Ryder System, Inc.
- Restaurants and bars
  - McDonald's Corp.
- Semiconductors
  - Intel Corp.
- Shipping
  - Alexander & Baldwin, Inc.
  - Overseas Shipholding Group, Inc.

- Soft drinks
  - Coca-Cola Company
- Software
  - Microsoft Corp.
- Trucking
  - Con-Way, Inc.
  - JB Hunt Transport Services, Inc.
  - Landstar System, Inc.
  - YRC Worldwide Inc.

Limit Total Stock Holdings

In addition to industry diversification, each stock should initially represent no more than 10 percent of a portfolio. If that stock exceeds 20 percent, sell down to 10 percent.

Buy Quality Stocks

Buying low-quality, speculative stocks is only for the foolish investor. In other words, beware of new, unseasoned issues of stock. One rule of thumb is to always use the Standard & Poor's (S&P) stock ratings. Never, except under exceptional circumstances, buy stocks rated lower than *A* (above average) in the S&P listing.

Limit Trading

Frequent trading of stocks often means settling for small short-term gains. Further, this eliminates the opportunity for double or triple long-term gains. Many small gains through trading also mean heavy commission costs and taxable events. This diminishes a portfolio's net profits.

Sell Losers

The most difficult question for many investors is when to sell. A good rule of thumb is to consider selling when something significantly negative has occurred to the company, something that changes the original reason for the purchase of the stock. Such an event would be an unpleasant surprise in earnings (a decline when a rise is expected), or a negative announcement on a promising new product.

You don't have to be right all the time. Sell the losers, keep the winners. Did your losers go up right after you sold them? So what? You buy fire insurance, and your house didn't burn down. Are you mad? No. You protected yourself. Learn to take losses. Don't let your losses go too far. That is how you lose money in the market. Cut your losses fast; do not wait to break even.

If the stock goes up and you see a fat capital gain, the question becomes one of overpriced stock. Although there are no strict rules here, I like the guideline that the P/E ratio should ideally equal the growth rate. When the P/E exceeds the growth rate, the stock may be too high-priced. Long-term portfolio management is normally a rigid buy-and-sell discipline. On the buy side, I rate a stock as exceptional when the P/E ratio is 50 percent or less of the projected growth rate.

For contrarian investing, the best opportunities for buying stocks are normally when markets are dull or depressed. When the economy is falling, and corporate earnings are turning profits to losses, most investors (both individual and institutional) become frightened and want to flee to the sidelines. Uncertainty usually spells opportunity and the time to buy. Buy when the economic outlook is bleak, and everyone else is full of fear and doom!

Use Dollar-Cost Averaging

This idea has been practiced widely by astute investors for years. Instead of trying to time the highs and lows for their purchases, they have learned the value of investing a fixed dollar amount of money on a regular schedule and letting the principle of dollar-cost averaging work for them.

This plan does not require brilliance or luck, but the discipline to save and invest over a long period. This approach can be very dull. Remember, though: the reason we are investing is to make money! We are not trying to make our adrenal glands surge, or bring a sparkle to our eyes, or share stories about our marvelous cunning in the stock market.

> The certain way to be cheated is to fancy one's self more cunning than others.
>
> —Charron

Let's assume that you are going to get your kicks in other ways, and that you believe becoming financially richer does have some compensating features. What is dollar-cost averaging? Why should you consider it as one method for building your financial estate?

Because dollar-cost averaging works.

Dollar-cost averaging requires investing the same amount of money in the same stock at the same interval over a long period. The reality is that the stock market will fluctuate and eventually go up. These two occur-rences have always happened in the past.

If you become paralyzed into a state of inertia by fear of when to buy, what to buy, and when to sell, skip buying a particular stock and choose a good no-load growth and income mutual fund. Select one that has an excellent reputation for good management and a commendable record of past performance. A fund is especially adaptable to dollar-cost averaging. Under an accumulation plan, you can buy fractional shares carried out to the third decimal point.

You also may invest monthly or quarterly in a monthly investment pro-gram (MIP) plan in a stock listed on the NYSE. However, you may find the MIP plan more costly in the end, and without sufficient diversification. The dividend reinvestment plan DRP (see Chapter 7) is less costly, with no or low commission.

A RELIABLE WAY TO INVEST

The most reliable way to invest in the stock market is dollar-cost averaging. In so doing, your average price per share is lower than the mean average price during the holding period. This is basic math: $100 buys 10 shares of a stock at $10, but only 5 shares at $20. The mean average price was $15. The investor owns 15 shares and paid just $200 for an average price per share of just $13.33.

Three examples of dollar-cost averaging:

In a Declining Market

Investment	Share Price	Shares Acquired
$300	$25.00	12
300	15.00	20
300	20.00	15
300	10.00	30
300	5.00	60
Total $1,500	$75.00	137

Average price per share ($75 ÷ 5) = $15
Dollar-cost average per share ($1,500 ÷ 137) = $10.95

This shows the importance of continuing your investment program throughout a declining market. When the share value dropped from $25 to

$5, that was when the greatest number of shares were purchased. So any recovery above the dollar-cost average of $10.95 would establish a profit.

In a Flat Market

Investment	Share Price	Shares Acquired
$300	$12.00	25
300	15.00	20
300	12.00	25
300	15.00	20
300	12.00	25
Total $1,500	70.00	115

Average price per share ($66 ÷ 5) = $13.20
Dollar-cost average per share ($1,500 ÷ 115) = $13.04

Even in a flat market, dollar-cost averaging can work to your advantage. As the example shows, the actual per share cost is 16 cents less that the average price of $13.20 per share.

In a Rising Market

Investment	Share Price	Shares Acquired
$300	$5.00	60
300	15.00	20
300	10.00	30
300	15.00	20
300	25.00	12
Total $1,500	70.00	142

Average price per share ($70 ÷ 5) = $14
Dollar-cost average per share ($1,500 ÷ 142) = $10.57

As the above example shows, the dollar-cost average per share of the five investments is $10.57, compared with the current $25-per-share value. This example shows the importance of fluctuations in prices to the success of dollar-cost averaging.

The practice of dollar-cost averaging does not remove the possibility of loss when the market is below the average cost. It clearly proves that successful pursuit of the system will lessen the amount of loss in a declining market. It will increase the opportunity of greater profit in a rising market.

This is an excellent approach for the smaller investor just getting started. Additionally, it works well with IRAs and diversified mutual funds.

Let's assume that you can discipline yourself to save $100 a month, or a quarter, or any regular interval. To make this work, you must have the earning capacity and the discipline to do this for a long period. Then get started immediately. We know it makes little or no difference in your results whether the market is going up, down, or sideways when you begin. Getting started does!

Truth has no special time of its own. Its hour is now—always ...

—Albert Schweitzer

The price is what you pay; the value is what you get.

—Warren Buffett

CHAPTER 11

Basic Investment
Guidelines

*The trouble is that clever people are not clever enough
and stupid people are not stupid enough. It is not
always easy to distinguish between the two. Intelligence is something that is better recognized than
defined.*

—Edward de Bono

For many investors, buying and selling stocks is done by sheer impulse—taking a flyer, as they say. Small wonder these investors often crash. They don't want to know the rules, and they refuse to learn by experience.

THE REALITIES OF INVESTING:
MIND OVER MATTER

We are experiencing a market decline as I write this; these are expected and a normal part of the investment process. History has shown that troubled markets eventually will rebound. Maintaining a long-term perspective through challenging economic times is not easy, but it can be rewarding. Over the years, the ups of the market generally have outweighed the downs, resulting in strong long-term growth opportunities.

DON'T PANIC

History has shown that while markets react negatively to shocking events or unfavorable news, they have regained value and grown over time. Long-term investors who have stayed the course and not withdrawn their money from the market have been rewarded for their patience and fortitude, even after significant market declines.

It is a natural instinct to follow the herd when the market is declining and investors are selling at a rapid pace. Sometimes, it is difficult to resist being overcome with emotion when investing.

Every investor should have an investment objective and a strategy. To reach your goals, you have to stick to that strategy.

DO NOT TRY TO PREDICT THE MARKET

It is nearly impossible to predict market movements. For this reason, it is a good idea to stay invested over the long term. Do not run the risk of missing the market's upward move by trying to time the market. While there are no guarantees of a quick rebound, history has shown that investors who remained invested were rewarded. Investors who remained invested versus those who missed the top 5 days in the market, missed the top 15 days in the market, and missed the top 25 days in the market over a 20-year period. No one can accurately predict market performance. Trying to do so by moving in and out of the market can be very costly to you and your portfolio.

Remember, diversifying portfolios over a wide range of industry groups can help reduce and smooth the effects of normal volatility and market conditions. Diversification works, because when some industry groups fall in value, others tend to perform well. Again, I must say that a drop in value is the opportune time to invest more funds at bargain prices.

If you were looking for the perfect investment, you would probably want its attributes to include high returns with little risk. The truth is that such an investment is next to impossible to find. It is not enough to look at the risk and reward of one particular stock. By investing in more than one stock, an investor can reap the benefits of diversification, also known as not putting all your eggs in one basket. Diversification reduces the risk in your portfolio.

For most investors, the risk they take when they buy one stock is that the return will be less than they expected. The risk in a portfolio of diverse individual stocks will be less than the risk of holding any one stock. Consider a portfolio that holds two risky stocks, one that is dependent on cotton harvests and the other on rice. Cotton has to be dry, with no rain, to grow, but rice has to have lots of rain to grow. A portfolio that contains both crops will always pay off, regardless of whether it rains or shines. Adding one risky crop to another can reduce the overall risk of an all-weather portfolio.

In other words, investment is not just about selecting diverse stocks, but about choosing the right combination of stocks in which to distribute one's nest eggs.

How many stocks for portfolio diversification? Mutual funds can contain many dozens of stocks. Some say even 100 stocks is not enough to diversify away disorganized risk. Others conclude that you would come very close to achieving optimal diversity after adding the 20th stock. I personally prefer 30 in different industry groups.

The following principles will give you an excellent foundation for successful investing. I employ these principles and strategies for my portfolio, and have benefited from them:

- Strive for stocks and markets that offer the potential for positive results and the least disappointments.
- Avoid the madness of crowds or herd instinct that prevails in the stock market; this often causes rises or falls to entirely unreasonable and unsustainable price levels. Stock prices become over- and undervalued because of this and other irrational emotional factors.
- Don't marry a stock! Don't grow so attached that you would not sell the stock for any reason.
- Understand that a stock or market can be swayed by more than just fundamentals for a period of time, which may have minor negative or positive surprises that will temporarily alter expectations.
- Study, analyze, and decide for yourself; do not guess or listen to self-proclaimed experts. Prepare a plan for both good and bad news and promptly take action.
- Recognize that correct fundamental analysis can often give positive results, but these results can take more or less time than originally expected.

Withstand the temptation to sell during a bear market. Use this opportunity to buy undervalued stocks for your portfolio. This can create a handsome reward when the market goes back to previous highs.

Remember, you are not buying the market, or the Dow Jones Industrial Average (DJIA). You are buying shares of ownership in a successful company.

Buying stock in a company, based on proper study and prudent judgment, lowers the risk of general market volatility. Market risk is highest for securities with above-average price volatility. Market risk is of little concern to a person who purchases securities with the intention of holding them for the long term.

Perception is very important, if not the pivotal factor influencing market movement, up or down. Wrong is not a dirty word. We are going to pick stocks that go down while markets go the other way. The ultimate mistake is to remain wrong.

Remember: You should always be fully invested. Classic bull market moves are so sudden and so powerful that missing even the first few days of one can wreck your long-term total returns. If you weren't already in when things were going down, you'll be afraid to invest in stocks that just went up.

I saw fear in others in 1987. The longer I look back on Black Monday, the more I am satisfied that I knew what to do and did it. I favorably affected my long-term capital gains. Many at the investor center were sad, nervous, lost confidence in their ability to trade, and lost a great amount of money.

The important point is that you absolutely have to buy during a *market down phase*. No one knows how far *down* is. You may lose money for awhile, buying stocks that are undervalued but have not yet reached the bottom. Don't wait, though; market down phases are few and far between. Buy, buy, buy. Always buy undervalued stocks. The reason is that you cannot tell a real bull market until stocks have already risen 25 to 50 percent.

CAPITALIZE ON STOCK MARKET ANXIETY AND EUPHORIA

Financial experts sometimes give wrong advice. Joseph Granville signaled "sell everything" and Howard Ruff preached "doom and gloom." The resulting anxiety and subsequent selling by their followers caused the market to drop. An informed investor capitalizes on that anxiety by buying those undervalued stocks whose prices fell below their fundamental values and very shortly thereafter recovered.

> They should try to be fearful when others are greedy and greedy only when others are fearful.
>
> —Warren Buffett

Warren Buffett is buying as I write this, in January 2009; is that simpleminded? No, it's simply his recognition of the fact that the crowd can become irrational, producing valuations that anyone who is not caught up in the frenzy can easily see are too high or too low.

Of course, when euphoria or market consensus causes most people to buy, the market rises. The informed investor capitalizes on the optimism or euphoria by selling the overvalued stocks and taking a reasonable profit. Never run with the herd. An informed contrarian buys when others are selling and sells when others are buying.

REMEMBER, NO ONE BECOMES POOR TAKING A PROFIT

Economic recessions and recoveries will always occur on a cyclical basis. Until the nature of human psychology changes, the devastating effect of a bear market will be as profound as the euphoric effect of a bull market. The resulting mania propels the market even further in either direction.

The antidote to market anxiety and euphoria are principles that I have experienced and studied. My stock market insights follow; but, remember safety first, rather than reward.

What is my investing style?

Value investing. Benjamin Graham introduced the idea of intrinsic value—the fair value of a stock, based on its future earnings power. Graham looked for securities with prices that were unjustifiably low based on their intrinsic value. Like bargain seekers, value investors seek products that are beneficial and of high quality but underpriced. I look in the trash heap for bargains that are really treasures overlooked by other investors.

> The worst trades are generally when people freeze and start to pray and hope, rather than take some action.
>
> —Robert Mnuchin

Like many successful formulas, it looks simple. But simple does not mean easy. To guide me in my decisions, I use key considerations categorized in the areas of business, management, financials, and value. These considerations may seem easy to know, but they can be very difficult to execute. Other considerations may seem complex, but are easy to execute.

My traditional style of investing is open to adaptation. I have modified Graham's methods to use covered call options. (Call options were first introduced in April 1973.)

UNDERSTANDING BANKRUPTCY

> What men want is not knowledge but certainty.
>
> —Bertrand Russell

Your greatest fear has been realized! The company in which you have invested has gone broke and is unable to pay its debts. This is the worst thing that could happen to you. What should you do? How could you have known?

Of course, you felt it was coming and should have sold the stock, but you didn't. How did you know? By the price of the stock falling to new lows, the report of the independent auditors contained in the annual report, and general economic conditions

In 2008, as the curtain fell on one of the most devastating financial years on record, business bankruptcies—both large and small—continue to soar. More than 63,000 U.S. businesses filed for protection under the Bankruptcy Code. Dealing with bankruptcy has become an important part of investing in today's environment. Investors need to understand some basic principles of the Bankruptcy Code.

The combination of massive job losses, stagnant consumer spending, tighter credit and the subprime mortgage crisis have hindered businesses nationwide if not worldwide. Some of the victims include Washington Mutual and Lehman Brothers, the two largest corporate bankruptcies in America's history.

Thousands of smaller companies also have been forced to liquidate or restructure through bankruptcy. They include natural gas markets, car dealerships, and many retail store chain store firms.

When the recession began, businesses nationwide were filing an average of 250 bankruptcy petitions a day. That average has increased steadily, reaching 350 per day in December 2008.

Things look even worse for 2009, when business filings are likely to increase 50 percent. The business experts expect a wave of retail bankruptcies in the first quarter of 2009, as struggling businesses run out of money after hanging on for the holiday shopping season. Circuit City was one of them.

Earlier, the nation's largest poultry producer, Pilgrim's Pride, sought Chapter 11 bankruptcy protection. The uncertainty shows no sign of lessening.

The federal bankruptcy code is federal law, administered by specialized bankruptcy courts. There are two kinds of bankruptcy: involuntary, when one or more creditors petition to have a debtor judged insolvent by a court, and voluntary, when the debtor files the petition. In both cases, the objective is an orderly and equitable settlement of obligations.

Chapter 7 Bankruptcy

Chapter 7 bankruptcy deals with liquidation. It provides for a court-appointed interim trustee with broad powers and discretion to make management changes, arrange unsecured financing, and generally operate the debtor business in such a way as to prevent further loss. Assets will be sold so that everything possible can be converted to cash in order to liquidate the business. Usually, a distress sale means assets will go for 25 cents or less on the dollar. After taxes, trustee fees, investigators, lawyers, and the creditors are paid, there usually is nothing left for the shareholders.

A prime example is the case of the International Gold Bullion Exchange, whose thousands of investors lost millions of dollars in one of the nation's biggest commodity scams. Investors claimed they were owed close to $80 million, but assets to satisfy them and the creditors only amounted to $1.6 million. After the IRS and state and local governments received their tax money and about 175 exchange employees were paid for their last weeks of work, there wasn't anything left for the investors.

Chapter 11 Bankruptcy

Chapter 11 bankruptcy deals with reorganization. It provides that, unless the court rules otherwise, the debtor remains in possession of the business and in control of its operation. Debtor and creditors are allowed considerable flexibility in working together. It makes possible the negotiation of payment schedules, restructuring of debt, and even the granting of loans by the creditors to the debtor.

Restructuring debt usually means the easing of debt and the time allowed to repay. Assets will be sold, but in a more opportune manner, giving the business a cash infusion to allow it to continue.

To accomplish all this, the stock will be watered, meaning the shareholders will suffer a total loss of their investment or certainly a large dilution of their stock's value. At least your investment is still alive, and you may still recover some of your investment with time. You should have sold before the company got into trouble.

Kmart is an excellent example of this. The stock was declared worthless, and the management reorganized the company. Kmart was allowed to keep most of their 2,000 stores, and used their equity to buy Sears. The stock went out at a loss and reopened, after purchasing Sears Holding, at a price of $175.

Persons and businesses that supply goods or services and financial institutions that lend money to a Chapter 11 debtor after the bankruptcy case has commenced typically receive priority to payment from the debtor. This priority usually leads to a full payment and answers the question, "Why is anyone willing to deal with a bankrupt corporation?"

Because of the priority given to ongoing suppliers, debtors can keep their businesses running long after a bankruptcy petition is filed. However, the vast majority of Chapter 11 reorganizations do not succeed. When it becomes evident that the continued operation of the debtor will only waste assets, the debtor ceases operation voluntarily or by court order. The Chapter 11 proceedings then become essentially a liquidation case and are formally converted to proceedings under Chapter 7.

For creditors, bankruptcy cases lead to one question: "How much will I get paid?" Creditors holding collateral can look to the value of the collateral for payment. After all the debtor's assets that have been pledged as collateral are sold and the proceeds distributed, the bankruptcy code has an elaborate system of priorities to distribute any remaining assets to creditors not holding collateral.

Suppliers, lenders, and others who help administer the debtor's business have first priority to payment. The bankruptcy code also gives priority to wage claims from the debtor's former employees and federal, state, and local tax claims. The last priority is given to the debtor's general creditors, which includes the typical suppliers. General trade creditors are often fortunate to receive a small percentage of their claim against the debtor.

Stockholders are owners of the business, and therefore usually will receive nothing. There are two good things that come from all this: You have a deduction for your income tax and you have some wallpaper (stock certificates) with which to decorate your den.

> An excellent monument might be erected to the Unknown Stockholder. It might take the form of a solid stone ark of faith apparently floating in a pool of water.
>
> —Felix Riesenberg
>
> No man can make another a debtor against his will.
>
> —Legal maxim

KEY CONSIDERATIONS

Business is a key consideration. You are not just buying stock; you are buying a piece of a business, ownership in a quality company capable of making earnings. First, analyze the business, not the market or the economy or investor sentiment. Look for a consistent operating history, profits, any competitors, and the products or services they all produce.

Secondly, consider the job that management is doing. Is management smart? Is management retaining earnings or returning profits as dividends to the shareholders? Is management doing a good job, as outlined in the annual report and verified by the independent auditors? How are they doing, businesswise, compared to competitors' new products or services?

When looking at a company's financials, I look for high profit margins, return on equity, return on assets, and amount of debt and equity, all of which can be found in the annual report.

Has the company performed well in the past five to ten years? Sometimes, return on equity (ROE) reveals the rate at which shareholders are earning income on their shares. ROE is calculated as follows:

$$ROE = Net\ Income \div Shareholder's\ Equity$$

Does the company have an excessive or manageable debt/equity ratio? This ratio shows the proportion of equity and debt the company is using to finance its assets; the lower the ratio, the more equity is financing the company. A high level of debt can result in volatile earnings and large interest expenses. Debt/equity ratio is calculated as follows:

$$Debt/Equity\ Ratio = Total\ Liabilities \div Shareholder's\ Equity$$

How high are profit margins, and are they increasing? The profitability depends not only on having a good profit margin but also on increasing this profit margin. To get a good indication of past profit margins, look back at least five years. Profit margins are calculated as follows:

$$Profit\ Margin = Net\ Income \div Net\ Sales$$

Lastly, consider value investing. Value investing is looking at companies that have a track record of at least 10 years and have withstood the test of time, but are currently undervalued. Never underestimate the value of past performance, which shows the company's ability or inability to increase shareholder value. Remember that past performance of a stock does not guarantee future performance. It is the investor's job to determine this.

Is the stock a value selling for less than it is worth? This is the hardest part of determining the stock's worth. You will have to analyze the intrinsic value of the company, checking earnings, revenues, and assets. Look at intangibles, such as a brand name or any character that a competitor would find hard to overcome to gain market share.

After determining the intrinsic value of the company, compare it to its current stock price (market capitalization), the current total worth. If this measure of intrinsic value is higher than the company's market capitalization, you have discovered a real value stock.

Markets cycle as much on people's emotions as they do on market fundamentals. When a stock you purchased goes up, you feel euphoric. When it goes down, you feel defeated. But making an investment decision based on emotions instead of reasoned analysis can lead to costly mistakes. As they say about roller coasters, you only get hurt if you jump off in the middle of the ride.

ALWAYS REMEMBER

- Do not panic and always do your research. Look for value.
- Always have patience. Ninety-five percent of the market moves are unpredictable and perhaps 5 percent are predictable.
- Always buy stock at or below the average of the year's high and low price.
- Always take your profit when the stock is overvalued.
- Always reinvest your dividends and capital gains.
- Always disregard "hot tips."
- Balance momentum, growth and value.
- Never buy stocks at market; always make them limit orders.
- Never buy a sympathy stock. Never buy a weak company because a strong one has started to move. Many do this, and it is rarely profitable. Buy the company that is going up.
- Never buy a stock that did not go up in a bull market. Smart money is never placed on a nonachiever.
- Never sell a stock that did not go down in a bear market. The smart money is in holding its position.
- Never sell an inactive stock just as it begins to move up.
- Never overpay for comfort, excitement, and sex appeal. These are traps for uninformed investors.

A writer writes, a reader reads. As a writer, I know who I am and what the material means to me. But I can't begin to know who the reader will be, or what background that reader will or won't bring to the page.

I have tried to write a book that will be useful and of value to both investors and prospective investors. It starts out simply and then grows in detail. It reflects my involvement over the years with the investment process.

The rest of the book explains in greater depth these techniques, practices, and strategies. Hold on to your money until you have a working knowledge of what follows. It is essential that you have a full understanding of the principles discussed in order to take advantage of them.

Then again, remember that portfolio theory is just that—theory. At the end of the day, a portfolio's success rests on the investor's skills and the time he or she devotes to the portfolio. Sometimes it is better to select a small number of out-of-favor investments and wait for the market to turn in your favor. Yes, luck happens.

Patience is power; with time and patience, the mulberry leaf becomes silk.
—Chinese proverb

Trust everybody, but cut the cards.
—Finley Dunne

CHAPTER 12

Options and the Stock Market

Money is like a sixth sense without which you cannot make a complete use of the other five.

—W. Somerset Maugham

You are now ready to be introduced to the real world of the stock market. A stock can do three things: it can go up, it can go down, or it can stay the same in value. Regardless of what the stock value does, it can be to your advantage. You will learn how to deal with this volatility and make money.

The brokerage industry has finally come up with a wonder weapon: Exchange listed options.

WHAT IS AN OPTION?

According to *Webster's New World Dictionary*, option is defined as "1. to wish, desire. 2. . . . choosing; choice. 3. the power, right, or liberty of choosing. 4. the right, acquired for a consideration, to buy or sell . . . something at a fixed price . . . within a specified time." The last definition applies to options in the stock market.

The following material is an introduction to the use of options as an investment tool. The material is divided into two sections. The first section describes the basic terminology of options, factors affecting option prices, and the ways options are bought and sold. The second section describes why an investor would buy or sell an option. It also deals with the basic concepts of options and how and why an investor would use them.

THE BUSINESS OF OPTIONS

Options of one kind or another are commonplace in the business world, such as the option to purchase real estate. The essential components of a securities option are: a description of the security the option buyer may purchase from, or sell to, the option writer; the price at which the security may be purchased or sold; and the time period during which the buyer of the option must exercise or lose his or her right. If the option buyer chooses not to exercise his or her right during the allocated time, the option simply expires. It ceases to exist.

For the time granted by the option, the buyer pays, and the writer receives, a sum of money. The money is kept by the writer whether the option is exercised or not. This is the option premium. Each option is normally for 100 shares of a specific, widely held, actively traded stock. The stock is the underlying security.

The price at which the option buyer may elect to exercise the right obtained with the purchase of the option is the exercise price, also known as the strike price. The expiration date is the last day on which the buyer is entitled to exercise the option to purchase or sell the stock.

An option is a legal contract that gives the right to buy or sell a specified stock at a specified price—the *strike price*—before a specified date—the *expiration date*. An option giving the buyer the right to purchase the stock at a fixed price is called a *call option*. An option giving the buyer the right to sell the stock at a fixed price is known as a *put option*.

The *premium* is the money the buyer pays to acquire the option. The option writer, the seller of the option, receives the premium money. The premium is mostly what options trading is all about.

Most buyers hope to purchase an option when the premium is low and later sell the same option for a higher premium, realizing a profit on the increase. Other buyers hope the market price of the underlying stock will rise above the exercise price of the option (in the case of calls) or fall below the exercise price of the option (in the case of puts) by an amount that enables the buyer to exercise the option at a profit. That is, the buyer will either acquire the stock from the writer of the call option below the stock's current market value or sell it to the writer of the put option at above the stock's current market value.

Writers of options regard the premiums they receive as a source of additional income or as a hedge against a possible decline in the market price of stocks that they own or wish to purchase.

Just as an option buyer may sell the option at any time prior to expiration, realizing a profit or loss on the increase or decrease in the premium, an option writer can *buy to close* an option that he or she sold (assuming that the option had not been exercised or expired). This offsetting transaction terminates the obligation to deliver or purchase the underlying stock. The profit or loss is the difference between the premium of the option initially sold and the premium of the option later purchased.

The ability of the option writer to terminate his or her obligation to deliver or purchase the stock by buying an offsetting option in no way affects the buyer's right to exercise the option he or she bought. The reason is that the Options Clearing Corporation (OCC) acts as the buyer to every seller and seller to every buyer. There is no continuing relationship between original buyer and seller. This feature helps to ensure the financial integrity of all options bought and sold on the option exchanges.

Listed options are securities that are regulated by the exchange on which they are traded. A *listed securities option* is a contract to buy or sell units of an underlying security at a specified price, at any time before the option expires. An option contract is for 100 shares (unless adjusted for stock splits or stock dividends).

Option buyers, or holders, pay a premium for the right to buy or sell the underlying security. The seller or writer of a call option is obligated to sell the underlying security to the option buyer if the call is exercised. The seller or writer of a put option is obligated to buy the underlying stock if the put is exercised.

The essential elements of an option contract are the strike price, premium, and expiration date:

- The strike price or exercise price is the price at which the underlying security can be bought or sold.
- The premium is the price the buyer pays in return for the rights conveyed in the option.
- The expiration date is the last day on which the option can be exercised.

OPTIONS SHARE MANY SIMILARITIES WITH COMMON STOCKS

Both options and stocks are listed securities. Orders to buy and sell options are handled through brokers in the same way as orders to buy and sell stocks. Listed option orders are executed on the trading floors of national SEC-regulated exchanges where all trading is conducted in an open, competitive auction market.

Still another similarity is the opportunity to follow price movements, trading volume, and other important information minute by minute or day by day. The buyer or writer of an option, like the buyer or seller of stock, can learn almost instantly the price at which the order was executed.

It is important to understand that an option is simply a contract involving a buyer and a seller willing to pay a premium to obtain certain rights and a seller willing to grant these rights in return for the premium. So, unlike shares of common stock, there is no fixed number of options. The number of options depends solely on the number that buyers wish to buy and that sellers are willing to write. What is a great opportunity for the option sellers is that there are always more buyers than sellers.

When the OCC is satisfied that there are matching orders from a buyer and a seller, it completely terminates the contractual obligations.

The buyer and the seller are free to act independently of one another. If a buyer sells an option he has previously purchased, and a seller buys back an option he has previously sold, the result is one less option. Most options are offset in this way, by a closing purchase or a sale, prior to reaching the expiration date. This is called open interest, the number of options that are outstanding. The OCC guarantees all options it has issued.

Like stocks, options trade with buyers making bids and sellers making offers. In stocks, those bids and offers are for shares of stock. In options, the bids and offers are for the right to buy or sell 100 shares (per option contract) of the underlying stock at a given price per share for a given period of time.

HISTORY OF OPTIONS

In the year 1694, put and call options were introduced in London, England. More than two and a half centuries later, put and call options continue to be an important addition to security dealings.

Introduced into this country about a century ago, put and call options soon became the favorite speculative tool of the old-time Wolves of Wall Street. The conventional shied away from them, and to this day, many cast a prejudiced eye upon options. The ordinary investor used to regard dealing in puts and calls as a special, complicated maneuver, tinged with evil. About 40 years ago, when threatened with the stopping of option trading, the Put and Call Brokers and Dealers Association instituted rules and standards that resulted in a degree of respectability for put and call options. Since then, these stock options have become better understood and more widely used by investors to hedge against price movements, to protect unrealized profits, and to gain potential tax savings.

Although the history of options extends over several centuries, it was not until 1973 that standardized, exchange-listed, and government-regulated options became available. In only a few years, these options almost displaced the limited trading in over-the-counter options. The options trading has become an indispensable tool for the securities industry.

FUNCTION OF OPTIONS

Standardized option contracts provide orderly, efficient, and liquid option markets. All stock option contracts are for 100 shares of the underlying stock. The strike price of an option is the specified share price at which the shares of stock will be bought if the holder exercises the option.

Options are an extremely versatile investment tool. Because of their unique risk/reward structure, options can be used with other financial instruments to create a hedged position.

A stock option allows you to fix the price, for a specific period of time, at which you can sell 100 shares of stock. For a price (premium) this option is granted. Unlike other investments where the risk may have no limit, options offer a known risk to buyers.

The OCC selects the companies to be listed on the option exchanges. Though most companies favor this listing because it adds interest in their securities, the choice is not theirs. Listing requirements state that trading of the company stock must be at a high volume and above $10 per share. If these requirements are not met, new option expirations are not traded, and when existing contracts expire, companies are delisted, or taken off of the options list.

The OCC guarantees that the terms of an option contract will be honored. There are no ifs, ands, or buts with options.

Before the existence of option exchanges and the OCC, an option holder who wanted to exercise an option depended on the ethical and financial integrity of the writer (or his or her brokerage firm) for performance. Also, there was no convenient means of closing out one's position before the expiration of the contract.

The OCC, as the common clearing entity for all SEC-regulated option transactions, resolves these difficulties. Once the OCC verifies that there are matching orders from a buyer and a seller, it ends the transactions. In effect, OCC becomes the buyer to the seller and the seller to the buyer, guaranteeing contract performance. The seller can buy back the same option he has written, closing out the transaction and terminating his obligation to deliver the underlying stock. This in no way affects the right of the original buyer to sell, hold, or exercise his option. All premium and settlement payments are made to and paid by the OCC.

FACTORS AFFECTING OPTION VALUATION

The importance of premium to buyers and sellers alike raises the question of what factors determine the amount of the premium and what causes it to increase and decrease.

As with any item traded in a competitive market, the price, or premium, is dependent on supply and demand. During times of rising stock market prices, there is usually interest in purchasing calls. Investors who own stocks when stock prices are rising prefer to hold their stock in the hope of further appreciation. When more investors interested in buying calls and fewer investors are interested in writing them, the result usually is to raise the level of call premiums.

In times of generally weak or declining stock prices, there is greater interest in writing call options but less interest in buying them. Correspondingly, premiums tend to decline.

The reverse applies to put options. Strong stock prices tend to reduce the demand, and thus the price, of puts. Weak stock prices generally increase the demand, and thus the price, of puts.

In addition, investors should be familiar with three other factors that interact to influence the level and movement of option premiums. The price or premium of an option is dependent on:

1. The price movement (volatility) of the underlying stock.
2. The period of time to expiration of the option (more time means more money).
3. The difference between the current stock price and the strike price.

Underlying Security

The underlying security is the stock, which can be purchased or sold according to the terms of the option contract and is the base upon which a sound option-writing program rests. The ideal stock for option writing would be one with medium volatility and a growth potential based on solid fundamental value. A dividend is also preferable but not a requirement.

Volatility

Volatility is a measure of stock price fluctuation. If a common stock traditionally fluctuates a good deal, the option is likely to command a higher premium than the option for a stock that normally trades in a narrow price range.

Look at the relationship between the exercise price and the current market value of the stock. As a general rule, premiums neither increase or decrease point for point with the price of the underlying stock. That is, a one-point change in the stock usually results in a less-than-one-point change in the option premium.

While premiums, for the reasons mentioned, generally do not increase point for point with stock prices, neither do they tend to decrease point for point when stock prices drop. The reason: time value. Even a sharp drop in the price of the stock over, say, three days has only a small impact on that component of the premium that reflects the option's remaining time value.

Time Value

Time value obviously affects option premiums during periods of rising and falling stock prices. All things being equal, the more time remaining until the expiration date, the higher the premium tends to be.

For example, in January, an October 50 call is sold on ABC Corp. The October 50 call commands a higher option premium than one for an identical July 50 call, because the buyer of the October option has an additional three months for the underlying stock to increase or decrease in price.

It should be evident that an option is a *wasting asset*. Common stock can be held indefinitely in the hope that it may eventually become profitable, or that an already profitable stock may become even more profitable. As the expiration date approaches, the time value will decline and eventually become zero. At expiration, the option's only value will be the intrinsic value, the amount that is in the money.

The Stock's Current Price and the Strike Price

The relationship between the current market price and the strike price of the option is a major factor affecting option premiums. In January, an investor purchases a July 50 ABC call, when the market price is $50. At this time the investor is paying for six months' time and the possibility that the market price will rise in value in this time. Let us assume that in April, the market value of ABC has climbed to $60. The investor who now buys an ABC July 50 with the stock at $60 will pay a higher price than the original investor, who only had an expectation that the stock would appreciate in value. With ABC stock at $60 the July 50 is called as in the money call option, because the market price of the stock is greater than the strike price of the call.

Option Valuation Example:
DEF Corp. stock is selling on the New York Stock Exchange (NYSE) at $32 a share today.

- Option 1 gives the buyer the right to buy DEF Corp. stock at $25 a share.
- Option 2 gives the buyer the right to buy DEF Corp. stock at $35 a share.

Option 1 is more valuable, since the buyer would rather have an option to pay $25 for a $32 stock. As a result, it costs more to buy Option 1 than to buy Option 2.

Sellers know this, so as the stock price rises and falls, the option price rises and falls with it. As time elapses towards the expiration date, the option price falls because of the wasting time value. Option investors, like stock investors, can follow price movements, trading volume, and other pertinent information day-by-day or even minute-by-minute.

There are some important differences between options and common stocks that should be noted. Unlike common stock, an option has a limited life. Common stocks can be held indefinitely in the hope that their value may increase, while an option has an expiration date. If an option is not closed out or exercised before its expiration date, it ceases to exist as a financial instrument, which is why it is considered a wasting asset. There is not a fixed number of options, as there is with common stock shares. An option is simply a contract involving a buyer willing to pay a price to obtain certain rights and a seller willing to grant these rights in return for the price. Thus, unlike shares of common stock, the number of outstanding option contracts, commonly called *open interest*, depends solely on the number of buyers and sellers interested in receiving and giving these rights.

Unlike stocks, which have certificates, option positions are shown on printed statements prepared by a buyer's or seller's brokerage firm. This procedure sharply reduces paperwork and delays.

While stock ownership gives the holder a share of the company, including certain voting rights and rights to dividends (if any), option owners' only benefit is from an upward price movement of the stock.

The *option contract* is defined by the following elements: type (a call or a put), underlying security (deliverable security), and strike price and expiration date. All option contracts that are the same type, cover the same underlying security, and have the same strike price and same expiration date are referred to as an option series and are fungible.

Fungibility is a very important word for option traders. All options in an option series are fungible. All fungible assets, such as commodities, options, and securities, are interchangeable. For example, investors' shares of GHI Corp., left in custody at a brokerage firm, are freely mixed with other shares of GHI stock options, and are freely interchangeable among investors, just as wheat stored in a grain elevator is not specifically identified as to its ownership. We use the concept of fungibility later to our advantage in investing with covered call options.

THE OPTION PREMIUM

The *option premium* is the cash price exchanged when buying or selling options. Premiums fluctuate depending on the duration of the contract, the strike price, and the current price of the underlying stock. Premiums can run as high as 25 percent of the value of the underlying stock; that is, for a volatile stock selling at $20 ($2,000 for 100 shares), the premium for a call to be exercised in 9 months might be $5 ($500) when the exercise price is also $20. Shorter-term options on more stable stocks carry smaller premiums, from 2 percent (for expiration in a month) to 10 percent for those with longer maturities. Commission costs will lower these returns.

The writer of an option is obligated to deliver the underlying security if the option is exercised. Whether or not an option is ever exercised, the writer keeps the premium.

Premiums are quoted on a per-share basis. Thus, a premium of 1 represents a premium payment of $100 per option contract ($1 × 100 shares). Premium quotations are stated in points and decimals.

An option buyer cannot lose more than the price of the option premium paid. The option will expire as worthless if the conditions for profitable exercise do not occur by the expiration date. Options are a wasting asset that go to zero with time.

In a stock option contract, the premium is the only variable. The number of shares, the expiration month, and the strike prices are all standardized.

There are three classes of people in the world. The first learn from their own experience—these are wise; the second learn from the experience of others—these are happy; the third neither learns from their own experience nor the experience of others—these are fools.

—Anonymous

THE OPTION STRATEGY

To some investors, the very mention of the word option evokes images of very speculative, highly leveraged trades. However, there is an option strategy that is quite conservative and appropriate for most equity investors.

The television advertisement that says "buying an option on stock offers the chance for unlimited profit with a limited risk" is the extent of the knowledge that most people have. Buying options is like buying lottery tickets. You could win big, but the odds are against your winning at all.

But if buying options is a risky endeavor, how about selling them?

Selling options is not risky, and though your winnings are small, you win more often. Option buyers could win big, but the odds are against their winning at all. The money makers in options trading are those who sell options; their winnings are never spectacular, but they are regular.

This strategy is *covered call writing*. The covered call writer does one of two things:

1. Buys stock and simultaneously sells an equivalent number of call options (buy-write).
2. Sells calls with stock that is already owned.

Benefits of Covered Call Writing
- Places money in the investor's account.
- Increases investor's probability of profit, often substantially.
- Allows investors to make a profit, sometimes 50 to 80 percent annualized, without worrying about the swings of stock prices.

What Is a Covered Call Option?

A covered call option is sold by the investor who owns the underlying stock. In case the option is exercised, the seller is covered by the stock that is owned. For example, someone who holds 100 shares of AT&T common is considered covered if they write one option on their stock.

What Is a Covered Writer?

A *covered writer* is the seller or writer of an option contract who owns the underlying stock. Option writers are normally conservative investors seeking additional current income.

Before we go any further, let's understand the first important point. We will always be selling, which means we will always be taking in money. The buyer is on the risky side. He or she must predetermine the value of the stock and the time period he or she wants. The buyer is always paying, which means giving money away. We, the sellers, are always going to be taking in money. Nice, yes?

Sophisticated traders use complex options strategies, such as combination spreads, strips, straps, and straddles. We will not be discussing these at all, as they do not matter to investors only following this one strategy, selling covered call options.

It is our intention to always be selling covered call options, making us the covered option writer. We are not concerned with the other techniques that are available in the option market. We will be using one strategy (i.e., buying an *optionable stock* and writing covered call options on that stock). An optionable stock is one listed on an option exchange (approximately 2,500 companies).

Of my investing, 90 percent involves the stocks of high-quality companies; 10 percent is done in slightly higher-risk companies with the potential for higher rewards. *All* my investing is done in covered call writing. I should add that 75 percent of my gains result from dealing in options.

I am conservative. As the saying goes, I am concerned less with the return on my money than I am with the return of my money. I wish to stress that neither I nor anyone else knows for sure whether a stock is going to go up or down. I do know the prices at which I am a happy buyer or a happy seller. If the stocks do nothing, I will be getting more than the return of a money market investment. Options allow me to own stock in a more conservative manner. Instead of trying for the big capital gain, I can get a good return, with some participation on the upside, through covered call options. I know what the rates of return will be if the stock is called away or if it stays unchanged through expiration. If the stock goes down, the option premium offers some cushion. The key is discipline, which I stress over and over.

> If you must play, decide on three things at the start: the rules of the game, the stakes, and the quitting time.
>
> —Chinese proverb

SOME QUESTIONS AND ANSWERS

Do you want increased cash flow from your investments?

Would you like to reduce the money investment of the stocks you buy?

Do you want to reduce the risk of owning stocks?

Are you puzzled about the right time to sell a stock?

Selling covered call options generates extra earnings from your blue chip securities. This approach solves the investor's most difficult problem—identifying the best time to sell a stock. In effect, that decision is made in advance.

The exercise price of the option helps you establish a target price at which you are willing to sell a stock. The money received by selling the option increases your cash flow. The immediate cash flow has the secondary benefit of reducing the cost of your security and, therefore, reducing the risk of owning stock.

In an article on covered call option writing, *Changing Times* magazine said, "It's popular among both individual and institutional investors. Many bank trust departments and pension fund managers use it to generate extra income on stocks in their portfolios and as a hedge against price declines." No matter whether the market environment is bearish, neutral, or bullish, the covered option writer will fare better than the investor who buys and holds only equities.

From now on we will refer to covered call options simply as *options*. Options are a powerful, mysterious segment of the financial market.

We shall be studying call options, the most popular and widely used option. We will ignore put options, which are a mirror image, the opposite of call options. Calls are for the right to buy stocks. Puts are for the right to sell stocks. I always prefer to deal with stocks that are going up than those going down.

The use of exchange listed options enhances returns in a variety of ways:

- By hedging downside risk.
- By combining risk protection with upside potential.
- By making tactical adjustments without having to buy or sell securities.
- By increasing liquidity through more risk-return alternatives.

GETTING STARTED

I am going to give you a method that will greatly increase the income that you receive from dividend paying stocks without adding significant risk.

Before you can start, you will have to be approved for option writing by your broker. You will submit an application entitled "Options Client Agreement and Approval Form." You will want the most limiting option level 1: Covered Equity/Call Writing. In this level, calls are fully covered by the underlying stock. If assigned, the client will be required to sell sufficient shares of stock at the strike price, which may be substantially lower than the current market price. Potential for loss on the stock position is substantial. The hedging benefit of the option is limited only to the amount of the premium received.

Now you will be prepared to implement this strategy, which involves the use of options or contracts that permit the sale of call options of a specific security at a set price (strike price). Just like options to buy in the real estate industry, these contracts have predetermined time frames.

The most important thing you need to know for this relatively simple option strategy is that options originate from investors themselves. This strategy is known as *writing the covered call* and is a very conservative approach.

> Experience is not what happens to a man; it is what a man does with what happens to him.
>
> —Aldous Huxley

WHY SELLERS SELL CALLS: SOME STRATEGIES

Writers (sellers) of calls likewise seek two basic objectives: additional income from their stock investments, coupled with protection against a decline in the market price of their stocks. The call premiums can help the option writer achieve these goals.

With the covered call strategy, you can use stocks that you already own, or you can purchase new stocks to sell covered call options on. In either case, you will not be overly concerned about the movement of your stocks up or down over a specific period of time. However, you will only write covered calls on stock you do own, the underlying stock. This approach gives you income with no risk of loss on the option transaction. (I will explain the one risk this does cause shortly.)

Now, we are going to apply this call option writing to dividend paying stocks. You will be getting two sources of income from the same underlying stocks: the dividends and the money you receive from writing the covered calls. Although we are not concerned with it, there is a third source of income, and that is if the underlying stocks were to rise in value. This is a great scenario. If we were to allow the stock to be called, on delivery we would receive the strike price in addition to the premium received.

As pointed out previously (but worth repeating), the call writer does not have to remain obligated to deliver the stock. The option writer can terminate this obligation (as long as the call has not yet been exercised) simply by purchasing to close an identical option at the current premium price, thereby closing out the position. Note that even if the call option is exercised, you do not have to deliver the original stock. You can purchase new stock to deliver, keeping your low-cost shares or, if you prefer, selling your high-cost shares and improving your portfolio by replacing these with low-cost shares. This process is covered in depth in the chapter on using an option income portfolio as a tax shelter.

Remember that when you write a covered call option, you still own the stock, so you continue to receive all dividends paid before the option is called or exercised. A rare, but possible, exception is that the call holder might want to receive the stock dividend. In this case, the option must be exercised before the underlying stock's *ex-dividend date* (companies check to see who owns the stock on the ex-dividend date to identify the person who should receive the dividend check on the dividend date, giving them time to allow processing and mailing of the checks). This is the only way for the call holder to purchase the underlying shares and be eligible to receive the dividend payment. Later, you will learn how to always avoid this happening to you and your portfolio. Another decision would be a stock that you wish to keep holding even though you feel it will decline in value in that specific time.

Understanding the fundamentals of covered option writing is essential to learning how to distinguish a good covered write. An option gives its holder the right to buy an underlying security. For example, an XYZ Corp. May 20 option entitles the buyer to purchase 100 shares of XYZ Corp. common stock at $20 per share at any time prior to the option's expiration date in May.

When you write (sell) options, you begin with an immediate, sure, limited profit rather than an uncertain potential greater gain. The most you can make is the premium you receive, even if the price of the stock soars. When you write options on the stock you own, any loss of the value of the stock will be reduced by the amount of the premium received.

The *underlying security* is the specific stock on which an option contract is based. Options are derivative securities, because their values are derived in part from the value and characteristics of the underlying security. A stock option contract's unit of trade is 100 shares of underlying stock, which are represented by that option. This means that one option contract represents the right to buy 100 shares of the underlying security.

The *strike price* is the price per share that the holder of the option must pay to buy the corresponding stock, if they choose to exercise their right. The strike price for an option is initially set at a price that is close to the current share price of the underlying security. Additional or subsequent strike prices are set at the following intervals: $2^1/_2$ points when the strike price to be set is $25 or less, or 5 points when the strike price is over $25. New strike prices begin when the price of the underlying security rises to the highest or falls to the lowest strike price currently available.

If the strike price of an option is less than the current market price of the underlying security, the option is said to be *in-the-money*. If the strike price of an option is more than the stock price, it is said to be *out-of-the-money*. If the strike price equals the current market price, the option is said to be *at-the-money*.

Example: At-the-Money Option

At-the-money options are written at an exercise price that is at or close to the current price of the stock. This approach is the one I prefer, as I do not have to predict the price movements of the underlying security.

In January, Paul Prudent buys 100 shares of Always Good (AG) at 20 and sells a July option, at the strike price of 20, for $2 ($200). Paul realizes that AG may move above $22 in the next 6 months, but he is willing to accept the $2 per share income.

Jane, the option buyer, anticipating that AG will move up well above $22, got the right to buy the stock for $20 at any time before the expiration date in July.

Paul will not realize a dollar loss until the price of AG goes below $18. At $22, the profit starts for Jane, the option buyer. Let's see what happens if AG stock rises to $30. At any time before expiration in July, Jane can exercise her option and pay $2,000 for stock that is then worth $3,000. After deducting about $300 (the $200 premium plus commissions), Jane will have a net profit of about $700.

If the price of AG stock moves up to only $22, Jane will call (exercise the option) and buy the stock, but she will not be even because of the premium and commission costs. Paul would have sold the AG stock for $22 ($20 for the stock and $2 for the option), plus two dividends of $25 each.

If the price of AG stock stays at $20 or less, Paul will still own the stock, keep the $200 premium, and can write a new option.

Example: In-the-Money Options

This is a more aggressive technique that requires more attention but can result in great profits and tax benefits.

In January, Joe Smart buys 300 shares of Fantastic Furs (FF) at $20 ($6,000) and sells three July 15 options at $7 each ($2,100). If FF stock stays at or below $15, Joe keeps the premiums and the stock. If it goes to $25, he can buy back the options for $10 (stock price $25 – strike price $15 = $10) or a total price of $3,000 ($10 × 300) to set up a short-term tax loss of –$900 ($3,000 buyback – $2,100 option money = –$900). Joe can sell the shares for $7,500 ($25 per share × 300 shares = $7,500), for a $1,500 gain ($7,500 sale price –$6,000 cost) –$900 option loss for a net gain of $600.

If FF stock drops below $15, Joe keeps the premiums and writes new options. He won't suffer a loss until his real cost of $13 ($20 stock cost – $7 option premium) drops to $13.

In-the-money options are sold at strike prices below the current price of the stock. Since the options involve a smaller investment, there is a higher percentage of return and, in a down market, more protection from loss. In the above example, Joe started with $6,000 worth of stock, with an actual cash outlay of $3,900, because of the option premium money received.

Example: Out-of-the-Money Options

These are written at an exercise price that is above the current price of the stock. In this example Sally Surething owned 300 shares of Safest Safes Industries (SSI), which she had bought at $10 two years earlier. Sally, anticipating a rise in the stock price, wrote an option at a higher strike price. In January, when SSI was at $20, she wrote three option contracts for July 25 at $3 ($900 premium, $3 × 300 = $900). In July, SSI was at $26 and she was exercised. Sally received $25 for the stock and had received $3 premium, for a total sale price of $28 when the stock was only $26.

Out-of-the-money options work best in an up-market with quality stocks that are bought when undervalued and when there are far-out options (six to nine months) with a rich premium. Of course, if the stock price was below $25 at expiration, the option owner would not exercise their right and Sally could rewrite the options again, for an additional new premium.

OPTION EXERCISE

In an option exercise, the option holder buys the underlying stock from the option writer.

If the holder of a call option decides to exercise his right, he must notify his broker or *exercise the option*. The brokerage firm, upon receiving an exercise notice, will assign one or more of its customers, either randomly or on a first-in first-out basis. They may assign the total to one seller. They may assign a part to several sellers' contracts to fill the obligation. This approach results in multiple commissions for the brokerage firm, and you should object strongly if this occurs. The assigned writer is obligated to sell the underlying shares of stock at the specified strike price.

OPTION FUNDAMENTALS

Cash Premium = Time Value + Intrinsic Value

The *cash premium* is the sum of the time value and the intrinsic value. It is received from the sale of the call, which effectively reduces the cost of buying the stock (but not the cost basis), providing a measure of downside protection for the investor against declines in the stock price. The cash premium effectively increases the yield on the investor's position.

Time value represents the value of the time remaining until the expiration of the option. Generally, investors want to sell calls with as much time value as possible. Time value is the part of an option's total price that exceeds intrinsic value. If the option has no intrinsic value, it consists entirely of time value. In general, the greater the time value on a covered write, the better the downside protection and the higher the total return will be.

For example, we sell an out-of-the-money option on a $17.50 dollar stock for a strike price of $20, and we receive $2.50 for a total of $250. (Remember, options trade on 100 share lots.) This is for time value of $2.50, as there is no intrinsic value on this trade. The $2.50 is all time value, as we did sell a $20 strike price.

For another example, let's sell an in-the-money option. The stock is $17.50, and we sell an option for a $15 strike price. We receive $5, $2.50 for time value and $2.50 for intrinsic value, as the stock is $17.50 and we are selling it for $15, $2.50 below the current value.

For an at-the-money option, we will sell a strike price of $17.50 and we will receive $2.50 time value; again, there is no intrinsic value in the option.

Intrinsic value is the in-the-money portion of an option's price. The difference between the strike price and the market value of the underlying security is the intrinsic value. Have your cake and eat it too.

Nearly all the time, covered call options allow you to do this. You can hold your stock for the long-term, collect any dividends, and receive option premiums also.

For example, you own a stock that is selling for $30, and you do not expect it to go higher than $33 in the next six months. The option writing is fairly straightforward; you can sell a contract for every 100-share lot you own at a strike price of $35 per share. You will collect the amount that is paid for the contract. Like a dividend, this payment is yours to keep no matter what.

Your only risk: if the stock rises above $35 and the option holder decides to exercise the option, the shares you own would be called away. You could lose the opportunity to make the profit from the stock's rise above the $35 level. Later in this book, I demonstrate how this does not have to happen, and how you can in fact achieve great results.

Remember, the option buyer has to be correct on the strike price and the time frame, which is a wasting asset, in order to win.

More complete summary of the possible outcomes:

- If the stock price fails to rise above the $35 by the end of six months, the investor who bought your call option will let it expire, worthless. You get to keep your stock, plus the premium money you collected for the option.
- If the stock price rises above the strike price, but the option holder fails to exercise the contract, and then the price falls back down below $35 at the end of the six months, you get to keep the premium money you collected for the option.
- If the stock price goes nowhere, you keep the premium money.
- If the stock price goes down, you keep the premium money. Your shares may be worth less, but you realized a gain from the option. You are free to write it again for a lower stock price, taking in additional premium money.
- If the stock rises above $35 and the option holder exercises his or her right to buy your shares, surprise execution is a possibility. Remember, options can be traded at any time that the option buyer desires. The shares will be called away from your account for the strike price. You have still received the premium money in addition to the stock sale; or, you could buy new shares to give to the exercise of your shares, keeping your lower cost basis shares. Remember, the option holder just wants your shares, and does not care how long you have held them. You could have gotten the shares years ago from your father, and the cost basis may be very low, or you could have just bought them today. It does not matter to the option holder. This is a more costly way to answer an assignment, as you have to rebuy the shares for another new stock commission.
- If the stock rises above $35, before the option holder exercises his or her right to buy your shares, you can buy back the shares in a closing transaction. This tactic enables you to keep your shares, especially if you have a low cost basis, and sell a new option at a higher price for

a new option premium. This is a less costly approach, as you do not have to sell your old called-away shares and replace them with another stock commission.

Assuming that the option expires worthless, you are now able to write a new call option with a new strike price and a new expiration date, and receive a new premium.

The most important consideration when developing a covered write strategy is the underlying stock. The investor must have a positive opinion of the stock. I look for stocks with solid value, and don't second-guess the market to find a high-flyer stock that is going to be a big gainer.

The second consideration must be the rate of return generated by the position. The combined return from the appreciation on the stock, the option premium, and the dividends received should exceed alternative investments with comparable risk/reward characteristics.

This is a conservative investment approach. The idea behind it is to earn added income from assets that are solid and productive in their own right. The stock selection process used is a defensive one. The stocks chosen are those that pay a good option premium. The emphasis in this approach is *not losing.*

By following a rigid discipline, we can overcome many amateur errors. There is absolutely no room in this approach for the latest hot tip or gut feeling. To repeat, the most important part of this investment program is the quality of the underlying security.

The stocks included in your options program should be evaluated using the standards already discussed. Criteria to review quickly would include dividend yields, the P/E (price/earnings) ratio, and the stock's market history. The stocks in your portfolio will be chosen because they are optionable and because they pay a high premium.

The successful investor should diversify his or her stock holdings as much as possible. Normally, the more stocks in your portfolio, the lower your risk will be.

Once you have analyzed what is available and how much contracts are selling for, you will be able to decide which contracts you will like to write.

Investing with covered call options requires the following four steps:

1. Buy a carefully selected optionable stock; find out what call options are available, how they are priced, and their open interest (the number of outstanding contracts.) We will learn about option chains to do this.
2. Sell options (collect a premium) for cash with a good return.
3. When an option expires, write another option (collect a premium).
4. When an option is exercised, sell the stock for the strike price.

The goal of option writing is to reduce risk and to generate extra income. After wincing over single-digit returns, it's no wonder that interest-starved investors perk up at talk of squeezing extra yield from their stocks. This extra yield is after commissions and on top of dividends paid by the stock.

The fascinating question is, why would someone be willing to give you extra profit? The answer is there are really two someones involved.

The most visible someone is the brokerage firm offering the chance for riches by enticing investors to buy options. The firm is willing to offer the chance for unlimited wealth because it gets a commission to act as broker.

The other someone is the option seller. Most of these people are professional traders, both on and off the exchange trading floor. They are willing to sell options for the same reasons as insurance companies and mutual funds: to increase their earnings and have a protective hedge against a downside in the market.

Option sellers are familiar with the markets; they know that the market will move, and they can balance potential risk against potential reward.

There are always opportunities for individual investors to use options as a part of a total plan. With careful selection and constant monitoring, selling options can:

- Boost annual income by 15 percent or more.
- Be used for tax benefits and low costs.
- Give a variety of choice (in underlying assets, strike prices, and time frames).

Remember: Never buy options, only sell them! Buying options is speculation! Selling options is investing!

Every dollar that option buyers lose goes into the pockets of option sellers. Since a majority of options—70 percent—expire worthlessly, it means that the seller of an option who waits for it to expire has a good chance of making profit. Investors with adequate time and the financial resources to operate on the seller's side of the options market can build a fortune with these odds.

Selling (or writing) options turns off most uneducated investors for a couple of reasons. To begin with, there doesn't seem to be much money in it. Most stock options transactions sell for $500 or less. Assuming the option expires totally worthless, the option writer can't earn more than the premium received for the option. Option writing doesn't deliver the instant returns of 200 or 300 percent on your investment that are possible when you buy options.

Even given the few transactions that go against you, the probabilities are that over the long term, you'll rake in far bigger profits as an option writer than as the speculator who buys options in hopes of making a quick killing. In the options market, the writers of options have 60 to 80 percent odds in their favor. Not bad, you say? It is the time premium that tips the odds in favor of the option seller.

While buying options offers the promise (and occasionally the reality) of big profits, selling options is the wonder weapon that holds the potential for getting interest-free loans, avoiding the concerns of price swings in the stock market, and getting a 25 to 40 percent annualized yield. Selling an option puts money into the investor's account.

Why is something this good kept almost a secret? Because it is more complicated than just buying and holding stocks, and most brokers do not really understand the full potential of covered call writing.

There are many individual investors who want to sell options and reap the benefits. Since the option seller is selling time value, he or she can frequently make money whether the market stays the same, goes up, or goes down, which increases the probability of profit and enables the option seller to reap the benefits.

USING OPTIONS AND MARGIN

Sell covered call options to hedge our position and make profits with possible tax advantages? Use margin to enhance our portfolio and ease our taxes? What?

I can hear you now: "In this book, you have the nerve, the audacity, to introduce me to dangerous investment methods while claiming to write about low-stress profitable investing?"

"Options? That is gambling! Margin? That is borrowing! What? You are suggesting that I borrow to gamble!"

Even some of Wall Street's savvy investors recoil at the mention of options. But the realm of puts and calls isn't reserved solely for speculators with ice in their veins. Options can be a part of a very conservative hedging strategy, and one of the best is covered call writing, a favorite of some investment professionals.

Others will tell you of the poor performance of the mutual funds that used options in their strategy. "If the pros can't do it, you can't do it." You will know why the option funds do not do well when you understand the correct method of selling options.

Others will tell you that the stock market is dangerous enough and it is no place to use borrowed funds to invest. It is important to understand the meaning of margin. The rational use of margin need be no more risky than buying a house with a mortgage.

> You cannot discover new oceans unless you have the courage to lose sight of the shore.
>
> —Anonymous

The ideas about options and margin are the most prevalent misconceptions in the stock market. In this book, I will teach you to understand the use of options and margin. You will learn what can be done with them, what mistakes to avoid, and how to protect yourself against their misuse and having to pay the consequences.

Options and margin can be effective tools for enhancing the total return of an undervalued, diversified, long-term stock portfolio. Not many stock market participants (investors, stockbrokers, bankers, lawyers, and accountants) really understand all the technicalities of margined and optioned portfolios, especially the underlying rational assumptions.

WHAT IS MARGIN?

What I want to impart to you is simply this: when, how, and where to seek (and hopefully profit from) the opportunities open to margin investors consistent with the risks involved. My aim here is to outline for you the many ways in which a margin account offers you a greater flexibility than a cash account; to explore some of the myths that surround the philosophy and practice of margin; to make clear the risks; and to present examples of additional purchasing power that the leverage of margin offers the investor.

Margin use is not a sure path to riches, but in Chapter 14 on margins, I hope to help you decide whether the opportunities, demands, restrictions, and risks of margin usage should become a part of your investment planning.

AVOID THE PREMIUM TRAP

Many investors who are hunting premium become elated by the high potential returns available on writes of volatile stocks, such as takeover issues, fad stocks, and the like. The time premium for options on these stocks is very hig, making them tempting to write. However, economic reasoning provides little basis for initiating writes on extremely volatile stocks. Profit from any dramatic gain in price of the underlying security may be limited to the strike price of the option sold. But participation in all losses past the net proceeds received from selling the option is not limited.

In short, there is no option premium big enough to protect you from a downside break in a volatile situation ... ask any investor who initiated an option write on a $20 stock because of the fat $4 premium that could be earned by selling an option, only to have the stock price drop to the $7 dollar level as the market saw through the phantom fundamentals propping up the stock's price.

Stick to fundamental value, and never write on a stock you wouldn't feel comfortable owning at the net price option chains paid for the optionable stock.

The Internet and the business pages open up a world of stocks from which to choose. The best way to do this may be through the process of elimination. Don't select stocks with fundamental characteristics you do not find attractive. From the remainder of the optional stocks, choose a diversified list of fundamentally sound companies that can be analyzed thoroughly and monitored easily. This will enhance familiarity with a company's earnings and a stock's trading patterns, therefore minimizing surprises.

PUT-CALL RATIOS

Put-call ratios are market-sentiment statistics that have been around for quite some time and enjoy a realistic following among option traders. This is based on the open interest and is readily available in the option trains listings.

A put-call ratio is the number of put contracts divided by the number of call contracts open. Put-call ratios are usually considered contrarian indicators, which means that a high ratio (more calls than puts) may be considered bullish on the underlying stocks. I use these indicators when determining the strike price of the option that I am considering selling. If there are more open calls than puts, I will sell the strike price higher than it is at the moment. If there are more puts, I would sell a lower strike price on my options. Remember, we are dealing with speculators. Remember that they are gamblers; they are not stupid, they are wise, and they are putting up real dollars to back up their opinions. The put-call ratio is a true indicator of option market sentiment. I rely on the put-call continuously and I find it very reliable.

OPTION QUOTES

Option quotes are data concerning the most recent trades. Following are some definitions related to option quotes.

- The *put-call* indicates whether the option being traded is a call or a put.
- The *expiration date* tells you what date the option is set to expire in.
- The *strike* shows you the strike price of the option.
- The *last bid* is the price for which the option last traded.
- The *bid* is the highest price any buyer is willing to pay for the option.
- The *ask* is the lowest price any seller is willing to accept for the option.
- The *high* and *low* show the range of transaction prices for the day.
- The *previous close* is the final transaction price from the previous day.
- The *change* and *percent change* show how much the last sale differed from the previous day's closing price.
- *Open interest* is the total number of contracts in existence for that particular option.

The option trade volume is the total number of contracts that have been traded for that day. The higher the volume the better for option sales. Remember the open interest of a specific equity, which represents the number of outstanding (or open) contracts in the exchange market on that particular option. It is updated at the end of each trading day. The higher the open interest, the better.

SELLING OPTIONS: PRUDENT INVESTING METHOD

Option selling has now become so established as a prudent, conservative method of investing that it has received official recognition by almost every regulatory body that has control over investments. The Comptroller of the Currency, who regulates the national banks, has ruled that option writing is appropriate for use by bank trust departments in investing their trust funds.

The insurance commissioners of all states have ruled that insurance companies may use option writing on a portion of their own investments. Various officials entrusted with seeing that pension plans are properly administered have given their blessings to the use of option writing for pension plans. In addition, an enormous number of conservative, professionally managed investment groups have begun using option writing, including church, university, and college endowment funds and union welfare plans.

Clearly, the time has come for the speculative stain of options to be completely and finally removed from the concept of selling covered options.

By its very definition, the word conservative means to be more concerned about protecting what one has than with increasing its value through changes in market prices. Option selling protects the investor from declines in the stock price up to the amount of the premium received from the sale of the options. Therefore, using options with stock ownership is more conservative than outright ownership of stock.

Selling options is one of the few forms of investing in which one can compute exactly what the return on investment will be if the position is successful. When an investor buys a stock, he or she can compute the dividend, but the result of that investment one year after purchase is going to be determined mostly by what has happened to that stock's price.

Here, the idea is to continue to own common stock, but to get some downside protection and to take in some profit if the stock stays still or moves up.

Everyone who owns securities should understand and use options. For investors, they can provide extra income, set up tax losses, make possible protective hedges, and usually limit losses. But to make money with options, you must work hard, research thoroughly, review often, and follow strict rules. Why bother with options at all? In case you have not noticed, there is risk in stock ownership.

Time is what we want most, but what, alas! we use worst ...
—William Penn

CHAPTER 13

Options and Potential Returns

Hindsight is always twenty-twenty.

—Billy Wilder

"I 'll have a Coke please."
"Classic or new?"
"New."
"Cherry or plain?"
"Plain."
"Regular or caffeine-free?"
"Regular."
"Diet or sugar?"
"Forget the whole thing. I'm not thirsty anymore!"

Having a lot of options could take away your thirst; sometimes it might even take away your appetite. We now have approximately 2,500 optionable stocks and more pending. With this great number, how can you decide which ones are best for your portfolio? Let's start with the well known KISS strategy—Keep It Simple, Sweetheart—and go on from there.

- *Keep it simple.* Don't sell uncovered options because they are "free money, the stock can't go up that far." This could produce losses that are fearsome in their magnitude.
- *Keep it safe.* Don't exceed your risk tolerance.
- *Keep it sensible.* Just because you read about some alleged mastermind making a killing with options doesn't mean that you should try to copy his operation. Don't try anything that will take you beyond your eating and sleeping points. Stay within your risk tolerance.

- *Keep it diversified.* Gain greater safety through buying different stocks rather than large trades of a single stock.

Finally, and most important:

- *Keep it disciplined.* Losses sometimes come because of the wrong stock, the wrong strategy, the wrong timing, or just bad luck. More often, losses occur and get larger because of a lack of discipline. Whenever you implement an option strategy, you should have two points clearly understood in your mind:
  1. First, set an approximate goal, the point where you expect the strategy to produce profits.
  2. Second, set an exit point to be used if the trade goes against you.

Don't forget that selling covered call options can be used in a protective capacity as an instrument for the transfer and/or reduction of risk. Keep in mind that writing calls against your stock holdings is safer than just holding the stock. Here, the concept is to continue owning common stock, but to give yourself some downside protection and to take in some profit if the stock stays still or moves up. This approach is not as glamorous as the more risky strategy of buying calls. However, our goal is the enhancement and the preservation of capital.

NAKED OPTION WRITING

No, it does not imply trading in the nude. Naked writing is when you sell an option on something you don't own. It is very risky and can be financially ruinous, because you must always be ready to buy the stock and then immediately sell it to the option buyer on demand . . . no matter how high the stock has risen in price. Avoid this very high gamble.

STARTING A COVERED CALL PROGRAM

If you already own 100 shares or more of an optionable stock, then your decisions are already partly made for you. Since there are always three time frames available, your first question is probably whether you should sell the three-month option, the six-month option, or the nine-month option. The way to decide is to compare the average monthly return for each time period. The shortest time frame pays the highest return on a monthly basis.

The longer-term options offer a commission savings that should be considered. Also, you may prefer longer-term options to avoid the necessity of multiple transactions for the same period of time.

THE PRICING OF OPTIONS

The most important factors that contribute value to an option contract and influence the premium at which it is traded are:

- The price of the underlying stock
- Time remaining until expiration

$$\text{Option Premium} = \text{Intrinsic Value} + \text{Time Value}$$

If the underlying stock price is in-the-money, there is intrinsic value. For example, if an option's strike price is $25, and that stock is trading at $35, the option has intrinsic value of $10. If underlying stock price is at-the-money or out-of-the-money, there is no intrinsic value.

For in-the-money options, the time value premium is the excess portion over the intrinsic value. For at-the-money and out-of-the-money options, the time value premium is the option premium.

These values are in dollars per share. For example, an option contract covering 100 shares of common stock, when trading on the options exchange at 2 points, has a total value of $200 (100 shares × $2 = $200).

$$\text{Intrinsic Value} = \text{Stock Price} - \text{Exercise Price}$$

The intrinsic value is always a positive number or zero.

$$\text{Time Value} = \text{Premium Value} - \text{Intrinsic Value}$$

The time value of an option premium is the difference between the dollar value of the cash premium and the intrinsic value in dollars of the option contract.

The longer the time remaining until an option's expiration date, the higher the option premium, because there is a greater possibility that the underlying share price might move to make the option in-the-money.

The time value of an option does not decrease at a linear rate. The time value falls off gradually until close to expiration, and then falls off rapidly.

Example of Time and Intrinsic Values

ABC Corp. on May 21

ABC common stock closed at 35
ABC August 30 option closed at 8
Intrinsic value: $(35 - 30) = 5$
Time value: $(8 - 5) = 3$
Total premium: 8

Option contracts have a maximum life of nine months. During this period the premium can vary widely, from very low to very high. Their values may be small when the time to expiration is very short, or when there is very little anticipation by option buyers that the market price of the underlying common stock will rise before expiration. Their value will be high when the time to expiration is long, or when the stock is above the strike price.

When the market price of the common stock is below or less than the strike price of the option contract, the intrinsic value is zero. In this instance, any value of the premium is entirely time value.

ABC Corp. on May 21

ABC common stock closed at 35
ABC August 40 option closed at 3
Time value $= 3$
Total premium: 3

In mid-August, with ABC valued at $32.50, the option buyer will not call your 100 shares of ABC from you. You keep the $300 premium money and write another option on your ABC Corp. stock.

ABC Corp. on May 21

ABC common stock closed at 35
ABC August 35 option closed at $4^1/_2$
Intrinsic value $= 0$
Time value $= 4^1/_2$
Total premium: $4^1/_2$

In mid-August, with ABC valued at $32.50, the option buyer will not call your 100 shares of ABC from you. You keep the $450 premium money (pretax) and write another option on your ABC Corp. stock.

ABC Corp. on May 21

ABC common stock closed at 35
ABC August 30 option closed at 8
Intrinsic value (35 − 30) = 5
Time value = 3
Total premium: 8

In mid-August, with ABC valued at $32.50, the option buyer calls 100 shares ABC from you at $30. Then you:

Sell 100 ABC common at 30
Premium received: 8
Total received (per share): 38

Your net profit is $300. This was the time value of the cash premium of $800 that you received three months previously. Your net profit can never exceed the time value of the option you have sold.

Other factors that give options value, and therefore affect the premium, are volatility, dividends, and interest rates.

Volatility

Volatility is the frequent large price fluctuations of a stock. The volatility of the underlying share price influences the option premium. The higher the volatility, the higher the premium.

Dividends

The regular cash dividend paid goes to the stock owner. Cash dividends affect option premiums through their effect on the underlying share price. Options reflect stock dividends and stock splits, because the number of shares represented by each option are adjusted to take these changes into consideration (e.g., one option at $40 becomes two options at $20).

Interest Rates

Higher interest rates have tended to result in higher option premiums. The portion of the time value attributable to the interest rate factor will be greater.

DETERMINING THE BEST TIME VALUE

In determining how long an option to write, one should remember that a three-month option will have a higher average monthly return than a six- or nine-month option.

If your analysis indicates that the stock price will be lower in three months, it would be to your advantage to write a nine-month contract, which would produce more premium than writing a three-month contract and, on its expiration, writing another three-month contract, and so on.

If your analysis indicates that the stock price will increase in three months, then it will be to your advantage to only write a three-month contract and on its expiration write another three-month contract, which would total more premium than would an original nine-month contract.

For this example, the stock price on May 21 is $50.00:

	3 mo	6 mo	9 mo
Aug 50 option premiums	3.00	5.00	6.50
Nov 50 option premium	3.00		
Feb 50 option premium	3.00	5.00	
9-month total premiums	9.00	7.50*	6.50

*Only half of second 6-month premium included in total.

If your analysis indicates that in three months the stock may be down 5 and selling at $45, you should sell the long-term option. For the stock price on May 21 at $50.00:

	3 mo	9 mo
Aug 50 option premium	3.00	6.50
Nov 50 option premium*	1.00	
Feb 50 option premium*	1.00	
9-month total premiums	5.00	6.50

*Stock price at $45.00.

When the stock price is $45, options with a strike price of $45 probably would have a premium for 3 months of $2\frac{1}{2}$. You could sell this option after the first option expired, but the risk is that if the price goes up to 50, buying back the $45 option for $5 would incur a $2.50 loss. Selling the November 50 option and getting a 6-percent return in three months, equaling 24 percent a year, is hardly losing. We are using averages and will expect to lose on 10 percent of the trades.

If you believe that your stock has an expectation of going up during the next three months, then you should sell the shortest term option. If the stock does as well as you expected, you will be assigned, sell your stock, and be free to reinvest in another option-able security.

If your analysis gives no indication of a stock price rise or fall, you can follow the rule of selling the option that gives you the highest return on a monthly basis.

DETERMINING THE BEST STRIKE PRICE

What are the results of choosing a high strike price, rather than a low one? Since your stock has options available at three or more strike prices, which one should you write?

Options with the highest strike price will be the most profitable if the stock goes up, but the option with the lowest strike price will perform the best if the stock goes down.

A lower strike price offers a higher premium. A strike price below the stock price provides a premium, including intrinsic value, which gives downside protection.

For example, when ABC Corp was selling at 39, its five-month options at that time were priced as follows:

Strike price	Premium
35	$5^3/_4$
40	$2^1/_2$
45	1

When ABC stock remains at 39 until the expiration date of the option, the seller of the 35 option will realize $35 from the exercise of the stock plus the $5.75 premium, making a total of $40.75. The seller of the 40 strike price will keep his stock and the premium of $2.62. The seller of the 45 strike price option will keep his stock and will keep the premium of $1.

If the price of the stock had risen to 45, the seller of the 45 option would have done the best. The seller of the 35 option would have $40.75 as above. The seller of the 40 option would receive $40 for his stock plus the $2.62 option premium, making a total of $42.62. The seller of the 45 option would have the value of his stock, $45.00, plus the premium of $1, a total of $46. It would appear that the best strategy is to sell the option with the highest strike price.

But what if the stock had gone down? Suppose the price of the stock fell from $39 to $34. None of the options would have been exercised, and each seller would be left with the stock and his premium. Now, each option seller has stock worth $34, and the 35 strike price writer has a premium of $5.75 in his account, the writer of the 40 strike price option has $2.62, and the one who did best in the previous example ends up with just $1.

Well, which strike price should one write?

The answer to this question is to go back to an understanding of the basic reason for selling covered call options. The reason is that the investor who invests *without fear* is willing to give up a large potential future gain that may never happen in exchange for a certain profit now, which is the option premium being paid.

The main reason we are selling covered calls is to obtain an assured income. The one big risk is that the price of the underlying stock will fall. Therefore, my general rule is: When selling an option, give first preference to the option with the lowest strike price.

This gives the most protection against a decline in the stock's price. If the price of the stock rises, you would have been better off selling at a higher strike price, but you are still making a profit with the lower strike price. The thinking to have when you sell a covered call option is that you are giving up possible future home runs for a steady stream of base hits.

> Common sense is the knack of seeing things as they are, and doing things as they ought to be done.
>
> —C. E. Stowe

In our example, when you sell the 35 strike price option you have made an extra $1.75 on your stock, which is 4.4 percent. Since this profit will be earned in five months, it means that you are earning an annual rate of 10 percent. This is great when you consider that the buyer of your option is giving you free insurance for every dollar that your stock could fall down to $35.

If you strongly believe that your stock has a good expectation of rising, you may wish to sell at the highest strike price. You get to keep part of the rise in your stock and only turn over to the option buyer the excess increase in your stock. Remember, though, that if the price goes down, you will be left with a loss on your stock and only a small premium to cushion that.

Each investor has an opinion of what return on investment is acceptable. This is based on financial condition and the amount of risk the investor is willing to assume. Option selling is no different.

An option writer accepts a certain amount of risk due to the potential volatility of stock ownership. Therefore, the likely returns from an option sale must exceed those that can be earned on a risk-free investment.

One general guideline, used to set minimum acceptable returns on an option sale, is to seek potential returns of at least double the selected risk-free rate on an if-exercised basis. Note: On high-yield stocks, attractive potential returns can be found in utilities and some major oil companies. The reason for the attractive return is the stock's dividend. Because these stocks have low volatility, option premiums are small. An option premium would only add marginal income. In such situations, it would be more sensible to buy the stock and own it outright (without selling an option). The option premium provides little in the way of income or downside protection, yet it will limit the upside potential in the stock.

DETERMINING THE BEST UNDERLYING STOCK

If you do not own any optionable stock and would like to sell a covered call option, you have to decide which stock to purchase.

First, you should select a stock that you personally will want to own and hold, using all the information already given to you in the first part of this book. For instance, if you decide that there will soon be a downturn in drug stocks profits and stock prices, there is no point in buying Merck stock just because it may have a high option premium. Select a stock that you would want to own as if you were not going to be selling options. Remember, if the price of the stock declines, you will still own the stock, and the only risk in selling options (as in owning stock) is that the price of the stock may go down.

Second, you will have to check the quotations to find what the option premiums are for the various stocks. The amount of the option premium varies depending upon many factors. For more details on this, please refer to the option pricing section of this chapter. You should select a stock whose option has a high premium. Usually the lower-priced stocks have the higher premiums.

Third, pay attention to the strike prices for the stock you are considering. As suggested earlier in this chapter, the safest option is the one with the lowest strike price. You are seeking less risk, so pick a stock whose option has a strike price below the current market price of the stock. If, after doing all your research, you are optimistic, you can pick a stock that has a strike price well above its current price, with the understanding that this will reduce the amount of your premium and provide little downside protection.

While checking the strike prices available, it would be a good practice to check not only the current option period but also those for the next three-month period, and the one after that, because not all strike prices may be available for future periods. If the price of the stock has declined substantially, then the highest strike price is not going to be offered for the longest timeframe options. If the price of the stock has increased substantially, then the higher strike price may not have opened yet for trading.

WHEN TO TAKE ACTION

Once you have written an option, you could wait until it expires and then decide which option to write next. In most cases, it will be to your advantage to decide whether there are changes that could be made before expiration that will enhance your profit or decrease your downside risk, or perhaps both. You will be watching your positions to see if you are earning the maximum amount from the time value of the options you have sold.

There are two situations that should alert you to action:

The first is if the current price of any option you have sold declines to a small fraction of its original premium. If any of your outstanding options are selling for 25 cents or less, it is time to act. No matter what happens, the maximum remaining profit you can make from that option is only 25 cents a share and your downside protection is also only 25 cents a share, which is nil. This low price of your outstanding options results from time decay or a decline in the price of your underlying stock.

The second situation would be if you notice that the time value of your outstanding in-the-money options has fallen to a small amount. When this amount begins to approach zero, there is no reason to continue the position. You still have the possibility of loss if the stock declines, but you no longer have the opportunity of a meaningful profit.

UNDERSTANDING PUBLISHED OPTION PREMIUMS

Premiums (prices) for exchange-traded options are published daily in many newspapers. Many investors have some difficulty in understanding the option tables. They are different from the stock tables with which most readers are more familiar.

The *Investor's Business Daily* introduced an alphabetical option listing and included the volume of contracts. Thank you, Mr. William O'Neil, for this innovation. The *Wall Street Journal* finally has started publishing an improved option listing that appears to be the best now available.

The listing below shows a portion of an option table for a trading day. This is only a small part of the total information, but it is sufficient for us to obtain an understanding of these listings. It also will allow us to introduce some frequently used option words.

To identify the items of information, let's look more closely at the listing for ABC Corp. options. Although we will not be using puts, it is very important to realize where they are listed and never confuse the cash premiums between the types of options.

Yahoo! Finance Page

Strike	Symbol	Last	Chg	Bid	Ask	Vol	Open Int
25.00	VPAE.X	25.33	0.00	25.40	26.50	1	13
30.00	VPAF.X	21.84	0.00	20.50	21.20	3	49
35.00	VPAG.X	16.30	0.00	15.70	16.60	3	20
40.00	VPAH.X	12.40	0.00	11.80	12.40	8	1,546
45.00	VPAI.X	8.70	↓0.50	8.40	9.10	1	348
50.00	VPAJ.X	6.00	↓0.30	5.70	6.30	9	2,452
55.00	VPAK.X	4.10	0.00	3.70	4.20	5	610
60.00	VPAL.X	2.85	0.00	2.25	2.60	120	1,394
65.00	VPAM.X	1.40	0.00	1.40	1.45	10	593
70.00	VPAN.X	0.85	0.00	0.70	0.85	34	795
75.00	VPAO.X	0.45	0.00	0.35	0.50	56	153
80.00	VPAP.X	0.30	0.00	0.15	0.30	12	360
85.00	VPAQ.X	0.20	0.00	0.05	0.25	30	102
90.00	VPAR.X	0.10	0.00	N/A	0.20	50	223
95.00	VPAS.X	0.15	0.00	N/A	0.20	0	50

The *Wall Street Journal* Format

Option/Strike			Vol	Exch	Last	Net Chg	a-Close	Open Int
ABC	Jun	$12^1/_2$	60	CB	$3^1/_2$	$+^1/_2$	16	72
ABC	Jun	15	200	CB	1_-	$+^1/_4$	16	570
ABC	Jun	$17^1/_2$ p	40	CB	$1^1/_2$	$-^1/_4$	16	660
ABC	Jul	15	800	CB	$1^1/_2$	$+^1/_4$	16	600
ABC	Jul	15 p	80	CB	$^1/_4$	$-^1/_4$	16	120
ABC	Jul	$17^1/_2$	200	CB	$^1/_4$	...	16	1,000
ABC	Aug	15	1300	CB	$1^3/_4$	$+^3/_4$	16	408
ABC	Aug	15 p	200	CB	$^1/_2$	$-^1/_4$	16	930
ABC	Aug	$17^1/_2$	10	CB	$^1/_2$	...	16	812
ABC	Aug	20 p	4	CB	4	$-^1/_4$	16	25

a-Close means underlying stock price.
c-Call p-Put

The published table reflects the previous day's trading.

Under *Option/Strike* is the name of the underlying security, the expiration month, and the available strike price.

- *Vol* (volume) is the number of trades.
- *Exch* is the exchange on which the option is traded.
- *Last* is the closing price of the option contract.
- *Net Chg* (net change) is the difference between the last trading price from one day to the next.
- *a-Close* is the closing price of the underlying security.
- *Open Int* (open interest) is the number of options outstanding.

Local Paper Format

Options & NY Close	Strike Price	Calls-Last			Puts-Last		
		Jun	July	Aug	Jun	July	Aug
ABC Corp	$12^1/_2$	$3^1/_2$	r*	r	r	r	r
16	15	$1^1/_2$	$1^1/_2$	$1^3/_4$	r	$^1/_4$	$^1/_2$
16	$17^1/_2$	R	$^1/_4$	$^1/_2$	$1^1/_2$	r	r
16	20	s**	s	r	s	s	4

*r = no option trades that day
**s = no such option exists

The published table reflects the previous day's trading.

In the first column is the name of the underlying security and its closing price. The second column lists the available strike prices. The next three columns (Calls-Last) show the closing premium for each of the closing months for which calls are trading. The last three columns (Puts-Last) show the closing premium for the each of the closing months in which puts are trading.

In these examples, the in-the-money ABC Corp. August 15 calls closed at $1^3/_4$, or $175 per contract. The out-of-the money ABC Corp. August $17^1/_2$ calls closed at $^1/_2$ or $50 per contract.

For purposes of illustration, commission and transaction costs and tax considerations are omitted. These factors will definitely affect a strategy's potential outcome, profit, or loss on your income tax return.

OPTION SYMBOLS

A specific optionable stock trades in only one of three expiration cycles. Each cycle is composed of four three-month periods.

Cycle 1	Jan	Apr	Jul	Oct
Cycle 2	Feb	May	Aug	Nov
Cycle 3	Mar	Jun	Sep	Dec

The maximum life of an option is about nine months. Expiration dates are the third Friday of the month. New nine-month periods commence on the Monday following the third Friday of the month. Options can be traded for the time remaining to their expiration. In addition to the cycles, prior to expiration, trades can be made for a period from one day to the end of the following month (e.g., on the third Friday in January until 4:15 P.M. Eastern time, a trade covering a period from one day through the end of February is possible). This creates a new short-term option expiration.

When using a computer or terminal for quotes, you will need the option symbol, composed of the stock symbol, the expiration month code, and the strike price code. It is also handy for you to use these when giving orders over the telephone to your broker. With use, these will become second nature to you.

The month and strike price codes are listed next.

Month	Call		Strike Price Codes			
January	A	A	5	105	205	305
February	B	B	10	110	210	310
March	C	C	15	115	215	315
April	D	D	20	120	220	320
May	E	E	25	125	225	325
June	F	F	30	130	230	330
July	G	G	35	135	235	335
August	H	H	40	140	240	340
September	I	I	45	145	245	345
October	J	J	50	150	250	350
November	K	K	55	155	255	355
December	L	L	60	160	260	360
		M	65	165	265	365
		N	70	170	270	370
		O	75	175	275	375
		P	80	180	280	380
		Q	85	185	285	385
		R	90	190	290	390
		S	95	195	295	395
		T	100	200	300	400
		U	$7\frac{1}{2}$			
		V	$12\frac{1}{2}$			
		W	$17\frac{1}{2}$			
		X	$22\frac{1}{2}$			

The ticker/quotation symbol for the stock is used first, followed by the month and the strike price codes. Examples: ABCLW is ABC stock, December, $17\frac{1}{2}$ call). ABCFF is ABC, June, 30. XYZHX is XYZ, August, $22\frac{1}{2}$.

The *option expiration months* are the two near-term months plus the two additional months in the January, February, or March quarterly cycle.

The *expiration date* is the last day an option exists. For listed stock options, this is the Saturday following the third Friday of the expiration month. That is the deadline by which brokerage firms must submit exercise notices to the OCC. The exchanges and brokerage firms have rules and procedures regarding deadlines for an option holder to notify his or her brokerage firm of any intention to exercise. Contact your broker for specific deadlines.

As a covered call option writer, you are ready to deliver the necessary shares if assigned. Before being assigned, you may cancel your obligation by buying to close (i.e., buying the same option that was sold). Remember fungibility. A covered call writer's potential profits are influenced by the strike price of the option sold.

- If one writes an at-the-money option, the maximum net gain is the premium received for selling the option.
- If one writes an in-the-money option, the maximum net gain is the premium minus the difference between the stock purchase price and the strike price.
- If one writes an out-of-the money option, the maximum net gain is the premium plus the difference between the strike price and the stock purchase price, should the stock price rise above the strike price.

THE STANDARD METHOD OF USING OPTIONS

If assigned, the profit or loss is the sum of the premium plus the difference, if any, between the strike price and the original stock price. If the stock price rises above the strike price, the stock will be called away, and the opportunity to profit from further increases in the stock price is lost. If the stock price declines, hedging protects against loss to the extent of the premium.

When the underlying stock stays the same, you win when selling out-of-the-money options or at-the-money options. You keep the premium and your stock.

When the underlying stock goes up in value, so does the option premium. In the standard or usual manner of option selling, your stock would be assigned.

MY METHOD OF USING OPTIONS

All the experts in the stock market field will say, "The writer of an option, in return for the cash premium received, forgoes the opportunity to benefit from an increase in the stock price that exceeds the strike price of the option. The option writer continues to bear the risk of a sharp decline in the price of the stock. The cash premium received will only slightly offset this loss."

That is not correct.

Using Fungibility

An option writer may cancel the obligation any time before being assigned by executing a closing purchase transaction, buying back the option that was previously sold—*a fungible action*. The writer of an option, in return for the premium received, uses the opportunity to benefit from an increase in the stock price.

Stock Price Is No Longer a Concern

With my method, you no longer care about the price of the stock that you bought. Investors normally watch their stock's price go up and down and sideways. With my method, when the stock does go down, we would buy back the option at a very inexpensive price and immediately write it again. Perhaps we took in a premium of $2 and could close it out by buying the option for 25 cents. If the stock price went down $5 we would write a new option at a $5 lower strike price. Since you already lost when the stock declined, using my method you are always taking in additional premium income, which will help offset the decline in the stock price.

When the stock does not reach the strike price, let the option expire, keep the premium income, and write a new option at the same strike price.

When the stock goes up, you could let the option go at a profit (as in the standard method). With my method, you would buy the option back and immediately write a new option at a higher strike price, reflecting the gain in the stock price. The second premium added to the first will help defray the cost.

During the months of existence of most option contracts, the option price and also the stock price will vary and fluctuate. The time value portion of the option always represents a judgment determined by the traders. Changes in the time value or the intrinsic value occur continuously during the market trading hours, either of which can affect the option price.

For the buyer, the option contract is a wasting asset to own; its value decays as time passes. The time value portion of the option premium value always is zero at expiration. Selling the time value repeatedly, for the same underlying stock, makes option income work for you.

> Once you are moving in the direction of your goals ... nothing can stop you.
>
> —Anonymous

Using the principles in this book, you will learn to react to the stock market. You will not be looking for the stock to go up to make money. You will be making money on the wasting asset called time value. Your plan is to get gains from the time values of options you have sold. Your philosophy about the stock market will be changed. You will be counting real cash premiums put into your account by the speculators.

On the plus side, death is one of the few things that can be done just as easily lying down.

—Woody Allen

Time: the stuff between pay days.

—Anonymous

CHAPTER 14

Margin: The Credit You Can Use

A bank is a place where they lend you an umbrella in fair weather and ask for it back when it begins to rain.

—Robert Frost

M *argin* is the amount a customer deposits with a broker when borrowing from the broker to buy securities. A brokerage account that permits an investor to purchase securities on credit and to borrow on securities already in the account is a *margin account*. Buying on credit and borrowing are subject to standards established by the Federal Reserve and subject to the firm carrying the account. Interest is charged on any borrowed funds and only for the period that the loan is outstanding.

With margin, you can have a larger portfolio and take advantage of downturns in the market to buy bargains. The interest cost of borrowing on margin is very low. Within certain limits, margin loan interest can be tax deductible, as well.

A margin loan against the value of your portfolio is set at 50 percent down. Since it is open-ended, there are no monthly payments. Interest is deducted from your account monthly. Which is safer? A loan made with 10 percent down or one made with 50 percent down?

Margin received a bad name thanks to horror stories about people being wiped out in 1929. Buying on margin does not deserve this bad reputation. Margin is the same as a mortgage. It is borrowing on something you own to help finance the purchase of a home or a car, or to meet cash flow or for long-term investing. Mortgages generally are accepted methods in America for buying a home or a car. Almost everyone has one. But margin is considered a terrible way to finance anything. To buy a home, most people borrowed 90 percent or more of the house's market value. This approach was certainly the case in the subprime market, where you could borrow more than the value of your house, and it was this situation that threw the nation into a financial turmoil.

You can take out too large a mortgage, experience an economic downturn, or have a run of bad luck. Under such circumstances, you would lose your home or car because you could not meet the monthly payments.

The only time in my life I borrowed money was to buy a home. I paid off the loan in 10 years. I do not like debt, and other than the home loan, I have been debt free. Most people do not know that you pay for your home *four times over* when using a 30-year loan.

I have been using margin in my option income portfolio since the crash of 1987. This year, 2009, is the opportunity for which I had been waiting . . . to buy common stocks at up to a 70 percent discount. The money to pay for the purchases came from my use of margin. Margin is the borrowing of money against the market value of a portfolio. The use of margin enabled me to buy more stocks than I could have otherwise. It is an investment tool I choose to use.

As an investor, you are in business, the business of investing in other businesses through the ownership of common stock. These shares are your inventory. When you add to your inventory at bargain prices, you will have more shares to sell options against, thus enhancing your earnings. It is a good business practice to purchase a widely diversified portfolio of good company stocks and, by borrowing against your stock portfolio, to buy more shares. Again, this approach enables you to sell more options, thus increasing your profits. Through diversification, you are spreading your risk among many companies whose stocks may advance or decline at different times. The average of rises and declines, over a long period, will tend to rise and make you profits.

Today I owe more in my margin account than I ever have owed in my entire life. I still believe in fiscal responsibility and have no other debt.

> Credit is like a looking-glass, which when once sullied by a breath, may be wiped clean again; but if once cracked can never be repaired.
> —Sir Walter Scott

Our great American economy is built on, is based on, and continues to grow on borrowed money. Federal, state, and local governments borrow and service huge amounts of debt. The debt takes care of the present and future needs of the citizens. Such borrowing is done with Treasury bills (T-bills), notes, bonds, and municipal bonds.

Every large corporation has debt for future growth, for expansion, and for research and development. Business people borrow to start and fund their companies, and use credit or loans to finance their operations.

Most of us buy our homes, cars, and other large purchases using our personal credit to do so. We get the benefit of using these items now, rather than waiting until we can pay cash. The people who provide and make the things we want have the benefit of employment. They in turn can go out and use credit to get the things that they want or need. Our economy, based on credit, has given us the high standard of living we enjoy.

With many, margin (credit) has a bad reputation. "What? Borrow to gamble on the stock market?" "Remember all those people who jumped from rooftops in 1929 because of margin!" "Every time a stock bought on margin drops in price, you have to put up more cash." These statements represent an uneducated viewpoint.

ADVANTAGES OF MARGIN

To use margin, you should understand it thoroughly. The use of margin generally incurs greater risk and portfolio volatility.

The reality is that you have more shares, with the safety of wider stock diversification. This provides increased total return and more safety than your cash alone would permit you to buy. During market declines, although your losses are leveraged, they are manageable and of a shorter duration than market rises, if you don't sell.

Greater rewards are possible with the prudently planned use of margin. Over a long time period, as the market goes up and margin is effectively employed, margin-buying gives the portfolio leverage. In financial terms, leverage means using your money and borrowed money to increase the total rate of return.

The margin loan is open-ended. It has no specific time limits. No specific installments are due nor principal payments required. The cost of borrowing on margin is very low. Margin loan interest rates are comparable to, if not lower than, the prime interest rate offered to a bank's best business customers. Within certain limits, margin loan interest can be tax-deductible, as well.

Depending on the amount requested, applying for other types of loans today can be a time-consuming process. Credit screening is a pain. Credit bureau errors can be embarrassing. When the loan is approved, you pay for loan origination fees, and interest rates are often high. Life and accident insurance may be required and can add extra monthly charges. Despite your ability to repay, there is a set schedule of payments extended over a predetermined length of time. Also, there can be penalties for early and late payments. If you cannot pay, you can lose the asset you purchased.

Applying to use margin is fast and easy. It is part of applying for a brokerage account. There is no credit screening, since the stocks in your account provide collateral. The margin loan is open-ended. It has no specific time limits. No specific installments are due or principal payments required. The cost of borrowing on margin is very low, and no other monthly charges are added. Until you use it, no interest is incurred. Margin loan interest rates are comparable to, if not lower than, the prime interest rate offered to a bank's best business customers. Within certain limits, margin loan interest can be tax-deductible, as well.

In theory, the margin debit is callable. You should carefully read the margin agreement papers you must sign to use margin. I have never heard of a margin debit called other than to meet the minimum legal requirement.

Margin, in a word, is trading on credit. The customer makes only part payment for the deposits with a broker when borrowing from the broker to buy securities. A brokerage account that permits an investor to purchase securities on credit and to borrow on securities already in the account is a *margin account*. Buying on credit and borrowing are subject to standards established by the Federal Reserve, the stock exchanges, and the firm carrying the account. Not all securities are marginable. Interest is charged on any borrowed funds and only for the period that the loan is outstanding.

Member firms have their own margin requirements and may place higher minimum percentage requirements on certain securities. Your brokerage will be glad to inform you of the current margin requirements.

THE MARGIN ACCOUNT AND BUYING POWER

Assuming you put up cash in the amount of $10,000, under Exchange and Federal margin rules you could buy 50 percent on margin: $20,000 worth of marginable stocks. Higher margin percentages are also usually placed on low-priced stocks by member firms and may be required when an account consists of one stock. Over the years, the initial margin requirement has ranged from 45 percent to 100 percent; however, in recent years the Federal Reserve has maintained the requirement at 50 percent, always subject to revision.

Brokerage firms are also guided by the Exchange's minimum initial equity requirement of a cash deposit of no less than $2,000 or an equivalent in securities. On a purchase of $3,000, you would have to deposit 66⅔ percent, or $2,000, rather than $1,500, or 50 percent. In addition, your broker may ask for a higher initial margin than the Exchange's $2,000 startoff minimum. In any case, your credit will cost you at the current rate for interest. As with any credit transaction, the cost of money will be influenced by the size and activity of your account. Ask your broker for the interest costs.

You can also deposit securities instead of cash; the amount of credit will be determined based on the value of the securities, typically at 50 percent of the current market value.

All brokers hold your margin account in street name and credit you with all dividends received on them. It is still your stock. You can sell it, vote on company proxy matters, and receive any stock splits. I hold all of my stocks in street name, which enables me to sell a stock without the bother of getting it to the broker; many of my clients sometimes have problems finding their certificates, or they have them at the bank in the vault—what a bother. Street name is the way to go.

Using margin can increase the percentage of profit on your investment by a surprisingly large amount, as you can have a larger portfolio and take advantage of downturns in the market to buy bargains. The cost of borrowing on margin is very low. Within certain limits, margin loan interest can be tax deductible as well.

A margin loan against the value of your portfolio is limited to 50 percent. Since the loan is open-ended, there are no monthly payments. Interest is deducted from your account monthly. Which is safer, a home loan made with 10 percent down, or a margin made with 50 percent down? You could take out too large a mortgage and then experience an economic downturn or have a run of bad luck. Under such circumstances, you would lose your home or car by not meeting the monthly payments. That is exactly the situation in which we are today as I write this; many are experiencing the results of the subprime financial mess.

MARGIN ACCOUNT MAINTENANCE

Now that you have opened your margin account, further factors become effective. The equity status of your margin account includes additional purchases and sales, withdrawals of cash or securities, and interest chares.

The most obvious charge affecting your margin account is the price movement of the stocks in your portfolio. Should they start to decline, you will be getting in financial trouble. Should they fall below the 50 percent margin level, you are flirting with failure to meet the maintenance margin for your account. Remember, in a cash account a decline means a real or paper loss. With a margin account, you will also be accountable for the monies the broker advanced to you, plus interest and commissions.

A margin account assures you of all the net profit you realize, but it cannot protect you against declining stocks, poor investments, or bad advice. Most brokerages will lend you up to 70 percent of your account; this amount varies, but at 70 percent, you would own only 30 percent of your portfolio. A maintenance margin call will be in effect. This is a reminder that your account does not meet the margin maintenance requirements.

When you receive this call, you either deliver more funds or marginable stock or sell part of the portfolio to reduce your margin debit in the account. You have one day to correct this debit, or the broker has the right to liquidate stocks in your account. The bad thing is that the broker can sell positions, without consulting you. This occurrence could really affect your portfolio strategies, as you might lose stocks you wished to keep.

Most portfolios have more than one stock in their accounts; one stock that declines rapidly might not affect the entire account if the rest of the portfolio did not decline as well. If your portfolio should rise, you can decide how much profit you want. You can withdraw funds or buy more stocks and do more option trades, using margin to gain an even larger portfolio.

> Those who think profit is a dirty word should try to make one.
>
> —James Cook

The cost of borrowing on margin is based on the *broker call rate*, a figure published daily in the financial press, plus a percentage added by your broker. For example, the broker's call rate can be found under *money rates*. It is listed as *call money*. A brokerage representative can tell you the current margin rates.

MARGIN INTEREST

Margin interest is based on the total amount of the margin loan. Avoid having more than one margin account; it will save you interest, because the larger the loan, the lower the interest rate. If you have multiple margin accounts, you can transfer into one account, without having to sell anything. This makes consolidating margin accounts easy.

Margin interest is calculated with the following percentages added to the broker call rate. An example:

Amount of Loan	Broker Add-On
0–$9,999	2.00%
$10,000–24,999	1.50%
$25,000–49,999	1.00%
$50,000+	0.50%

Brokers will add on from .50 percent to 2.0 percent over the broker loan rate, depending on the size of the margin loan.

Comparison of Margin Rates to Other Interest Rates (Jan. 2009)

Broker Call Loan Rate	5.00%
$10,000 Margin Loan	6.50%
Prime Rate	6.00%
Credit Card Rate	18.00%

Your brokerage statement will report your current margin buying power (the amount of securities you can purchase with available marginable securities), your outstanding margin debt, the interest incurred for the period, and the interest rate for the period. You can get an up-to-the-minute report by calling your broker.

It is beneficial to have a margin account. You will be ready to take advantage of market opportunities. There is no cost to open a margin account, and interest charges only begin upon settlement of your purchases.

Once you decide to use margin, the interest rate (based on the broker's call rate) will be charged each day until you pay off the loan, or until you sell some of the securities used as collateral.

Interest is calculated daily and posted to your account. Payback on the loan is at your convenience, and there is no fixed payment schedule. Any dividends or interest from the securities used as collateral will be applied to reducing the balance.

A benefit of using margin is that it allows you to use the value of your assets without selling them. You don't have to consider liquidating stocks that are doing well when another attractive investment opportunity comes along. You don't have to realize a profit and pay tax on the sale of stock to use the money.

IMPORTANT MARGIN PRINCIPLES

- *Borrow less than the full loan value*: By limiting borrowing to 25% of the full loan value of your securities, you can still employ leverage and low-cost borrowing. You reduce the chance of having dramatic market fluctuations place you in a *margin call* (maintenance) situation.
- *Borrow against conservative investments*: Borrow only against sound stocks, those with proven track records and dividend payment histories. The risk of margin call situations can be lessened considerably.
- *Borrow against a diversified portfolio*: It is highly unlikely that all stocks would go down substantially and simultaneously. Some stocks may be lower, some stocks may be higher, and many would retain the same values.

> I hear and I forget. I see and I remember. I do and I understand.
>
> —Chinese proverb

OPENING A MARGIN ACCOUNT

There is no charge for opening a margin account. Margin is an additional feature of a brokerage account. If you already have one, adding margin requires only that you read, understand, complete, sign, and return a margin agreement.

Once approved, you may purchase or deposit eligible securities in your account to be used as collateral. Instruct your brokerage representative to deposit your securities in a type 2 margin account (type 1 is a cash account). Ask your brokerage representative the amount of cash available, or the additional buying power you have.

BASIC IDEAS AND TERMINOLOGY

- *Market value* is the price at which a security is currently trading.
- *Mark to the market* is the revaluing of a margin account to ensure compliance with maintenance requirements. Daily gains and losses are reflected by this process.
- *Debit balance* is the money a margin customer owes a broker.
- *Credit balance* is the money a broker owes a customer.
- *Market Value – Debit Balance = Equity*

- Market price fluctuations increase or decrease market value and equity.
- Margin interest increases debit balance and decreases equity.
- Expired options and dividends increase equity and decrease the debit balance.

PORTFOLIO VALUATION

Having opened a margin account with $7,500 cash or marginable securities, if you borrow $2,500 and buy more stock, you will then have $10,000 in stock, a $2,500 debit balance, and an equity value of $7,500.

Marginable stocks market value	$10,000
Debits (loans, margin interest)	2,500
Equity (net worth)	7,500

PORTFOLIO FINANCIALS

Marginable stocks market value	$10,000
Dividend income $10,000 @ 3.5%	350 annual
Margin interest $ 2,500 @ 7.00%	−175 annual

(Broker call loan rate 5% + 2% broker add-on.)

The annual dividends will more than cover the annual margin costs.

Market Value − Debit Balance = 75 percent Account Equity

The seasoned margin user spends appreciated gains to buy more stock to bring the portfolio to a 25-percent margined level. This presents no more risk than the original decision to use margin.

The decline in the price of one stock will not by itself create a margin call, since evaluation of a margin account is based on the entire portfolio. Securities valued at less than $5 per share have no loan value. Certain over-the-counter stocks are also not marginable. Call your broker for details.

MARGIN OR MAINTENANCE CALL

The margin call is literally a call from your broker asking you to add assets to your margin account. The Federal Reserve policy governing margin requires a call when the amount owed is more than 50 percent of the current value of your margin account. Brokerage firms may set their own higher margin levels.

Your equity (Market Value – Debit Balance = Equity) must drop to 30 percent before there will be a margin call. Generally, you are given five business days to meet a margin call. With some brokers, the margin call is met if the market value of your portfolio increases.

As we are investing, we do not anticipate ever receiving a margin call, since we never borrow more than 25 percent of our portfolio.

> We cannot direct the wind, but we can adjust the sails.
>
> —Anonymous

CONVERTING DIVIDENDS INTO CAPITAL GAINS

Margin interest is deductible against dividend income. Generally, the dividend yields gained from a total portfolio will tend to offset the margin interest. The use of margin provides the opportunity to own a larger stock portfolio, which results in the opportunity for greater capital gains. Upon selling the stock, the growth in value is taxed at the favorable long-term capital gains rate, whereas the dividends would have been taxed as ordinary income.

USING MARGIN FOR PERSONAL PURCHASES

Your stocks can act as security when borrowing money for any purpose through your margin account. However, using your margin for purposes other than your investment portfolio could be hazardous to your wealth by jeopardizing your investment plan.

The simple fact is that the use of credit in buying and selling stocks can be no worse or no better than the use of credit in any other business. The skill and judgment of the user of the credit are what is important.

If you would know what the Lord God thinks of money, you have only to look at those to whom he gives it.

—Maurice Baring

Money and time are the heaviest burdens of life, and ... the unhappiest of all mortals are those who have more of either than they know how to use.

—Samuel Johnson

CHAPTER 15

Managing an Option Income Portfolio

Half of our life is spent trying to find something to do with the time we have rushed through life trying to save.

—Will Rogers

T he option income portfolio approach to selling covered call options endeavors:

- To minimize risk.
- To provide diversification.
- To maximize capital gains potential, dividend income, options premium income, and downside protection.
- To create option portfolios with the objective of earning consistent returns on investment throughout the stock market cycle.
- To increase long-term capital appreciation and income from stock ownership.

The option income portfolio is a continuous investment strategy. Stock should be owned and options sold. Dividends and option premiums can be earned and capital gains increased. This is another step toward successful investing.

Using covered calls is a conservative strategy; professional investors write covered calls to increase their investment income. Individual investors can also benefit from this simple, effective option strategy by taking the time to learn it. Investors can add to their investment finances and give themselves more opportunities.

The way you participate in options depends on four factors: your knowledge and previous experience in trading; how much time you are able to devote to trading; the amount of capital you can commit; and your individual personality and risk tolerance. If you have watched the markets for years but have not taken the plunge, there are three factors to consider so you do not fail.

1. Research is the first step in trading. If you are trading options, understand the contract you are trading. Be wary of things that sound too good to be true on the Internet or in published materials. Anything that indicates that learning to trade or trading successfully is easy is a huge red flag.

   If you are trading options, education is especially important because options, while technically less risky, are more complicated than stocks. Controlling risk is one of the largest advantages to trading options versus stocks, but you must first understand how they work. Once you understand options, they are a much more sensible investment tool than everything else, because you can control your risk better than with any other financial product. Research is critical. The Options Industry Council web site, www.optionseducation.org, has an extensive educational library for option investors.

2. Create a trading plan that you can stick to. The plan should include how many funds you are willing to risk for a trade, what contracts you are going to trade, how much loss you are willing to take on each contract, and how you are going to keep track of all your trades.

   Even the best trading plan is useless if you do not stick to it. The reason most people lose in trading is that they to do not have a plan, and if they do have a plan, they do not follow it. If you have a plan and you follow it, you are ahead of the other starting traders.

   Discipline is very important in trading, and so is the need for money management. You could have the best trading strategy, follow it completely, and foul it up with poor money management.

   Take responsibility for your money management; do not leave it to someone else or take it for granted. Money management should fit the investment style and risk tolerance of the individual investor. Consider how much time you have to trade, how frequently you trade, and what kind of risk you are taking.

3. Learn risk management; practice makes perfect. Never paper trade; although many propose this, the results will not help you. You need the real-life experience of feeling in the dumps when you lose, as well as feeling the great euphoria when you win. Paper trading, since it is

not real, does not give you these feelings of despair and happiness. Real trading is never what it looks like in the books. The amount of difference you can expect is often based on how you enter and exit the market. Are you entering on limit orders, or market orders? Limit orders provide certainty, but can result in you missing an entry. Market orders will always get filled, but the price can surprise you. With a market order you are saying, "I do not care what the order costs, I must have it." I always use limit orders and will change the price, if need be, to get the price I am willing to pay. If you do not want to do this point by point, use good till canceled (GTC) orders. Your order may not be filled instantly, but you will only get a fill when it is at your price.

Find a brokerage that will give you the tools for pricing, portfolio management, and optimal execution.

I recommend starting with $10,000 in your account, but whatever it is, it needs to be a fixed amount. You should figure out how you are going to start trading with X number of dollars. Start with small trades in a variety of industries.

Option accounts can be smaller, because you are dealing with a known risk with selling (taking in money) to expand your funds. For beginners, trading in highly liquid stocks tends to be truer to the technical and the chart patterns. The more volume there is in a market, the more the market flows in a predictable way.

Beginners should keep the following in mind: Think small, do not get too emotional, and be patient. The largest trap is overdoing it, diving in head first, and not recognizing the value of experience. Have finite risk in the beginning of option trading. If your worst-case scenario can only lose 10 percent of your nest egg, that is a great way to start. Keeping your emotions in check is important. No one likes taking losses, but is something you have to understand if the market decides not to cooperate with your trading plans.

As a stock owner, you are entitled to several rights. One of these is the right to sell your stock at any time for the market price. Covered call writing is simply the selling of the right to someone else in exchange for cash paid today. The buyer of this right pays the seller a cash premium on the day the option is sold. It is the seller's money to keep, regardless of whether the option is exercised.

Selling options with the strike price near the current market price of the stock usually results in the most balanced combination of potential returns and downside protection. The potential will exist for stock appreciation. Meanwhile, a substantial amount of option premium will be earned, providing downside protection.

Investors generally have two objections to option selling: They may lose if a stock's price declines past the breakeven point, and they may limit the upside potential if a stock's price appreciates more than the premium.

Limiting an account to one or two option positions increases the odds that one of these unfavorable events will occur. A diversified portfolio permits losses on one position to be offset by gains on another.

Assuming the portfolio of stocks selected performs about equally to the stock market, continuous option selling as described above should do better than the market. In addition, total returns will be greater over time.

The asset base for an option income portfolio should consist only of common stocks for which option contracts are routinely traded on option exchanges.

There are many stocks from which you might generate 25 percent per year (gross) regularly using options. This gross income can be captured by the conservative investor. The buyer of the options will pay a cash premium for the right to buy stock at the strike price until the option contract expires.

The option contract is a wasting asset. Its value decays as time passes. It is only the time value component of the option contract, not the intrinsic value, that wastes as the time of expiration grows near. At expiration, the time value is zero.

Time value becomes a money machine as a new option is sold on the same underlying stock. Because the time value sale can be repeated continuously and indefinitely, the profit from time value is a certainty. As one contract expires, a new contract is sold on the same round lot of stock.

Though an option income portfolio can be operated with as few as one to five different stocks, for safety it is advisable to increase the number of companies represented in a portfolio. The number of stocks owned would probably not exceed 20. At this level, diversity and reasonable safety are achieved. As with all businesses, when initial funds are lower than they ought to be, you must make compromises. You must accept some higher cost and risk. The next chapter deals with the problem of insufficient investment money and how to overcome it.

There are rarely more than 20 optionable stocks that will have options selling with acceptable time value in their option premiums. Most time values are too low. Always be on the lookout for higher time values.

As opinions become more favorable on the outlook for a specific stock, the time value in the option premium becomes larger. Sell stocks that no longer have large enough time value premiums compared to the ones with which you could replace them, and buy stocks that have larger time values. Follow these changing time values in the financial press.

THE WRITING POSSIBILITIES

- *At-the-money*: The strike price and the stock price are the same. The buyer pays for time value only, as there is no intrinsic value.
- *In-the-money*: The strike price is below the stock price. The buyer pays for intrinsic and time value.
- *Out-of-the-money*: The strike price is above the stock price. The buyer pays less for time value, and there is no intrinsic value.

Time Value = Strike Price + Premium − Stock Price

To help screen the option chains rapidly, just look at the three-, six-, and nine-month option columns. Look for premiums in which the time value is 5 to 10 percent of the stock price.

With a little practice, you can quickly scan the option chains and identify the good writes. Make note of each, and go on. In a short time, you will have five to ten candidates. Now use the stock and option selection formula below:

Strike Price − Today's Stock Price + Option Premium ÷ Today's Stock

Price × Sales per Year = Annualized Percentage

Example

XYX stock price today = $20
three-month $20 option premium = $1.90
six-month $20 option premium = $2.80
nine-month $20 option premium = $3.60
$20 − $20 = 0 + 1.90 ÷ $20 = .095 × 4 = 38%
$20 − $20 = 0 + 2.80 ÷ $20 = .14 × 2 = 28%
$20 − $20 = 0 + 3.60 ÷ $20 = 1.18 × 1.333 = .24%

The annualized percentage will serve as a realistic guide to select the most profitable writes. At this time, you may wish to do your fundamental buy-and-hold analysis on each marked stock. Select the finalists for your option income portfolio.

Stocks and their options tend to rise and fall over the weeks and months. At times, there may be no stock candidates to study. At other times, there will be more candidates than you can possibly buy. There is never a rush in this business; if you miss one today, there will be ample time to find another. This permits you the time to do the investment study on your candidates. Everything is constantly changing. The stock market is a living and breathing enterprise. Yesterday's closing prices will be different when you call your broker the next morning. Remember, don't chase stocks and their options!

On almost any weekend, people cram into hotel rooms for seminars on how to trade stock options. The sponsors hold such educational seminars frequently. Most are free to attendants.

To brokerages, seminars are just part of the cost of luring the online stock trading crowd into the Internet options pits and keeping them there. It has been very successful—for the brokers, anyway.

Who are the believers? Investors who want easy money and believe the notion that options are a ticket to wealth unavailable to people who just buy plain old stocks. Most are looking for wealth without work. Sell options and you win.

There are many such believers. A financial publication just published a column advocating a covered call strategy, in which you just buy stocks and then sell call options against them, pocketing the premiums. They did not mention any of the work that goes into the process.

There are all kinds of retail investors: those who call into a broker (via the phone) or online traders who use the Internet; those who use the Internet feel they can gain an edge trading options. The edge is receiving the lowest commission (fees), better stock prices, and the ease and convenience of the transaction.

Options are not a free lunch. Used properly, they are similar to insurance policies in that they transfer risk. You have to work at this, staying aware of what is happening.

It would be great if there were some clever option strategy that made the same profits as a pure stock portfolio but at reduced risk, or earned more but at the same risk. Nice, but very unlikely. Wouldn't the investors on the other side of these option trades be getting bad deals?

The covered call strategy looks great. Buy Microsoft at $20, sell a covered call exercisable at $30, and pocket many dollars of options income. Sure enough, a covered call writer will do better than a pure stock investor. Is this a formula for beating the stock market over time? No! It is true that market volatility has driven option premiums to attractive levels. But you have to work at it. You will have to follow the instructions I am giving you. This is why you are studying this book.

An option quote usually contains the following information:

- *Name of underlying security*: Microsoft, Pfizer, Citigroup
- *Expiration date*: January, April, November
- *Strike price*: $10, $25, $55
- *Class*: call or put

Another important element is the option premium, which is the amount of money that the seller of an option receives.

The above elements work together to determine the worth of an option. Understanding the basics of options can be said to be part science and part art. It is vital to understand where profits originate in order to optimize option trading profits.

OPTION SELECTION FOR OPTION WRITING

Throughout the day, a person makes hundreds of decisions. Paper or plastic? Salad or French fries? One of the hardest decisions for any new option trader is which option to select among the large list.

Option selection can be difficult for the novice investor. Do you play a short-term or long-term option? Do you play it safe and sell an in-the-money, or do you take a risk and use an out-of-the-money call? The process of selecting the option that fits the investor's style but also the situation does not have to overwhelming. The process can be broken down to three questions.

1. Which direction do you think the underlying stock is going?
2. What is your risk tolerance?
3. What are your expectations for the stock?

The first step can be the easiest or the most difficult. As contrarians, we are looking for a sign that sentiment is running counter to the stock's technical and fundamental trend. The use of the put/call ratio on the open interest table helps with this. Are there more calls than puts? That indicates that the players feel the stock will rise. If there are more puts than calls, the players feel the stock is going to decline. I use the put/call ratio to help me with my decision. The players are speculators, gamblers, and they are putting their money in what they believe is the direction of the stock price.

The risk inherent in the second step of selecting an option is choosing a strike price. To start, there are three prices of options: in-the-money, at-the-money, and out-of-the-money. Which one should be done?

An in-the-money has the highest price, because it has intrinsic value. An option is considered in-the-money when the stock price is higher than the strike price. For example: STU stock is trading at 50; the 45 call would be considered in the money. An in-the-money call is more expensive, because it has the value above the stock's price and has time value as well. The intrinsic value provides a spread for the option buyer, making it less risky.

An at-the-money option is when the strike price and the stock price are the same or very close. The price paid for the option is all time value. The benefit of this option is that it costs less than an out of the money option; if the stock price does not move above the strike price, the option buyer loses all their premium money.

The riskiest option is an out-of- the-money-option. This is when the stock price is trading below the strike price. The stock has to move up in value to above the strike price before the option gains intrinsic value. This option has only time value. If the stock price does not go above the strike price, the option buyer loses all his money.

On the positive side, an out-of-the-money option costs the least to buy. These have the highest chance of expiring worthless. When the stock does rise, they will make the most profit of the three.

Now to the third question: We have to decide which option time to sell. The more time, the more premium money. Selecting the right time to sell is up to you to decide. Most option buyers want to put up as little premium money as they can. You have to decide how much time premium you would like to receive. Regular options are for up to nine months; time in LEAPS (long-term-equity anticipation securities) is for 2-year options.

SELLING TIME VALUE

You will use a different philosophy than the average stock investor, who is looking for a stock that will go up in price. Your planned gains arise from the time values of the options you will sell. This approach to stock selection is unusual. Most investors select stocks on either fundamental analysis or technical analysis. You will use the time values of a stock, tempered by fundamental analysis and the long-time hold principles as discussed.

Deciding to trade a stock option requires choosing an expiration month. Option strategies require making modifications during the life of an option trade; you need to know in what months the options will expire. The expiration month you choose will have a significant impact on the success of any option trade. It is important to understand how the option exchanges decide what expiration months are available for each stock.

There are at least four different expiration months available for every stock on which options trade. The reason for this is that when option trading started in April 1973, the Chicago Board Options Exchange (CBOE) decided there would be only four months when options could be traded at any given time. Later, when LEAPS were introduced; it was possible for options to be traded for more than four months.

When stock options first began trading, each stock was assigned to one of three cycles: January, February, or March. Stocks assigned to the

January cycle are January, April, July, and October. Stocks on the February cycle are February, May, August, and November; stocks in the March cycle are March, June, September, and December.

Under the newest rules, the first two months are always available, but for the later months, the rules use the original cycles. It is this month and next month and then we go to the later regular cycle months. For example: in the middle of January, the next month will be February; since we need four trading months, we go back to the January cycle months, so it will be April and July.

When January expires, February is already trading, so that becomes the near month, but because four months must trade, March will be opened for trading, making the list February, March, April, and July.

Next comes March (the current month); April is the second month, July will be the third, and since we need four, we add October, because it is in the March cycle.

To select a stock for your option income portfolio, you must have available a current option chain list. Select a stock from the option chain list that has the most profitable time value in its option premiums. If this stock meets your selection criteria, buy it as an underlying stock.

To get an annual return of 20 to 40 percent, you must find available option premiums with time value that will produce a return of 5 to 10 percent in three months on the price of the stock. Using the option chain page, you mentally calculate the percentage of the stock purchase price that the time value represents. Of the more than 2,500 optionable stocks, in all probability, you will only have identified some 5 to 10 stocks to consider. If the time value seems attractive, then turn to fundamental and technical analysis to make your decisions.

There are about 28 investment strategies using stocks and options. You will be using only one. You will be writing option contracts. At expiration, you will sell a new option contract on the next 90-, 180-, or 270-day maturity.

SELLING A COVERED CALL OPTION

When you sell a covered call, you get money the next day in exchange for some of your stock's future upside.

As an example, let us assume you pay $40 for your LMN stock and you think it may rise to $50 within one year. Also, you would be willing to sell at $45 within six months, knowing you were giving further upside, but making a nice short-term profit. In this scenario, selling a covered call on your stock position might be an attractive option for you.

After looking at the stock's option chain, you find a LMN $45, six-month covered call position selling for $5 per share. If you did this, you would obligate yourself to sell the LMN shares at $45 within the next six months if the price rose to this amount. You would still get to keep your $5 premium, plus the $45 from the sale of your shares, for a grand total of $50—a 25 percent return over six months.

On the other hand, if the stock falls to $30, you will have a $10 loss on your original position. However, because you get to keep the $5 option premium from the sale of the LMN call option, the total loss is $5 per share, not $10. In this case, you would resell a new option at a striking price of $30, receiving a new option premium.

Scenario No. 1

January 2: Buy LMN shares at $40.

January 2: Sell LMN $45 call option for $5 today.

January 2: Expires on June 30, strike price $45.

June 30: Stock closes at $50; option is exercised because it is above $45.You receive $45 for your shares.

July 1: Total profit $5 capital gain in the stock + $5 premium received from sale of option $10 per share, or 25 percent.

Scenario No 2

January 2: Buy LMN shares at $40.

January 2: Sell LMN 45 call option for $5 today.

June 30: Stock closes at $30; option is not exercised because it is below 45, and option is worthless because stock is below strike price of $45.

July 1: Total loss – $10 + $5 = $5 on stock price; keep the $5 premium and sell shares or do a new option at $30.

Selling covered call options can help offset downside risk or add to the upside return, but it also means you trade the cash you get from the option premium for any upside gains beyond $50 per share over the next six months. You could come out worse; if the stock goes above $50, you would not share in the upside.

As long as you have sold options on your stock, you have to hold the shares. If you wish to sell your shares before expiration, you must buy back to close the open option position.

This will cost you premium money, and some of your profit.

You can use covered call premiums as a way to lower your out-of-pocket costs for stocks, (not your cost basis, which remains the same), or to gain income even if the stock does not pay a dividend. This strategy can serve you in an additional way to profit from stock ownership.

This investment strategy will attempt to get the maximum gross profit while keeping your expenses down and will generate as great a net profit as possible. The main expenses will be stockbrokerage commissions.

STOCKBROKERAGE COMMISSIONS

Commissions for option trading are higher than for the purchase and sale of common stocks. Keep stock turnover at a minimum. Sell stocks only when there is a real reason; the time value of the premium is smaller than can be had with another stock option.

Commission expense with options, as with stocks, is less per trade when you are dealing with more volume or value. There are savings on commissions when you do multiple contracts on options. Five contracts cost very little more than one. There is an economy of size that you will want to consider when doing options.

BUY AND WRITE STRATEGY (BUY-WRITE)

Do you now own the stock, or would you buy it?

When you own an optionable stock, make your time value comparison. If the stock's option rates poorly, sell it and buy a more promising one. Otherwise, immediately sell an option to protect yourself against a price decline and to generate current income.

On buying an optionable stock, you should be protected immediately against a price decline. *Buy-write* is the investment strategy of purchasing stock and writing options simultaneously. This is a conservative approach to generating maximum current income by use of option premiums.

An example: Tell your broker, "Buy 200 shares of ABC common stock, and write (sell) to open two contracts of the ABC September 10 call options with a net debit to me of $9."

By doing a buy-write order, if the stock price was $10 and the three-month call was $1, the amount owed would be the difference of $9 per share, or $1,800 plus commissions. The stock price could vary from $9 higher or lower, but combined with the option premium price you would still get a fill.

When buying a stock and selling an option, a cash premium is received that has two components—intrinsic value and time value. The strike price is the agreed upon selling price of the option for 90 days.

Buy ABC for $10.00 a share	-$10.00
Sell an ABC 10 option for 90 days	+1.00
Out of pocket	-9.00
Total agreed price and premium	11.00

You made 10 percent in 90 days (40 percent annualized). You can figure the desirability of stock/option choices from time values alone, as derived from the option premium, stock cost, and strike price. You do not need to add the dividends, stockbrokerage commissions, and margin interest, as this often complicates a simple procedure.

You will need to learn to read the Internet option chain tables or the quotation page as it appears in the financial press. Time is what we are selling. When an option contract expires, the contract is void forever.

The option maturity months show as an integral part of the quotations. A typical quotation for a specific option appears below. At a strike price of $20, this option is in-the-money by $.87 cents.

Date: April 21 (April options have expired); Stock price is $20.87

	July	Oct	Jan	NY Close
ABC Corp 20	2.87	4.375	5.50	20.875

Option Premium = Intrinsic Value + Time Value

Intrinsic value is $.87, time value is $2 for July, $3.50 for October, and $4.625 for January. The stock closed that day at $20.875. If you sold one ABC Corp. July 20 option contract at $2.875 per share for the 100-share contract, you would receive $287.50 gross income. You would receive $437.50 for October, and $550 for the January option contract.

It is advantageous to do three-month time frames on option contracts, instead of six- and nine-month contracts. The premium money looks larger at first for a nine-month contract, but note the results below, if the time value remained the same.

	Three-Month Contract	Nine-Month Contract
First contract	$287.50	$550.00
Second contract	287.50	
Third contract	287.50	
Gross	$862.50	$550.00

You will realize $312.50 more ($862.50 − $550.00 = $312.50) by writing consecutive three-month contracts. Other advantages will be discussed later. You will incur commission costs on the extra trades.

On buying a new stock and selling a short-term call, if you are midcycle for the 90-day contract, do not sell a call for the next expiration date, but go to the second expiration.

FORMULA FOR STOCK AND OPTION SELECTION

When an option is written at-the-money or out-of-the-money, the option premium is all time value. The in-the-money option will have time value plus the intrinsic value above the strike price.

The formula for computing estimated annualized rates of return in percent is:

Strike Price − Today's Stock Price + Option Premium ÷ Today's Stock

Price = Percentage

Percentage × Sales per Year = Annualized Percentage

For example, using three-month option periods, we could affect four sales per year. Using the April 21 example above, for the July, October, and January options the percentages are as follows:

July 20 − 20.875 + 2.875 ÷ 20.875 = .10 or 106
Oct 20 − 20.875 + 4.375 ÷ 20.875 × 2 = .34 or 346
Jan 20 − 20.875 + 5.50 ÷ 20.875 × 3 = .66 or 666

Four three-month options can be sold during a year, two six-month options, and $1\frac{1}{4}$ nine-month options. Using this formula will permit you to do your percentage calculations rapidly.

Within the last two or three days of an expiring option, if the stock price is below the strike price or even with it, the option will expire worthlessly. If your stock price is above the strike price (in-the-money) at expiration, you can either let the option buyer have it (normal method) or you can buy the fungible option back before expiration, keep the stock, and write it again at a higher strike price. After the expiration in July, assuming we wrote the option in April, we would now look at the October expiration. The October expiration is the next one available on the three-month cycle after July. You must learn to react prior to the option expiration.

Remember a stock can go up, go down, or stay the same. The whole essence of operating an option income portfolio is employing a method that guarantees a steady income by simply selling time, not trying to make our profit in the irrational market. We are no longer stock pickers. We are not trying to capture those elusive stock price swings by being a market timer. We are just cashing in on the decaying time values that we are selling.

THE OPTION BUYER

After years of selling options, I still marvel that such an opportunity exists. I still want to pinch myself when I see the option monies come in. I have to thank the option buyers who make all this possible. There are more option buyers than there are option sellers, which helps keep the option premiums up.

You must understand that the option buyers are speculating. They plan for the stock price to rise sharply beyond the premium value that they paid to you and for the option contract to be sold at a profit before expiration without buying or calling the underlying stock.

The contract that you sold once may be traded dozens of times. You will not know or care about this fact. The buyers are gambling with small amounts of money and do not have the cash to buy your stock from you. They do not want the stock. They want the rapid leveraged gains that can occasionally be made.

PROOF THAT AN OPTION INCOME PORTFOLIO IS A WINNER

With options we have a win–win–win situation; with stocks only a win–lose–draw.

Underlying Stock Price	Declines	Increases	Unchanged
Stock with options	win	win	win
Stock only	lose	win	same

If the stock price increases, you keep the time value portion of the premium received, even if the option-holder exercises the right to buy your stock. The intrinsic portion of the option goes to the buyer of the option. Though it may appear that you give up the gain in a large price rise that you would have had if you had not sold an option, we will use it to our advantage. In a small price rise, if the cash premium received is larger than the rise in the stock price, your gain will be larger than the gain in the stock price.

If the stock price stays the same, the option will expire and you keep the option premium received.

In a price decline, if the option premium received is larger than the decline, you have no loss and possibly still have a gain. The only risk is when the stock price goes lower than the cost of your underlying stock and the cash premium received. It is precisely at this time that you should buy back the option for pennies on the dollar and immediately write a new option. You will always be taking in money, and this income will act like a parachute in a stock price decline.

This approach will protect you. You have reduced the possibility of a loss but not eliminated it. The stock market is irrational, and any stock price has an equal probability of going up or down. Using the guidelines of this book, you can react to the market and use the various stock market basic principles for profitable investing.

You have just learned how to protect your option income portfolio from a decline in stock market price value while you sell covered call options.

FOLLOW-UP ACTION

Once an option is sold, it must be monitored, since follow-up action must be taken at or before the expiration of the option, even if it is just a decision to allow it to expire.

Some investors prefer a passive approach. They allow the stock to be called if its price is above the strike price at expiration. They rewrite an option if the stock price is below the strike price at expiration. This approach is simple and functional, but more active management creates greater profits.

Follow-up action on an option is guided by movements in the underlying stock's price and by the passage of time. Consideration is also given to the stock price in relation to the strike price of the option sold.

Option selling is a strategy designed to provide a balance of returns, consisting of the potential for stock appreciation, income, and downside protection.

As time passes, or the underlying stock fluctuates in price, this balance will be disrupted. Once the balance is disrupted, it is time to consider action to restore the position to its original balance or liquidate the stock.

The man on top of the mountain didn't fall there.

—Anonymous

PERIODICAL REVIEW OF PORTFOLIO EQUITY HOLDINGS

Buy more stock? Sell the stock? Hold the stock?

Informed investors agree that periodical reviews of their portfolio equity holdings are part of the investment process. In the simplest form of review, the investor looks at each equity holding and asks whether it should still be held. Are the fundamental and other reasons for which this stock was purchased still in effect? Should the stock be sold? Has the stock met a set objective or changed to the point where holding it can no longer be justified?

A more elaborate review process would add a fourth question: Should we be adding to our current holdings because the stock has moved down to an attractive buying range? This simple review process can be summarized by questioning whether a holding should be bought (adding to positions), held (doing nothing), or sold (liquidating).

Some investors might answer the triple question as follows:

1. Would I add to this position? Yes, but at a lower price.
2. Would I sell this stock? Yes, at the current price.
3. Would I sell this stock? Yes, but at a higher price.

Let us refine our review process and ask our questions as follows:

1. Would I be willing to add to this position if my costs were 10 percent below the current market price?
2. Would I be willing to liquidate my stock at a price 10 percent above the current market price?

Investors who answer yes to both questions can wait for the stock to move up or down 10 percent before taking action. Or they can use options, take immediate action, and create an opportunity to increase the return of their holdings, even if the selling or buying target is not realized.

Here is how it works. Investors who are willing to sell a holding at a higher price can write call options against their holdings. At expiration, if the stock price exceeds the strike price, the stock is sold.

TABLE 15.1 October calendar date and January option quotes

Stock	Stock Price	Series	Price
ABC	$43^1/_4$	Jan 45	2.62
LMN	$90^1/_2$	Jan 95	2.81
XYZ	$23^1/_4$	Jan 25	1

Investors who add new stock could write calls at the stock price or lower. The premium received could be thought of as getting a discount on the stock.

For investors who are willing to sell their holdings at a higher price and add to their positions at a lower price, this is a key strategy to consider. Table 15.1 shows a hypothetical portfolio and options for an October calendar date and January option quotes. For simplification, taxes and commissions have not been factored in.

Now assume the holders of the portfolio in the table are willing to sell any of the holdings at 10 percent above the current market price. They would also be willing to double up at a cost of 10 percent below the current market price.

With ABC stock at $43^1/_4$, this implies an effective selling price of $47.62 and a purchase price of $38^3/_4$, which is required to meet these objectives.

Should the investor sell the stock at $45, he will get to keep the premium. Thus the effective selling price will be $47.62, which was the target.

If the price of ABC fell to $41.62, the investor could buy more at that price and, with the premium received, reach the target of $38.88.

As you can see in Table 15.2, the 10 percent above, 10 percent below objectives can easily be met.

With covered call options, investors can increase the return of their holdings when neither the buying or selling targets are met. Looking again at ABC stock, if at the January expiration the stock is trading at the same price, it is highly unlikely that the option will be assigned. It will expire worthlessly. In this case, the investor keeps the $2.62 per share and repeats the operation selling the April 45 calls.

TABLE 15.2 January expiration: Required prices to reach target

Stock	Stock Price	Sell Price	Buy Price
ABC	$43^1/_4$	47.62	40.62
LMN	$90^1/_2$	97.81	87.62
XYZ	$23^1/_4$	26.00	22.25

TABLE 15.3 January expiration: Annualized returns in a flat market

Stock	Stock Price	Option Premium	Total Premium	Annualized Percent
ABC	$43^1/_4$	2.62	6.0%	24%
LMN	$90^1/_2$	2.81	3.2%	12.8%
XYZ	$23^1/_4$	1	3.3%	13.2%

The returns for our stock portfolio in a flat market can be seen in Table 15.3. They would be enhanced further by any dividends received on the stocks held.

As illustrated, the mechanics of covered calls are quite simple, and the strategy offers excellent returns in flat and rising markets while letting the investor average down in falling markets. The following four points should be taken into account before establishing a position.

1. *Ten percent up/down targets:* There is no magic to the 10 percent targets selected in these examples. These are realistic expectations for stocks with average volatility. Wider targets can be established for more volatile stocks (whose option premiums are normally higher). Narrower targets should be considered for lower volatility stocks. Targets may be established for longer or shorter option periods.

2. *Time horizon:* A three- to five-month time will let investors set targets that meet their realistic expectations. This time horizon may provide an adequate return in flat markets. Investors must remember to ask themselves when they establish the strategy: "Would I be willing to sell/buy my stock 10 percent above/below the current market price during the next three to five months?

3. *Future stock value:* In our examples, when selling a call, the strike prices were close to the current stock price. You will probably sell a call at a higher strike price if you are bullish on the stock and sell at a lower strike price if you are bearish on the stock.

4. *New positions:* Covered calls need not be limited to stocks already in the portfolio. An investor can use a buy-write to simultaneously purchase a stock and sell covered calls against these shares.

Follow-up action mainly consists of monitoring the prices of the stock and the option, taking no action if the underlying stock and its option price go up or remain the same until option expiration week. It is at this time, option expiration week, that you must make the decision either to do nothing and have your stock assigned, or to buy the option back and keep your stock (closing out the option). If the underlying stock and its option price go down, wait until expiration and let it expire worthlessly. A better strategy is to buy it back early in the option period, canceling the contract and rewriting a new lower strike price option for the next expiration cycle.

How can we determine when to do this buyback? The following three questions must be considered:

1. Is the time premium remaining on the option less than one-fourth of the time premium received? If so, it is time to consider writing a new option, as most of the profit from this position has been made.

2. Is the price of the option less than one-fourth of the premium received? If so, it is time to consider writing a new option, as there is minimal downside protection remaining.

3. Is the stock about to go ex-dividend? If so, action may be necessary; you must buy back the option to protect the receipt of the dividend.

An affirmative answer to any of these questions should trigger a review of the position and consideration of follow-up action.

OPTION INCOME PORTFOLIO REVIEW

-   Do not wish, pray or hope for a profitable trade. Always make trading decisions based on sound financial analysis, fundamental or technical.
-   Ideally, own several common stocks in different industries. Diversify, diversify, diversify! This cannot be stressed enough!
-   Do not let others influence your trading decisions. Stick with your decision.
-   Attempt to select stocks with options that expire in different months.
-   Use limit orders in your operation.
-   Let dividend income pay the margin interest costs and option premiums reduce the margin debit balance. Then borrow more on margin to buy more stocks and write more options. Remember the 25 percent rule.
-   Do not trade just to trade. Many people enjoy trading for the excitement of the action. Maintain your present position when there are no definite trading opportunities. Be patient and disciplined, and opportunities will appear.
-   Do not expect option trading to make you a millionaire overnight. Traders get into options investing and think it is going to be easy. They believe it is going to be like learning tennis or something, but it is much more complicated. However, you can ease the

complications of trading by doing your homework. Research and a little planning go a long way towards trading experience and trading success.

A scissors grinder is the only person whose business is good when things are dull.

—Anonymous

If thou wouldst keep money, save money; if thou wouldst reap money, sow money.

—Thomas Fuller

CHAPTER 16

Option Income Portfolio as a Tax Shelter

In 1790, the nation which had fought a revolution against taxation without representation discovered that some of its citizens were not much happier about taxation with representation.

—Lyndon B. Johnson

Treat your option income portfolio as a business. It is. What you have left after taxes is your real income. By employing the described techniques, you can reduce, defer, or eliminate taxes on investment income.

Never ignore the effects of taxes on your decision. Investments that produce only income are not only exposed to inflation, but are also fully exposed to taxation. Protect yourself from the tax consequences of your success. If you have even modest income or profits, you will be forced to consider tax planning and tax sheltering. Tax factors will affect your buy and sell decisions in operating your option income portfolio.

INVESTMENT DEFINITIONS

So that there is no confusion, several widely accepted investment definitions are presented in the following list:

- *Capital asset* is a long-term asset that is not bought or sold in the normal course of business. The IRS considers both stock and options to be capital assets.

- *Capital gain* is the amount by which the proceeds from the sale of a capital asset are more than the cost of acquiring it.
- *Capital loss* is the amount by which the proceeds from the sale of a capital asset are less than the cost of acquiring it.
- *Capital loss carry-forward* is the capital loss that exceeds capital gains and the allowed annual limit of $3,000 against ordinary income. It may be carried forward to subsequent years as an offset to capital gains or ordinary income. There is no limit to the amount of capital losses that may be used to offset capital gains in any one year. Only losses exceeding gains may be used to offset ordinary income.
- *Cost basis* is the original price of a stock, including stockbrokerage commissions.
- *Earned income* is income from wages, salaries, bonuses, and commissions generated by providing goods or services.
- *Fungible* means something of identical quality that is interchangeable. (Commodities, such as soybeans or wheat, common shares of the same company, and dollar bills are all familiar examples.) A fungible unit is any unit that can replace another unit, as in discharging a debt or obligation.
- *Fungibility* is the interchangeability of listed options, by virtue of their common expiration dates and strike prices. Fungibility makes it possible for buyers and sellers to close out their positions by using offsetting transactions through the Options Clearing Corporation (OCC).
- *Long-term and short-term* for taxes is the holding period required to differentiate short-term gain or loss from long-term gain or loss.
- *Offset (accounting)* is the amount equaling or counterbalancing another amount on the opposite side of the ledger. Capital gains can be offset by capital losses.
- *Offset (options)* is the purchase of an equal number of identical contracts to those previously sold, resulting in no further obligation.
- *Ordinary income* is income from the normal activities of an individual or business, as distinguished from capital gains from the sale of assets.
- *Realized or unrealized profit or loss* is the profit or loss resulting from the sale or other disposal of an asset. If you sell the asset at a gain, you will have a realized profit. Before you sell, your profit is unrealized.
- *Tax avoidance* is the reduction of a tax liability by legal means. For example, investors who itemize deductions may avoid some taxes by deducting the cost of this book and similar books.
- *Taxable event,* as used here, means any sale that results in a profit or loss that would affect taxes.
- *Unearned income* is individual income, such as dividends, investment interest, option premiums, and capital gains realized from invested capital.

Taxing profits is tantamount to taxing success in best serving the public.
—Ludwig von Mises

THE OPTION INCOME PORTFOLIO AND TAXES

Capital gains or losses can come from many sources, such as the sale of stocks, options, real estate and other items. Once a taxable event results in a capital gain or loss, it may be included with all other capital gains and losses for tax purposes. The IRS requires you to net or offset these gains and losses against each other to produce a net capital gain or net capital loss for your tax year. Long-term and short-term gains and losses must be totaled and netted out against each other. Your payback will be lower taxes.

Net capital losses can be used to reduce ordinary income to the extent allowed by the IRS. Capital losses can be offset dollar-for-dollar against capital gains and $3,000 of ordinary income.

There is preferential tax treatment of long-term capital gains for certain taxpayers by fixing a maximum tax rate of 25 percent on net capital gains (net long-term capital gains minus net short-term capital losses). Thus, in some (but not all) cases, individual investors with profitable positions may have an incentive to hold such positions for an extended period of time.

The long-term holding period will generally be more than one year. If stock is acquired and held for more than one year, the resulting gain or loss on a sale is a long-term capital gain or loss. If the stock is purchased and sold in one year or less, any resulting gain or loss is short-term. Any Congress may change these provisions at any time.

Net capital losses (long-term as well as short-term) can be used to reduce ordinary income to the extent allowed by the IRS. The capital loss carryover can be used when you have a greater capital loss than allowed to deduct for the tax year. This excess of unused capital loss is carried over to the next tax year. In this way, accumulated capital loss can be used, even if it takes several years.

Avoid unpleasant tax surprises. Keep careful track of both gains and losses, so that there is still time for year-end transactions. If there is a net gain, it is advisable to take a year-end loss to balance against it, thus reducing or eliminating taxes.

Tax planning requires knowing where you are concerning taxes and what tax liability will be incurred from your investment transactions. Any investment strategy that ignores tax consequences is not well-planned. Tax planning is for all investors, not just the wealthy, and next April 15 is not the time to do it.

OPTION CONTRACT CLOSING TRANSACTION

When an option contract (opening transaction) is sold, neither the profit or loss nor the tax consequences can be determined until the option contract ends. There are three possible outcomes:

1. *Exercise:* The holder of the option contract calls your stock away. You will sell the stock at the strike price to which you had previously agreed.
2. *Expiration:* The holder of the option contract does not call your stock. The expiration date passes.
3. *Purchasing an offsetting option:* Buying an option contract to close one previously sold. This closing buy ends your obligation to deliver or sell the stock.

Note: Until the opening transaction (the selling of an option) has ended by exercise, by expiration, or by purchasing a closing offsetting transaction, the option will remain open.

The premium received for writing a call is not included in income calculations until the contract has ended.

When an option is sold on stocks and it is not exercised, the premium is a short-term capital gain. If the option is exercised, the premium plus the strike price received become the sale price of the stock. The resulting gain or loss depends upon the holding period of the underlying security used to satisfy the assignment. It is possible that previously owned stock will be long-term and thus may result in a long-term capital gain or loss for a short-term option.

Gain or loss on buying an option offset closes the option obligation, either as short-term or long-term depending on the length of time the call was outstanding.

TAX DEFERRAL

Premium money received is not considered taxable until the option ends. Until that time, the final outcome of the option contract cannot be determined as a capital gain or a capital loss.

If you have stock that has appreciated in value but want to defer the gain until the following year to save on taxes, consider writing an option with an expiration date for the following year.

If the purchaser of the option doesn't exercise it until next year (or it expires), both the amount you received from selling the option and the proceeds from selling the stock will not be reported until the following year. For example: In 2009, you sell an option that expires in 2010. It is reported as 2010 income, not payable until April 15, 2011.

TAX GAINS OR LOSSES

Gain or loss in some cases can be determined by the writer of options. When you have an option gain or loss, the option is treated as having been sold or exchanged on the date it ends.

Pete purchased 100 shares of ABC stock for $20 per share on November 22. On December 1, the stock was selling for $50 a share, but Pete wanted to defer the gain until the following year and protect himself against a market decline. Pete wrote an option for $40 per share expiring in three months. He received $11 per share for selling this option. Pete has acquired protection against a market decline (he has $11 premium in his account). If the buyer of the option does not exercise it, Pete reports the $11 per share as a capital gain. If the option is exercised, the $11 per share is added to the $40 per share exercise price, making a total sale price of $51. A gain would have been realized when the option position was closed. Total gain is $31 ($51 − $20) per share cost basis.

If the ABC stock had continued to appreciate, the option would have been exercised. Pete could have bought other shares of the stock in the open market to deliver against the call, or he could choose to prevent an exercise by purchase or buyback of the option. A loss would have been realized when the option position was closed in either of these two ways. Buying back the offsetting option contract creates a capital loss, a taxable event. It also produces a gain in unrealized equity, which is nontaxable.

When buying new shares to deliver to an option assignment, a choice is presented. The buyer of the option does not care how long the stock was held, be it 10 years or a single day. All they want is the stock you are obligated to deliver to them at the strike price. Since all common stocks are fungible, you can deliver old or newly acquired shares.

It is at this time that you can decide to have a realized gain or loss on the delivery of these shares of stock.

If the cost basis is higher than the current market price, buy new shares at the lower price and deliver the old higher priced shares. Now you will have a lower cost basis for these shares in your portfolio and, at the same time, have a larger realized loss on this transaction.

If the cost basis is lower than the current market price, buy new shares at the higher price and deliver these. You will keep your lower cost basis shares in your portfolio and avoid a capital gain, a taxable event. By delivering the new higher priced shares, you will have a larger realized loss on this transaction.

Of course, if there are capital losses to use, the lower cost basis stock could be used for delivery in both cases and a larger capital gain would be realized for these transactions.

CAPITAL LOSS OR GAIN BANK

It is important to keep a running total on the capital losses or gains in your option income portfolio. Only by having this information available can it be determined which of the closing option strategies to use. If there are losses, take gains; if there are gains, take losses. Remember, capital gains plus up to $3,000 of ordinary income can be offset by capital losses dollar-for-dollar.

For all profits and losses realized as *short-term*, you will pay the highest tax rate.

Your decisions should be made considering your total tax liability. With careful planning and operational procedures, you can realize long-term capital gains on one side and a short-term loss on the other.

Remember that a tax shelter program helps to reduce, defer, or eliminate taxes on personal income. While the program offers reasonable economic gains, the first and second possible outcomes of an option plan are both taxable events. We retain the cash premiums after the option contract expires. The third possible outcome is not a taxable event: An unrealized gain on increased stock value is nontaxable.

There can be tax benefits when the option is exercised. The length of time you have held the underlying stock decides the holding period, not the option.

When you own the stock short-term, the option tax consequences are short-term. When you own the stock long-term, the option tax consequences are long-term. The premium becomes part of the selling price of the stock. It adds more net gain to the transaction (and lowers the real cost, out of pocket).

When ABC Corp. is bought in January at $20 (cost basis), the investor writes an April 20 option for a premium of 2 (the out-of-pocket cost is $18). The call is exercised in April for $20, and the profit on the ABC Corp. transaction is a $2 short-term gain. With options, the premium increases the amount realized by the writer on the sale of the underlying stock.

Now let's assume that the investor has owned ABC Corp. for a long-term holding period. In January, the investor writes an April 20 option for a premium of 2. If the stock is exercised in April, the tax sale price is $22 ($20 cost plus $2 premium). The $2 profit is long-term gain.

At year end, if the price of the stock has increased, buy back the option and take losses on this year's tax return. Sell a new option with an exercise date in the next year. This premium will not be taxable until the next year's tax return after the option has ended. By buying back the option, you could extend the holding period of a short-term underlying stock until it becomes a long-term holding.

Taxable events can be decreased and nontaxable events increased with a high degree of control in an option income portfolio. They are an excellent means of tax-sheltered income.

Most writers in the financial press and magazines never discuss this opportunity available to you, using the exchange-traded options. This buy-back capability exists because of the OCC. In the prospectus of the OCC, you can study the mechanics. The OCC makes the option contract fungible. All options for the same underlying stock, having the same exercise price and the same expiration date, are fungible, one to another.

The buying back of fungible option contracts will be done regularly, which benefits both your option income portfolio and your tax consequences. The one thing that hurts more than paying an income tax is not having an income to pay an income tax on.

Patience is not only virtue—it pays.

—B.C. Forbes

CHAPTER 17

Options: Standard Operating Procedures

The ladder of success doesn't care who climbs it.

—Frank Tyger

et us assume that you purchased 100 shares of ABC Corp., an optionable stock, for $35 per share at a total cost of $3,500 on February 21. On the same day, you sold an opening option for three months to expire on May 20, at a strike price of $30, for which you received $850. On that day, your out-of-pocket cost is $3,500 − $850 = $2,650 ($26.50 a share).

This is option investing. Because of the option hedge, you are protected in a price decline until the stock price drops below $26.50 per share.

You know that when we buy a stock, the price can go up, down, or stay the same. You also know that for the three-month period, there will be a related price movement between the stock and the option contract that you sold.

Here is what can happen to the market price of the option value at expiration due to stock price movement.

Price Feb. 21 $30 Prices on May 20th (expiration day)

ABC Corp stock	35.00	25	30	35	40	45
ABC Corp May $30 option:						
Intrinsic value	5.00	0	0	5	10	15
Time value	3.50	0	0	0	0	0
Option value	8.50	0	0	5	10	15

The preceding chart reflects five possible market prices for the stock on May 20. For each stock price you can see the related prices of the option contract. There is no time value remaining. The intrinsic value is zero if the stock is selling at or below the exercise price of $30. The intrinsic value is the difference between the higher stock price and the strike price.

If the option is exercised (called away), you would receive $3,000. You already received $850 for the option, so the total cash would be $3,000 + 850 = $3,850. You paid $3,500 in stock cost. Your gross profit would be $3,850 − 3,500 = $350. If called, you would have the $350 gross profit plus your original $3,500.

Your stock will not be called if the stock price is below the exercise price of $30. Stocks are rarely called during the life of a contract. Options are exercised the last few days, when the time value component of the option premium is very small.

RULE OF THUMB

It is advisable to buy back your option if the price is one-half or less of the premium received, and sell a new option for the next full option expiration cycle.

If it were midway (45 days), we could buy back the option for $1.75, resulting in your retaining $1.75 of the time value as well as the $5 intrinsic value. By selling the new option, you bring in more new money.

NO TIME = NO TIME VALUE

In our example, the time value on February 21 is $3.50 per share. At expiration, the time value component of the option premium is always zero. It is the understanding of this fact that permits you to make money in your option income portfolio. You always realize the time value as a gross profit.

The opening sell is controlled by you. The cash received for the sale, less the commission, will be credited to your brokerage account on the next trading day. You get your money in one day, and if you just bought the stock, you will have three days to pay for it. You will be using other people's money, since the proceeds of the option sale will apply toward the purchase of the stock you just bought.

The net cash you receive from this opening sell transaction falls into the option premiums received category. This income increases the cash amount carried in your account. When you sell an option contract, you cannot determine the tax consequences until the option has expired in one of the three following ways:

1. *Exercise:* The owner of the option calls the stock away.
2. *Expiration:* The option may expire worthless with the passage of time.
3. *Buyback:* When the option is bought back with a closing buy, it eliminates the obligation to deliver or sell the stock.

There are three ways to create a taxable event:

1. *Exercise:* You cannot control.
2. *Expiration:* You cannot control.
3. *Buyback:* You certainly control this method.

Most professionals will promote waiting until expiration if the option is not exercised, totally ignoring the buyback method.

In the example of the three-month ABC May 30 option, on May 20, since the stock was under the $30 strike price, no option holder would force you to sell the stock. Clearly, the same shares could be had for less on the open market.

At expiration, what action would you take if ABC Corp. stock was trading at one of the following five closing prices: $25, $30, $35, $40, or $45?

If the stock price is at or below the strike price of $30, you take no action. The option contract will expire worthless. This expiration is a taxable event.

If the stock price at expiration is above the strike price of $30, and if you wish to keep the stock, the action to take is to buy the offsetting option contract with a closing-buy transaction. Do this just before expiration, at the prices illustrated in the table's total option value row. On May 20, with the stock price at $35, you would pay $35 − $30 = $5 to buy the option back. At $40, you would pay $40 − $30 = $10. And at $45, you would pay $45 − $30 = $15.

To take these actions, instruct your stockbroker to "buy one ABC Corp. May 30 to close at the market." Any one of these closing buy transactions is a taxable event.

To explain tax implications further, let's look at the three things a stock can do after you optioned it. It can go down, up, or stay the same.

STOCK PRICE GOES DOWN

Let us consider a worst-case scenario: ABC Corp. stock declines from your purchase price of $35 (February 21) to $25 per share on May 20. (The very worst case would be if the company went broke and its stock fell to zero. Remember, diversify the portfolio to minimize the risk of a bankrupt stock.)

In this example, the tax consequences are not good. There is a realized capital gain of +$8.50 taxable as ordinary income. The unrealized capital loss in the stock of −$10 per share is a reduction in your equity. The only comfort is the pretax hedge given to you by your receipt of the cash option premium of +$8.50. This cash flow reduced your pretax loss in equity to −$1.50 when the stock value went down $10.

This stock is only one of some 20 stocks you should own in your option income portfolio. You would expect to have some short-term losses from other options that you sold and then bought back at higher prices. These net realized capital losses can be applied against the $8.50 net capital gain you received.

Clearly, buying stock at $35 and selling options for $8.50 is a more conservative way to own stock than if you simply purchased stock and then waited for its market price to rise. On a pretax cash basis, your invested capital would not be reduced until the stock price declined from $35 (your cost basis) to $26.50, a 24-percent decline.

STOCK PRICE STAYS THE SAME

If the stock price on May 20 was $35, the same you paid, you would pay $5 to buy the option offset. You would then have a net realized gain of $3.50, taxable as ordinary income. You would have no change in unrealized gain for the stock itself. Let's see how you did, when the stock price remains unchanged.

Strike Price − Today's Stock Price + Option Premium
÷ Today's Stock Price × Options per Year = Annualized Percentage

$$\$30 - \$35 + \$8.50 \div \$35 \times 4 = 40\%$$

With the stock price unchanged, we made 10 percent in three months and 40 percent annualized, before commissions. Not bad!

STOCK PRICE GOES UP

Despite how high the stock price may go, you agreed to sell your stock for $30. Actually, you are selling for the $30 strike price plus the $8.50 option premium.

Let's consider the net effect of buying back the option offset when the stock price is above the strike price (when the option is trading in-the-money). When you buy the option offset, your obligation to sell stock at the exercise price has been canceled. Now you can use the new higher market value of your stock to sell a higher strike price option.

If the stock price on May 20 is 45, you will pay $15 for the option buy-back (option offset). This produces a realized short-term capital loss of $6.50 ($15 − $8.50 = −$6.50). Your unrealized capital gain in your underlying stock becomes +$10 ($35 up to $45). You have an unrealized gain of $10 in your portfolio equity and have a realized loss of $6.50.

What you have done is shift assets from one position to another. You picked up a nontaxable equity gain and realized a tax loss benefit.

In rising markets, you will generate year-to-year tax loss carryovers, normally short-term. Any unused capital loss remaining after taking the maximum deduction allowable against ordinary income can be carried over indefinitely until used. Many investors build a loss carryover account, which allows them to realize tax-free cash in the future. Your trading gains realized on a future trade can be offset by losses in the loss carryover account.

This loss carryover account is valuable because it comes from your option buyback activities, which can produce nontaxable gains in your portfolio. You actually gain equity while receiving a short-term tax loss. You make money while generating a tax deduction.

Exercising an option may be to your advantage. If you wish to sell the underlying stock at expiration, you simply do nothing. When it is in the money, it will be called. This is a welcome exercise that you control. In fact, rather than just selling stock, I often will give it the last write (rite, as for the dead).

I sell an option deep in-the-money, knowing that it will be called. It usually does the trick. If the stock should drop below the strike price, after writing it deep in-the-money, you can keep a large premium and do it again.

The welcome exercise is of greater value because of the favorable tax treatment of capital gains. Normally, cash option premiums are short-term gains. When the underlying stock is called away, the option premium received assumes the status of the stock's long- or short-term characteristic.

The adjusted sales basis of the stock called away is the strike price plus the call option premium. If the stock is a long-term holding, the option premium will be considered a long-term holding. This gives you the opportunity to turn a short-term capital gain (the option premium) into a long-term holding for tax purposes.

The unwelcome exercise happens suddenly. You receive an unplanned demand from the holder of the option to exercise his right to buy your stock at the agreed-upon strike price. You do not have any control of the unwelcome assignment. OCC procedures require that on the same day you are called or assigned, you must comply with the terms of the option contract. You must deliver the stock.

Please pay close attention! Notice I said you must comply with the option holder's request and deliver stock. It does not have to be your shares . . . just the same number of shares for the same strike price. Yes, here is the time for *fungible* and *fungibility*. You can buy shares on the open market and deliver these if you want to or let them have your shares.

Whether the exercise against you is welcome or not, it is essential that you understand in responding to an exercise that you do not have to sell your originally optioned shares. Your choice is (1) to deliver shares you already own or (2) to buy and deliver new shares purchased on the open market at the prevailing price. Selling the new shares to the option holder at the strike price fulfills the terms of the contract, using fungibility.

It will be easier to understand if we go back to the last trades we did with ABC Corp. On February 21, we bought 100 shares of ABC Corp. at $35, and on the same day, we sold an option (ABC Corp. May 30 for $8.50). On May 20, the ABC Corp. stock is selling for $45, and your broker informs you that your 100 shares of ABC Corp. stock was exercised for $30.

The adjusted sales basis of the stock called away is the strike price plus the call option premium. If the stock is a long-term holding, the option premium will be considered a long term holding. This gives you the opportunity to turn a short-term capital gain (the option premium) into a long-term holding for tax purposes.

Your decision is to retain your shares. For whatever reason, you do not want to sell them. Maybe you want to hold them long enough to realize a long-term capital gain. Another consideration is that the stock has gone up from $35 to $45 a share and you would prefer to keep the lower-cost shares in your portfolio and avoid a taxable event if possible. You bought the shares at $35. You wrote the call for $8.50. Now you have been assigned at $30. The tax implications: $-35 + \$8.50 + \$30 = +\$3.50 \times 100 = \$350.00$ short-term taxable capital gain.

Your decision is to buy new shares today at $45 and sell these for $30 in cash. You wrote the option for $8.50 to sell stock for $30 and buy stock to deliver at $45. The tax implications: $+ \$8.50 + \$30 - \$45 = -\$6.50 \times 100 = -\$650$ short-term capital loss.

Cost basis of 100 ABC Corp @ $35	$3,500
Market value of 100 ABC Corp @ $45	$4,500
Gain in stock value	$1,000 (nontaxable)
Short-term capital loss	−650 (deductible)
Net after-tax gain	350

You received a net nontaxable gain of $350, 10 percent in 90 days on your equity of $3,500. Plus ... your tax savings are used at tax time. Your annualized, after-tax return on your applied equity is 40 percent. Note that the gain in equity resulted from the time value of the cash option premium at the time of your opening sell.

There has been no decrease in your equity by these trades, because you owned the underlying stock. Your after-tax equity increased. As part of the transactions, you obtained a realized short-term capital loss. These losses are not reductions in your equity. These losses from option buybacks may be accumulated during the tax year. If you do not use all the losses in one year, you may carry the unused losses to later tax years. Such totaled option buyback losses become the source of the tax-loss carryover account discussed previously. We are realizing tax losses without equity losses. Under decision two, you bought 100 shares of ABC Corp. at $45, or $4,500 cash outlay. You sold these 100 shares of ABC Corp. at $30 or $3,000. This totals to −$15 (−45 + 30 = −15) or you paid out $1,500 in cash. Your cost basis of the stock is $45, and your sale basis of the stock is $30, for a net loss of $1,500.

The sale of the ABC Corp. in response to an option assignment creates a taxable event by closing the formerly open position of your option contract. IRS rules require that you increase your sale basis ($30) by the cash option premium you received for selling the opening transaction ($8.50). In this example, your adjusted sales basis is $30 plus $8.50, equaling $38.50. You sold the stock for a loss of $15 per share, received $8.50 for the option, so you lost $6.50 per share. The out-of-pocket loss is $650. Your equity has gone up more than enough to cover this amount.

The loss for tax purposes is your cost basis ($45 minus your adjusted sale basis of $38.50). This produces a net realized short-term loss (−45 + 38.50 = −6.50). This loss is exactly what the loss would have been if you had done the options buyback.

Your decision was to keep your original stock and buy and sell the new stock on the same day. You have a gain and a tax situation that is the same as though you had used the option buyback offset. Common stock commissions are somewhat larger than option commissions. Thus, the unwelcome option assignment is slightly more costly than the option buyback offset.

Buying new shares when you are exercised (either welcome or unwelcome) gives you the opportunity to selling the higher priced shares to the option holder. In this example, the new shares were higher, so we sold the new shares and kept our lower cost basis. If our cost basis in the original shares was higher, we would sell the older higher cost shares and retain the newer lower cost shares in our portfolio.

Remember, if you sell options on shares of stock that you have held for years and your cost basis is very low, you can always substitute newly acquired shares to comply with the terms of the option contract. You never have to sell your original, low cost basis shares in response to an unwelcome assignment.

You had earlier declined decision one and now you must give an order to your broker. "Buy 100 ABC Corp. at the market and sell those shares just purchased at $30 to satisfy the assignment I have received."

Now that you have satisfied the call, the underlying stock in your possession is available for writing again. Any stock that went up 28 percent in three months will have caught the eye of the speculators. If you wrote the next period (August calls), and wrote it in-the-money as before, you would get a rich premium. The ABC Corp. August 40 probably would bring in $5 for intrinsic value and $4.50 for time value, so you probably would get $9.50, or $950. We now have a fresh $950, which more than offsets our previous $650 loss.

SELLING AND BUYING BACK CALLS: ONE STOCK FOR ONE YEAR

To obtain the best results, all blocks of stock should be working for us at all times. Therefore, upon closing an option on a block of stock, we immediately open another. Table 17.1 is a simulation of potential results of an XYZ Co. The purpose is to show the type of results from varying stock prices and actions.

In addition, there were $300 in annual dividends. Simultaneously using a spread order, we wrote the July $17\frac{1}{2}$ options at $1\frac{3}{4}$ to net $875. In May we bought these back at $\frac{3}{4}$ for a profit of $500.

We continued to sell and buy back until November. Then, anxious to set up a tax loss, we bought back the January 15 options at a cost of $4, or $2,000, for a short-term loss of $500. This loss would be applicable against other income. The same day we recouped the dollar loss by selling 5 April 15 options.

At year end, the price of the stock was at $15. We had a paper loss of $2,500, but we had received $6,125 income and spent $3,125, for a net profit

TABLE 17.1 Results of XYZ Co. for varying stock prices and actions.

Date	Action			Income	Cost	P/L
1/15	exp 5 Jan	$22\frac{1}{2}$				1100*
1/15	sold 5 Apr	20	@ 2	1000		
3/3	bought 5 Apr	20	@ $\frac{1}{2}$	250	750	
3/3	sold 5 Jul	$17\frac{1}{2}$	@ $1\frac{3}{4}$	875		
5/24	bought 5 Jul	$17\frac{1}{2}$	@ $\frac{3}{4}$	375	500	
5/24	sold 5 Oct	$17\frac{1}{2}$	@$1\frac{3}{4}$	875		
6/22	bought 5 Oct	$17\frac{1}{2}$	@ $\frac{1}{2}$		250	625
6/22	sold 5 Jan	$17\frac{1}{2}$	@$1\frac{3}{4}$	875		
8/23	bought 5 Jan	$17\frac{1}{2}$	@ $\frac{1}{2}$		250	625
8/23	sold 5 Jan	15	@ 3	1500		
11/29	bought 5 Jan	15	@ 4		2000	−500
11/29	sold 5 Apr	15	@ 4**	2000		
			Totals	7125	3125	3100

*Last year option expired this year
**Next year's settlement

of $3,000. If we had not taken a loss, our return would have been higher. Without the tax loss, our taxes would have been greater, because all gains, with all options, are short term.

OPTION INCOME PORTFOLIO PROCEDURE

Pfizer Incorporated engages in the discovery, development, manufacture, and marketing of prescription medicines for humans and animals worldwide. Pfizer's history illustrates the operational ideas we have covered. It shows the actual transactions made in my option income portfolio from 1/24/05 to 4/22/09. All dollar amounts include sales commissions. Remember, the margin interest and commissions are paid by the dividends generated from the stocks in the account.

52-week range: $11.62 to $20.13
Price-earnings ratio: 12.55
Earnings per share: $1.19
Dividend yield: 0.64 to 4.3 percent

Pfizer is in the process of acquiring Wyeth, a research-based pharmaceutical and health care company in the United States and internationally.

This is a great opportunity for Pfizer, as the two companies will complement each other in their respective fields.

- Pfizer Incorporated stock came into my portfolio on 1/24/05. I purchased 1,000 shares at $24.71 ($24,713), did a buy-write, and sold to open the January 07 25 for $3.50 ($3,480).
  - On the upside, I had $25 + $3.50 = $28.50.
  - On the downside, I had a cost of $24.71 − $3.50 = $21.21.
- 11/17/05: Sold to open 10 Pfizer December 22 .50 at $.40 for $384.98.
- 11/19/05: Buy 1,000 shares of Pfizer at $21.54 ($21,544).
  - The strategy was to sell a one-month option and give the buyer our higher-cost shares.
  - On the upside, I had $22.50 + $.40 = $22.90.
  - On the downside, I had $21.54 − $.40 = $21.14.
- 12/19/05: Buy to close Pfizer December 22.50 for $.30 ($315) with a net option gain of $384.98.
- 12/19/05: Sold to open Pfizer January 08 25 for $2.50 ($2,484.90). The stock price was $25.
  - The strategy was to keep 2,000 shares of Pfizer, and I sold a new LEAP option.
  - On the upside, I had $25 + $2.50 = $27.50.
  - On the downside, I had $21.54 − $2.50 = $19.04.
- 1/9/06: Buy to close 10 Pfizer January 07 25 at $1.95 ($1,965) with a net option gain of $1,514.90.
- 1/9/06: Sold to open 10 Pfizer January 08 25 for $2.85 ($2,835).
  - The strategy was to buy back the 07 option and sell an 08, joining it with the other one. I now had 2,000 shares of Pfizer and 20 contracts for January 08 25. The stock price was $26.
  - On the upside, I had $25 + $2.85 = $27.85.
  - On the downside, I had $24.71− $2.85 = $21.86.
- 8/22/06: Buy to close 20 Pfizer January 08 25 at $4 ($8032) with a net option loss of $2,712.
- 8/22/06: Sold to open 20 Pfizer January 09 30 at $2.40 ($4,768).
  - The strategy was to buy back the January 08 option for an option loss and sell the January 09 30 since the stock price was $27.50. I raised the strike price of the option from $25 to $30.
  - On the upside, I had $30 + $2.40 = $32.40.
  - On the downside, I had $24.71 − $2.40 = $22.31.
- 8/20/07: Buy to close 20 Pfizer January 09 30 at $.95 ($4,768) with a net option gain of $2,836.
- 8/10/07: Sold to open 20 Pfizer January 10 25 at $3.22 ($6,407).

- The strategy was to buy back the 09 option for an option gain and sell the January 10 25 since the stock price was $24. I took the strike price down from 30 to 25.
- On the upside, I had $25 + $3.22 = $28.22.
- On the downside, I had 23.13 − $3.22 = $19.91.
- 5/13/08: Buy to close 20 Pfizer January 10 25 at $.77 ($1,572) with a net option gain of $4,836.
- 5/13/08: Sold to open 20 Pfizer January 10 20 at $2 ($4,107).
  - The strategy was to capture the net option gain and sell the strike price of 20 since the stock price was now $17.50.
  - On the upside, I had $20 + $2 = $22.
  - On the downside, I had $23.13 − $2 = $21.13.
- 9/25/08: Sold to open 20 Pfizer December $17^1/_2$ at $1.25 ($2,468).
- 9/26/08: Buy 2,000 shares of Pfizer at $18.01 ($36,027).
  - The strategy is to sell a short option December, and when called, to sell our higher cost basis shares.
  - On the upside, I had $17.50 + $1.25 = $17.75.
  - On the downside, I had $18.01 − $1.25 = $16.76.
- 12/22/08: Pfizer December $17^1/_2$ expired with a worthless net option gain of $2,468.
- 12/24/08: Sold to open 20 Pfizer January 11 $17^1/_2$ at $2.70 ($5,168).
  - The strategy was to rewrite the 2,000 shares we owned unwritten. The stock price is now $17.
  - On the upside, I had $17.50 + $2.70 = $20.20.
  - On the downside, I had 18.01 − $2.70 = $15.31.
- 1/29/09: Buy to close 20 Pfizer January 10 20 at $1.08 ($2,192) with a net option gain of $1,916.
- 1/29/09: Sold to open 20 Pfizer January 11 $17^1/_2$ at $2.62 ($5,208).
  - The strategy was to capture the net option gain and rewrite Pfizer at a lower strike price since the stock price was $17.50.
  - On the upside, I had $17.50 + $2.62 = $20.12.
  - On the downside, I had $18.01 − $2.62 = $15.39.
- 2/23/09: Buy to close 40 Pfizer January 11 $17^1/_2$ at $1.33 ($5,357) with a net option gain of $5,219.
- 3/13/09: Sold to open 40 Pfizer January 11 15 at $2.15 ($8,543).
  - The strategy was to capture the net option gain and rewrite Pfizer at a lower strike price since the stock price was $13.62.
  - On the upside, I had $15 + $2.15 = 17.15.
  - On the downside, I had $21.54 − $2.15 = $19.39.
- 4/20/09: Sold to open 20 Pfizer September 15 at $.85.
- 4/22/09: Buy 2,000 shares of Pfizer at $14.22.

- The strategy is to write a short call and sell our higher-cost basis if called.
- On the upside, I had $15 + $.85 = 15.85.
- On the downside, I had $14.22 − $.85 = $13.37.

I presently own 6,000 shares of Pfizer Incorporated. Today's price is $15. My cost basis for Pfizer:

2,000 shares at $20.00
2,000 shares at $18.02
2,000 shares at $14.22
Total = $104,480

Using my methods, I have sold the Pfizer shares that I bought for $24.71. My yearly option net gains are:

2005	$49.95
2006	$1,515
2007	$2,835
2008	$8,670
2009	$7,135

This is after just four months. It will be a banner year for Pfizer.
Total option net gain: $20,204.95
My yearly dividends are:

2005	$760
2006	$1,440
2007	$2,320
2008	$3,200
2009	$1,280
Total	$9,000

Cost of shares: $104,480.00
Option net gains: −$20,204.95
Dividends: −$9,000.00
Cost (out-of-pocket): $75,275.05
Value of 6,000 shares at $15: $90,000.00
Unrealized gains in Pfizer shares: $14,724.95

Even with the stock declining drastically in price by using covered calls and dividends, I am still ahead in my portfolio. The prognosis for the Pfizer shares in the future looks fine to me.

SO WHY AREN'T YOU SELLING OPTIONS?

Over 70 percent of all options held through expiration will expire worthless.

In selling (or writing) options, you do not have to predict where the market is going to go. You simply have to decide to take action as demonstrated above. You can select a strike price above or below the current price. You sell the option at this price and collect the premium for doing so. If the time period elapses and the market has not attained this price, the option expires worthless and the writer who sold it keeps the premium collected as a profit.

One of the hardest parts of option trading is deciding when to take profits. With option selling, if the market behaves favorably towards your position, you will not have to make this decision. The market makes it for you. As time value decays your option, the market will make this decision for you. Upon expiration, if the option is still out-of-the-money (i.e., has not reached the strike price) the entire premium for which you sold the option is yours. At this time, your option position automatically closes out.

Option sellers then have a decided advantage in that they do not have to be absolutely correct in predicting market direction. If the option seller is trading with the trend of the market, this advantage increases substantially. Should the trend change after the option is sold, it does not mean the trade will be a loser. Therefore, the need for perfect timing of trade entries is also eliminated.

Remember you can liquidate your position at any time whether it is a profit or a loss. You can then sell a new option for a lesser or higher price or just more time. While you are now trading with percentages in your favor, the risks of writing options should be respected; any option writing approach should be respected and still carry the same disciplined trading plan and risk management rules as any traditional trading. This is accomplished by properly utilizing time value and by becoming familiar with core fundamentals that ultimately drive the prices of individual stocks.

While fundamentals will ultimately determine the price of an individual option, there are other factors that can drive prices beyond where normal fundamentals might direct them. Speculator and fund buying or selling is the primary example of this. Hedge funds and large mutual funds often use computer signals to determine when to buy or sell. Often, many of these fund managers may be using the same signals, or the same points of support or resistance. Prices trading through a particular level can trigger large buy-and-sell orders that can push a market outside of the base fundamental value. These can be opportune option writing events for those that know the true fundamentals.

More attractive are markets that have attracted the eye of the small speculators. Markets that are garnering a lot of media attention can often touch off a wave of speculative buying or selling that can drive prices beyond the stock's true value. Markets that have made extreme moves because of public interest offer some of the best writing opportunities. Why? The public is usually wrong and loves to buy options. This means that near the tops and bottoms of these moves, there will often be strike prices and option premiums available at what we term ridiculous levels.

How do you know if a market has reached these levels? You do not. However if the market has just made a big move due to some recent news event and there are rich premiums available, you can be pretty sure the market has achieved ridiculousness.

The history of the Pfizer trades illustrated the situations where options were bought and sold effectively, and the reasons explained. The objective was to give you an experience of trading and the utilization of option trading strategies in an irrational market.

I did not plan the above scenario, nor could I. You have to learn to react to the irrational market system and use it to your advantage. The subject of reducing and controlling risk to the portfolio is the theme of this book.

Give me the luxuries of life and I will willingly do without the necessities.
—Frank Lloyd Wright

What we call luck is simply pluck, and doing things over and over; Courage and will, perseverance and skill are the four leaves of luck's clover.
—"The Four Leaf Clover," unknown

CHAPTER 18

LEAPS

Money doesn't bring happiness, but it calms the nerves.

—French proverb

In the 1929 crash, people really did leap from rooftops and upper-story windows. My mother cautioned me as a young fellow about never investing in the stock market. She witnessed personally the awful 1929 event. What a contradiction that now the latest options being sold are called *long-term equity anticipation securities,* or LEAPS®. Just in case, remembering what my mother told me, I will no longer go up on a roof.

If you had sold options in 2008, you could have greatly limited your losses. In my Contrarian Investment Club, we made taxable gains of $260,000 on a $1 million portfolio. Of course, the portfolio went down in value to $850,000, but with limited risk because of our LEAPS option sales.

With LEAPS options you can design investment strategies that will profit regardless of what the stock market does. Besides, you can design strategies with extremely attractive risk-rewards that are much superior to any other investment. LEAPS options are an extremely valuable risk-reduction, profit-maximizing tool. In fact, for all option investors, options are an extremely valuable tool and can be used with all your trades.

Options are a wasting asset. They are not unending investment instruments. The closer you get to expiration, the faster the option decays, due to less time value. Think about why that is: why the more time is available on the option, the higher its time value is.

Look at two options contracts, both for the same equity and at the same price but with different expirations. Option A is for three months; Option B is for three years, using a LEAPS option.

In the three months, Option A will end by exercise or by running out of time. Time decay is intense in these options. Option A received 80 cents and Option B received $3.70 time value. Option sellers who find that they are frequent winners rather than losers are selling short-term options with more commissions and have to be wary of the ex-dividend date. They are collecting small-time values though.

In almost all situations, I want to have many months or more to save on commissions expense, not to have surprise executions on ex-dividend dates because of the time value, and, best of all, to collect large option premiums to use in my account. This is very similar to a long-term interest-free loan.

The LEAPS options market is one of the best opportunities for the individual investor, giving you your turn as the house (as in a casino). When I visit Las Vegas, it never ceases to amaze me how large, extravagant, and busy that city is as I walk through the lobby, sports book, casino, and shopping areas! I do not gamble or shop; walking at a brisk pace, it took me 25 minutes to go from the entrance to the end and back! I saw moving statues, fountain displays, and thick rich carpets and drapes. The gamblers who fill these spectacular casinos along the Strip ought to consider: They do not build these palaces because the house loses!

Occasionally, I speak to option buyers, and they complain that they do not win (make money) as often as they should. They do counter by saying, "At least the casinos give you drinks and free food as you lose." This is true, but the option buyers did it to themselves; they stacked the odds against themselves. They wanted wealth without work by betting small amounts for large rewards. They did not give themselves enough time to be right, and they mistook cheap options for inexpensive options. Remember, options sellers win 70 percent of the time.

LEAPS OPTIONS FOR A LONGER TERM

LEAPS options are long-term options available on many of the well-known stocks of companies with large interest. LEAPS options began trading October 5, 1990. They enable the owner of the underlying stock to sell an option with expiration up to three years in the future. Investors find the longer maturities provide additional time for investment forecasts to happen. Daily time decay is less significant than for a short-term option. For current options users, the option exchanges are finding that many of these customers are not replacing regular options with LEAPS. Instead, many are doing LEAPS options in addition to regular options.

Talk about time value! Around 20 to 30 percent of the stock price is readily available. The higher time value premium reduces the chance of being exercised early. This is because of the cost of buying LEAPS options versus an option call with a few months left.

You may want to use LEAPS if you are ready to carry your positions for a longer term. Having a longer amount of time for your position to work brings in larger premium monies and lets the speculators have more time, which is attractive to them in many ways. Selling LEAPS, which is selling (writing) a call against a stock, is a conservative option strategy. This strategy is used to increase the return on your stock and to provide a limited amount of downside protection.

To determine whether LEAPS options are available on a stock that interests you, look at the Directory of Listed Options LEAPS, provided at www.optionseducation.org/basics/leaps/leaps_3.jsp.

Exchanges listing the shorter-term options may decide to list LEAPS if the interest warrants it. Companies are desirous of being listed with LEAPS, as it brings interest in their securities, but it is not their choice. LEAPS are not available on every stock that has options traded on it. LEAPS, when they are offered, open with three strike prices: the current price and 20 to 25 percent above and below the current price of the stock. Strikes will be added as the underlying stock moves up or down. LEAPS are always listed for January expirations and for two succeeding years.

It is necessary to list new LEAPS series as they approach their expiration; they continue to be listed and traded until their expiration date, trading as ordinary short-term options. At this time, they lose their LEAPS symbol as new LEAPS are added for the next ensuing year.

LEAPS provide an investment vehicle that permits option trading with as little as 100 shares of a stock. Trading in regular stock options would not be possible because of the commission cost, which would eat up the entire premium. The greater time premium with LEAPS enables you to grow your portfolio with more optionable stocks.

Take the money and run.

—American dictum

LEAPS PRICING

Options pricing contains three main factors that I use to determine a value for a LEAPS option: the stock price, the strike price, and the time to expiration.

As before, the stock price determines which strike to employ. If you feel the stock price may go up, sell an out-of-the-money LEAPS call. The profit is equal to the appreciation in the stock price (the difference between the stock's original purchase price and the strike price of the call) plus the premium received for the call.

An investor uses an out-of-the-money LEAPS covered call strategy. DEF is currently trading at $29.50, and a DEF LEAPS call option with three-year expiration with a strike price of 35 is trading at $4.25.

The investor owns 500 shares of DEF at $29.50 and sells five DEF LEAPS calls with a strike price of $35 at $4.25 each, for a total of $2,125. The goal is to obtain profits without selling the stock. The break-even point is $25.25—the stock price of $29.50 minus the $4.25 premium. This is downside protection of $4.25. Loss can be realized if DEF falls to below $25.25. The possible outcomes at expiration are explained in the following paragraphs.

If the stock is above the strike price at $40, the covered call LEAPS writer, upon assignment, will obtain a net profit of $550 per contract—the exercise price of $35 less the stock price when the option was sold, plus the option premium of $4.25 × 100.

If you feel the stock price may go lower, sell an in-the-money LEAPS. The seller of the option cannot realize additional appreciation in the stock above the strike price, since the seller is obligated, upon assignment, to sell the stock at the call's strike price. The downside protection for the stock provided by the sale of the call is equal to the premium received in selling the option. The premium would be larger, since you are selling the option below the stock price and that intrinsic value would be added to the premium received. The writer will suffer a loss if the stock price continues to decline by an amount greater than the premium money received.

If the stock price at expiration is $24, the unexercised LEAPS calls would expire worthless, and the writer would have a stock loss of $2,750 on the stock price, less the $2,125 LEAPS option premium money received. This investor could lose more money if the underlying stock continues to decline.

If DEF advances to $34 at expiration, the LEAPS call will be out-of-the-money by $1. Therefore, the call will not be called, and the writer would retain his or her 500 shares of DEF and the option premium of $4.25 per share or $2,125, and resell the option.

If you do not know or have no inclination, sell an at-the-money LEAPS. I always sell LEAPS options at the closest strike price to the stock price. If the stock price is $11.50, I would sell a $12.50 strike, because that is closest to the current price. The other option would be a $10 strike.

- *Unit of trade:* 100 shares of stock per unadjusted contract. If there is a stock split or buyout, the number of underlying shares can change.

- *The premium (price) quotations:* Stated in points and decimals; the minimum contract price change for series trading below 3 is .05 ($5) and for all other series is .10 ($10).
- *Time to expiration:* Now we are considering LEAPS, as these can be sold for up to three years. I always sell the longest time that I can to gather in as much money as I can. This money goes right into your account; in one day it helps with your margin balance and provides funds to finance more stock purchases.
- *Expiration cycle:* Equity LEAPS expire in January of each year.
- *Expiration date:* Expiration occurs on the Saturday following the third Friday of the expiration month.

As LEAPS options approach within the one year of expiration, it becomes necessary to list new LEAPS series; the open LEAPS continue to trade and are listed as ordinary shorter-term options, losing their LEAPS symbols. New LEAPS options with expiration dates for one additional year are listed.

LEAPS SYMBOLS

To identify them as different from shorter-dated options, which have fixed symbols, LEAPS use different symbols that change to show the expiration year. The following is for Merck & Company, Inc.:

Option	Symbol	LEAPS	Symbol
Mar 09 30 call	MRKCF	JAN 10 30 call	WMRAF
Jul 09 30 call	MRKGF	JAN 11 30 call	VMKAF

This makes it easy to tell a long-term option from a shorter-term option shown in the option chains.

The following shows a complete option chain for Tyson Foods on February 9, 2009:

Symbol	Last	Change*	% Change*	Bid	Ask	B/A Size	Open Volume
TSN	9.45	−0.27	−2.78 %	−9.44	9.45	632 x 61	9.66

*Calculations (change and percent change) based on previous day's close.

And the calls:

Symbol	Last	Net	Bid	Ask	Vol	Open Int
.TSNBZ FEB 2009 2.50	0.00	0.00	6.80	7.10	0	0
.TSNBA FEB 2009 5.00	0.00	0.00	4.30	4.60	0	0
.TSNBU FEB 2009 7.50	+2.35	+0.10	1.90	2.10	10	268
.TSNBB FEB 2009 10.00	−0.20	−0.15	0.15	0.25	38	2,981
.TSNBV FEB 2009 12.50	−0.10	0.00	0.00	0.05	0	217
.TSNCZ MAR 2009 2.50	0.00	0.00	6.80	7.20	0	0
.TSNCA MAR 2009 5.00	0.00	0.00	4.30	4.70	0	0
.TSNCU MAR 2009 7.50	+2.10	0.00	2.05	2.20	0	445
.TSNCB MAR 2009 10.00	−0.55	−0.15	0.55	0.65	66	433
.TSNCV MAR 2009 12.50	−0.06	0.00	0.05	0.15	0	159
.TSNDZ APR 2009 2.50	+4.60	0.00	6.80	7.20	0	1
.TSNDA APR 2009 5.00	−3.70	0.00	4.40	4.60	0	184
.TSNDU APR 2009 7.50	+2.70	+0.20	2.25	2.40	5	3,586
.TSNDB APR 2009 10.00	−0.70	−0.25	0.75	0.85	61	5,459
.TSNDV APR 2009 12.50	−0.19	−0.05	0.15	0.25	10	1,014
.TSNDC APR 2009 15.00	−0.05	0.00	0.00	0.10	0	910
.TSNDW APR 2009 17.50	−0.15	0.00	0.00	0.10	0	1,865
.TSNDD APR 2009 20.00	−0.05	0.00	0.00	0.10	0	551
.TSNDX APR 2009 22.50	−0.15	0.00	0.00	0.10	0	219
.TSNGZ JUL 2009 2.50	+5.10	0.00	6.70	7.20	0	4
.TSNGA JUL 2009 5.00	+3.86	0.00	4.50	4.90	0	18
.TSNGU JUL 2009 7.50	+2.75	0.00	2.65	2.90	0	95
.TSNGB JUL 2009 10.00	−1.30	−0.25	1.25	1.45	13	2,431
.TSNGV JUL 2009 12.50	+0.60	+0.05	0.50	0.65	20	388
.TSNGC JUL 2009 15.00	+0.20	0.00	0.15	0.30	0	210
.TSNGW JUL 2009 17.50	−0.15	0.00	0.05	0.15	0	11
.YGKAZ JAN 2010 2.50	+6.90	+0.90	6.60	7.70	10	53
.YGKAA JAN 2010 5.00	−4.20	0.00	4.60	5.60	0	371
.YGKAU JAN 2010 7.50	+3.20	0.00	3.00	3.60	0	1,972
.YGKAB JAN 2010 10.00	+2.05	+0.05	1.75	2.10	2	439
.YGKAV JAN 2010 12.50	−1.30	0.00	0.95	1.35	0	328
.YGKAC JAN 2010 15.00	−0.61	0.00	0.50	0.85	0	464
.YGKAW JAN 2010 17.50	−0.35	0.00	0.20	0.50	0	846
.YGKAD JAN 2010 20.00	+0.60	0.00	0.10	0.35	0	712
.YGKAX JAN 2010 22.50	−0.25	0.00	0.00	0.25	0	78
.YGKAE JAN 2010 25.00	+0.10	0.00	0.00	0.20	0	2,658
.YGKAF JAN 2010 30.00	−0.05	0.00	0.00	0.20	0	289
.OGYAZ JAN 2011 2.50	+6.01	0.00	6.80	7.80	0	78
.OGYAA JAN 2011 5.00	−3.30	0.00	5.00	6.10	0	325

(Continued)

(*Continued*)

Symbol	Last	Net	Bid	Ask	Vol	Open Int
.OGYAU JAN 2011 7.50	−3.58	0.00	3.80	4.20	0	371
.OGYAB JAN 2011 10.00	+2.74	0.00	2.65	3.60		141
.OGYAV JAN 2011 12.50	+2.50	0.00	1.90	2.60		35
.OGYAC JAN 2011 15.00	−1.05	0.00	1.10	1.85		51
.OGYAW JAN 2011 17.50	−1.75	0.00	0.70	1.30		40
.OGYAD JAN 2011 20.00	+0.75	0.00	0.50	0.90		10
.OGYAX JAN 2011 22.50	+0.65	0.00	0.25	0.65		15

A good way for an investor to get started with safety is with the purchase of 100 shares of a blue chip stock and the sale of a LEAPS contract with a large premium for time. Until the introduction of this new product, I had a problem suggesting how an investor with limited capital could get started by using my methods.

Buying 100 shares of a blue chip stock and receiving a large cash premium up front does not diversify a portfolio. However, LEAPS options work, using all the other operating methods discussed in this book.

Writing high cash premium LEAPS options gives much downside protection and provides attractive returns to maturity, whether called or not. For conservative investors in dividend-paying blue chip stocks, selling LEAPS options is a viable and attractive strategy.

Of course, you should still add additional funds to your account, as it is your goal to become diversified as soon as possible. A second LEAPS in a different equity is a start. You will get there quickly using additional funding, the cash premium, and dividends. These should be invested in a brokerage cash account that draws money market interest.

> Success is a science. If you have the conditions, you get the result.
> —Oscar Wilde

LEAPS can be bought or sold with an expiration date as far as three years in the future. Starting in 1994, all LEAPS expire in January. The expiration date is the Saturday following the third Friday. The exchanges add new LEAPS as they deem significant. LEAPS strike prices will be in-, at-, and out-of-the-money. New series are added when the underlying stock reaches the exercise price. One LEAPS contract represents 100 shares of the underlying stock, as in equity options.

Daily price information is published in *Investor's Business Daily*. *Barron's* prints the data weekly. Literature and quotes on LEAPS can be obtained by calling the Chicago Board Options Exchange (CBOE) at 1-800-OPTIONS, contacting your broker, or looking at Yahoo! Finance.

Let's look at an example: Having used a buy-write, 100 shares of ABC Corp were purchased at $52.62 ($5,262) and one contract of the January 2010 70 LEAPS was sold. The 4\frac{1}{8}$ cash premium ($412) protects down to $48.50. The strike price is $70, which means that if the option is exercised, the stock will be sold for $7,000. The total of the value rise in the stock sale price over the stock purchase price plus the premium is $21.50, or $2,150. In addition, there would have been six dividends of $25.00, bringing the total to $2,300 on an investment of $5,262—about 44 percent. If the stock goes up above the $70 strike price, in order to keep the stock with its lower cost basis, purchase a closing option and immediately sell a new LEAPS opening transaction at a higher strike price, taking in a new cash premium to help finance the buyback.

If the market price of the stock goes down before January 2010, buy an option offset and cancel the obligation. Immediately sell another LEAPS option at a lower strike price, taking in a new cash premium.

If the market price of the stock stays the same until January 2010, let the LEAPS contract expire worthless. At this point, the return would be $412 (cash premium) plus $150 (dividends) for a total return of about 11 percent on a flat investment. The non-LEAPS owner of a flat investment would only have the dividends ... about a 2 percent return. At expiration, sell another LEAPS option at the same strike price, taking in a new cash premium.

The following are examples of some LEAPS contracts that I was doing as of February 9, 2009. Please note: These are all sold for the strike price closest to the stock price at the time. See the gain you will make if the underlying stocks go to the end of their time, unexercised.

Stock	Price	LEAPS	Strike	Premium	Strike + Premium
Altria	$16.81	Jan 2011	$17.50	$2.16	$19.66
Annaly Mtg.	$15.22	Jan 2011	$15.00	$2.49	$17.49
AT&T	$25.85	Jan 2011	$25.00	$5.35	$30.35
Archer Dan.	$29.05	Jan 2011	$30.00	$7.40	$37.40
Bank America	$6.89	Jan 2011	$7.50	$3.20	$10.70
Bristol-Myers	$22.86	Jan 2011	$20.00	$5.20	$25.20
CBS	$6.22	Jan 2011	$5.00	$2.30	$7.30
Cemex	$8.88	Jan 2011	$10.00	$3.50	$13.50

(Continued)

(Continued)

Stock	Price	LEAPS	Strike	Premium	Strike + Premium
Cisco	$16.85	Jan 2011	$17.50	$4.15	$21.65
Citigroup	$3.95	Jan 2011	$5.00	$1.68	$6.68
Corning	$11.87	Jan 2011	$12.50	$2.80	$15.30
Comcast	$14.38	Jan 2011	$14.40	$4.10	$18.50
Conagra	$16.90	Jan 2011	$17.50	$2.20	$19.70
D. R. Horton	$9.05	Jan 2011	$10.00	$3.30	$13.30
Dow Chem.	$10.59	Jan 2011	$10.00	$3.91	$13.91
Halliburton	$19.58	Jan 2011	$20.00	$5.85	$25.85
Hanes Brands	$8.32	Jul 2009	$7.50	$2.25	$9.75
E. Kodak	$4.66	Jan 2011	$5.00	$1.30	$6.30
Ericsson	$8.79	Jan 2011	$7.50	$2.90	$10.40
Ford	$1.89	Jan 2010	$2.50	$.64	$3.14
GE	$12.64	Jan 2011	$12.50	$3.55	$16.19
Goodyear	$7.24	Jan 2011	$7.50	$3.00	$10.50
Hewlett-P.	$36.33	Jan 2011	$40.00	$7.30	$47.30
Key Corp.	$9.03	Jan 2011	$10.00	$3.30	$13.30
Kraft	$25.89	Jan 2011	$25.89	$4.50	$30.39
Lorillard	$64.30	Jan 2011	$65.00	$8.80	$73.00
Microsoft	$19.44	Jan 2011	$20.00	$3.87	$23.87
Motorola	$4.15	Jan 2011	$5.00	$1.21	$6.21
Novell	$3.60	Jan 2010	$5.00	$.45	$5.45
Occidental P.	$58.61	Jan 2011	$60.00	$14.90	$74.90
Oracle	$18.05	Jan 2011	$17.50	$5.10	$22.60
Olin	$14.90	Jan 2011	$15.00	$3.90	$18.90
Pepsi	$51.43	Jan 2011	$50.00	$8.40	$58.40
Pfizer	$14.71	Jan 2011	$15.00	$2.63	$17.63
Philip Morris	$36.72	Jan 2011	$35.00	$6.60	$41.60
Qwest Comm.	$3.37	Jan 2010	$2.50	$1.15	$3.65
Sara Lee	$9.49	Jan 2010	$10.00	$1.15	$11.15
Schering P.	$20.09	Jan 2011	$20.00	$4.00	$24.00
Shaw Gp.	$29.42	Jan 2011	$30.00	$11.80	$41.80
Teco Energy	$11.88	Jan 2011	$12.50	$1.00	$13.50
Tyson	$9.45	Jan 2011	$10.00	$3.00	$13.00
United Online	$5.88	Jan 2011	$5.00	$1.40	$6.40
Verizon Com.	$31.39	Jan 2011	$30.00	$5.72	$35.72
Vodaphone	$20.34	Jan 2011	$20.00	$3.80	$23.80
Wells Fargo	$19.06	Jan 2011	$20.00	$6.80	$26.80
Xerox Corp.	$7.02	Jan 2011	$7.50	$1.60	$9.10
Xcel	$18.81	Jan 2011	$20.00	$.90	$20.90
Yahoo!	$13.90	Jan 2011	$15.00	$3.45	$18.45

LEAPS create exciting new opportunities for investors to achieve their intermediate-term trading goals by receiving the large time premiums. You will learn to *react* to the market. Instead of doing shorter three- to nine-month options, you will be doing longer options, up to three years. Your annualized premium will be less than with short-term option contracts, but you will find that it is possible to achieve your goals, even with a smaller investment.

> If a man empties his purse into his head, no man can take it away from him.
> —Benjamin Franklin
>
> Successful man: One who earns more than his wife can spend. Successful woman: One who finds such a man.
> —Anonymous

CHAPTER 19

Conclusions

"One can survive anything these days, except death..."

—Oscar Wilde

Your reason for investing is to make money.

Successful investing is like marshaling forces on a battlefield; all the pieces must be working together. Tactics that are misaligned can produce chaos over a long period of time. A well-thought-out plan and goal with discipline can be undermined by investing in the wrong stock at the wrong time, or by dollars lost through taxes and inflation. Every chapter in this book contains important points.

Your investing must be businesslike. In spite of running a successful business operation, some capable businesspeople operate their investment portfolios with complete disregard for sound business principles and practices. Trying to make profits from investing is a business venture and requires the use of accepted business principles and practices.

Know what you are doing. Know as much about investing as you know about the business in which you made your original capital.

Operate your investment business yourself. Have the conviction of your knowledge. If you have formed a decision based on the facts, and you know that your judgment is sound, act on it. If you make a decision and fail to promptly act on it, you have lost your time and opportunity. Be timely!

You are neither right nor wrong if the crowd disagrees with you. You are right because your research and reasoning are right. Remember, it is not what you think about a stock; it is what you *know* about a stock.

> Do not follow where the path may lead ... go instead where there is no path and leave a trail.
>
> —Anonymous

The main thing to remember with the stock market is to never put your money in just one company. Choose carefully. Spread your risk over a portfolio of stocks. You must do your homework before you invest. Become an authority on options before you sell any. There is no substitute for knowledge. It is both power and security.

To be sure, we cannot possibly know all the ins and outs of investment markets. Most of us made our money making products or selling services. Making money with money is an art that has to be learned, often the hard way.

FEAR, GREED, HOPE, AND ONE'S SELF

What prohibits us from approaching investing systematically, applying all of the lessons learned from our past mistakes?

The answer stems from the same elusive reason as when we broke New Year's resolutions, had that extra helping when on a diet, and never got around to fixing that leaky faucet ... human nature. The greatest obstacle to successful investing is one's lack of discipline and failure to act with that discipline.

Failing to control emotions causes one to keep a losing position too long, take profits too early, or take advice from uninformed people. Two enemies of the average investor are fear and hope. They are usually accompanied by another: greed. Controlling these hindrances to success, which exist in varying degrees within all of us, is essential for successful investing.

> Your attitude determines your altitude.
>
> —Anonymous

TRAITS OF THE WINNER

These characteristics are important in achieving success in the option markets. Nothing prevents an amateur from taking on the traits of the winner:

- *Attention to the market:* Scrutinizing market prices, news, and trends each day.
- *Capitalization:* Maintaining adequate funding to absorb reasonable losses.
- *Capital management:* Maintaining long-term purchasing power in your margin account.
- *Discipline:* Reacting to the market and the buy/sell signals with no hesitation or emotion.
- *Diversification:* Trading 15 to 25 varied industries, with never more than two companies in the same group.
- *Goals:* Having a long-term, well-tested trading system for profit.
- *Latest information:* Using reliable, current sources for research.
- *Margin calls:* Never!
- *Planned strategy:* Using sound business practices: cut losses and let profits run, and always look for a bargain undervalued stock.
- *Risk control:* Using option selling for protective hedges on all equity positions in the account.
- *Timing:* Reacting in a timely manner upon market knowledge.

TRAITS OF THE LOSER

By contrast, traits of the loser are:

- *Attention to the market:* Spending inadequate time on financial news, data, and trends.
- *Capitalization:* Being underfunded and unable to absorb losses or lessen risks by diversifying.
- *Capital management:* Being usually 100 percent invested and fully margined.
- *Discipline:* Acting on emotion; this results in big losses and small profits.
- *Diversification:* Building concentrated positions in only a few industries.
- *Goals:* Getting instant gratification.
- *Latest information:* Having imperfect knowledge and using hot tips.

- *Margin calls:* Very frequent.
- *Planned strategy:* Little planning; changing tactics and strategies.
- *Risk control:* None; frequently loses; takes high risks.
- *Timing:* Acting in haste on inadequate information, usually when broker calls.

> When you're afraid, keep your mind on what you have to do. And if you have been thoroughly prepared, you will not be afraid.
>
> —Dale Carnegie

With control of emotion and investment knowledge you will not merely hold your position, but make major capital gains. It should be repeated that investments are good in any economic climate.

You need not panic during a market crash. You can make an ally of panics and crashes by understanding their nature. You can avoid the mental upset and the emotional trauma if you grasp the patterns and learn the clues. You can preserve your capital while those around you are selling in terror when they should be buying, or you can buy in confidence in a declining market.

> Nothing in the world can take the place of Persistence. Talent will not; nothing is more common than unsuccessful men with talent. Genius will not; unrewarded genius is almost a proverb. Education will not; the world is full of educated derelicts. Persistence and determination alone are omnipotent.
>
> —Calvin Coolidge

THE SURPRISING NEW SHAPE OF THE ECONOMY

America has entered a period dramatically different from anything it has experienced before. Critical economic forces are now reshaping both the United States and the world at large:

- Long-term inflation, a rise in isolationism, resentment of the wealthy and powerful, and a lack of political resolve to control federal deficits.
- A rebirth in U.S. technological innovation and ability to compete.

- Massive restructuring of industry and banking, plus the North American Free Trade Agreement.
- The globalization of communications, technology, finance, and stock markets.
- The rise of capitalism and democracy in place of the discredited and crumbling beliefs of communism.

As a result, the decades ahead will not resemble any others. The alleged economic recovery has no parallel in American history, and neither will the performance of the stock market.

There are two schools of thought making up conventional wisdom. One holds that the sluggish recovery will be followed by a traditional boom in which inflation and interest rates will rise. However, some observers are forecasting a depression because of excessive debt levels, weak monetary growth, and lack of responsible decisions and actions concerning governmental fiscal matters.

I feel that neither of these extremes—a boom or a bust—is likely. We will not experience a return of 1970s inflation nor 1930s deflation. Something very different and more subtle is already unfolding.

It is a world of low inflation, relative price shifts, and restructured industries and financial institutions.

It is not surprising, then, that so few people understand what is happening behind the misleading government statistics. The statistics measure yesterday's economy, not tomorrow's, upon which the stock market is focused.

Most so-called experts see the future in terms of the past. They cannot make the creative leap required to envision a totally new kind of economy. Instead, they fall back on the old, traditional formulas and models because it is easier.

Investors, too, will be confused by unfamiliar signals and be led into dangerous and expensive traps. Consider, for example, the dramatic fall in stock prices in the face of largely negative signals from the economy. Most investors were unprepared for and have been puzzled by the pattern of stock and bond prices. They have been constantly warned by the bears that stocks were too expensive, interest rates would rise, and a depression would occur.

Expensive stock prices are not a sufficient reason for turning bearish, particularly at the beginning of a cyclical bull market. The key is in understanding the trend of valuation. Stocks have achieved a record low valuation and even higher levels are possible. The dangers are enormous because high stock prices always lead to big shakeouts. Low stock prices enable portfolio gains.

We are continually faced by great opportunities brilliantly disguised as insoluble problems.

—Lee Iacocca

MADNESS OF CROWDS RETURNS

Where will investors' money go? Returns on money market funds are now very disappointing. Meanwhile, confidence in the stock market has returned, so individual investors are likely to continue to build the equity portions of their portfolios. This phenomenon will further fuel the already evolving stock market mania of 2009.

For the first time in history, there is more money invested in mutual funds than on deposits in the banking system. But there is a danger: When people exaggerate the significance of such events and succumb to excessive optimism, as witnessed in the 1920s and 1960s, prices are driven to overvaluation extremes. Panics and crashes will always follow. Read Charles Mackay's book: *Extraordinary Popular Delusions and the Madness of Crowds*.

Such instability and volatility will be prevalent. Could the market double? Most people see the present crash as the end of a major bull market. I believe that there is compelling evidence that the crash was merely a pause in a long-term supercyclical mania.

Ultimately, like all madness, it will blow itself out. But before that happens, wise investors will have the opportunity to reap enormous profits. Investors who wish to profit from the mania should heed three important lessons:

1. When stocks are moving from under- to overvaluation, total returns are so high that a fully invested position strategy will almost certainly produce superior returns, compared with a market timing approach.

2. Contrary to popular belief, stocks can be good investments, even when they are expensive, as long as the trend to overvaluation is intact. But when they are overvalued and the correction has begun, those stocks must be sold.

3. Money and inflation trends are critical. The ideal breeding ground for a mania is when inflation is falling and money growth is accelerating. Liquidity, rather than business activity and general prices, then pushes up stock prices.

Surprisingly, even during manias, most investors lose money! Why? Because they cannot cope with the high level of volatility and risk that is an inherent element of the mania climate. However, investors who understand the mania process and who can follow a sound strategy can capitalize on a unique opportunity. They can profit handsomely while managing and minimizing the risks by practicing my precepts in this book.

Note well that a long-term, nonspeculative, disciplined strategy is essential. To endure the high volatility possible in any mania environment requires patience and determination.

Investing in this manner has demonstrated itself as a superior strategy to investors and has rewarded those who followed its reasoning with higher profits while helping to minimize risk and alarm.

We have looked at the basic principles of investing and the advanced usage of these ideas. If you expect to succeed, you must have a goal, a plan, and discipline. Lack of any one of these will seriously hamper any investments you may make.

> No one can predict to what heights you can soar. Even you will not know until you spread your wings.
>
> —Anonymous

There will be times when everything goes well, and there will be disasters when everything goes wrong. Everything cycles.

The only way to tell if you are getting anywhere in the long run is to see how you are progressing on the road toward your target. If you are really serious about this business, the first thing you have to do is establish goals and objectives. Then plan how to reach them.

> Eagles don't flock; you have to find them one at a time.
>
> —A plaque in H. Ross Perot's office

There are two types of people when it comes to investing. One group knows where their tennis balls are at any time, and they are always looking for more return, more bounce for their dollars. They read the financial press diligently and study and understand the annual and quarterly reports. They go to stockholder meetings if possible. Their favorite TV station is CNBC, the financial channel. They know the ticker symbols of their stocks and options, and like to trade them. To them this isn't work . . . it's fun. It is like a hobby and business, all mixed together. It fills much (or all) of their spare time. Their friends are from the investment world, and they never tire of talking stock market with each other. Most of them do pretty well in their investment activities.

If you are this type of person, you don't need this book. (If you are this type of person you could have stopped reading this book 200 pages ago, but you didn't.)

Most aren't like this. They either totally ignore investments or view them as a necessary evil. They become slightly interested in developing and maintaining an investment program, but fail to sustain that interest. It is a confusing and intimidating world out there. It is little wonder that most of them prefer to spend their spare time on something they really enjoy.

THE GOOD NEWS

If you are the second type, there is good news. You don't have to spend much time and effort to establish and maintain a sound option income portfolio program. Once committed, all you have to do is keep a supervisory eye on the whole process.

You have to manage your money. It isn't that difficult. It does take time and attention. Once you have established a planned program, this should not amount to more than two or three hours a week. We have found that the vast majority of investors can easily manage a personal investment program with very little guidance from outside sources. It requires reading the financial pages, watching daily financial news programs, reading the mailed business reports from the companies in which you own shares, and occasionally calling your broker.

It doesn't require riding a roller coaster of emotion and trepidation as the financial markets cycle. It permits you to view a Black Monday (or Wednesday, or Thursday) with a serene detachment. This simplicity is crucial.

By going for the long term, the small investor is free from getting caught up in the day-to-day market frenzies that lead to whipsaws. It frees the small investor from the trap of investment news. This information reports what has happened, not what will occur; it is out of date when you see it.

Have discipline! You have done the hard work. You have set your investment goal and decided to fund your option income portfolio. By applying the principles we have laid out, you can construct a basic financial goal and generate a plan for attacking it. Since each of us is different, you must fine-tune and individualize your plan. You will have some successes and undoubtedly you will have some failures. The important thing is to remain flexible and learn from past mistakes, so that you don't repeat them.

> The difference between a successful person and others is not a lack of strength, not a lack of knowledge, but rather is a lack of will.
>
> —Vincent Lombardi

What will ultimately decide your success is whether you have personal discipline and make regular cash infusions to build your option income portfolio.

REMEMBER TIME PLUS MONEY FOR SUCCESSFUL INVESTING

Achieving satisfactory investment results is easier than most people realize; achieving superior results is much more difficult.

I could conclude this book by saying, "The best of luck to you in your stock market adventure," although we all know that the element responsible for success is much less elusive and far more tangible than anything closely resembling luck.

Only results count. Remember that time is your most important ally. An individual mistake here or there won't sink your ship. Know you will never reach your destination if you do not leave the dock.

You earn your money the hard way, and you now have a safe, methodical way of investing and a solid foundation for building your wealth. You now have the knowledge to strip the mystique from investing. You now have a clear method from the very basics to a degree of sophistication on a par with the pros in the business. On the way, you learned to avoid the traps that constantly frustrate others who attempt to make a fortune in the stock market.

Now it is time to begin.

> Don't gamble! Take all your savings and buy some good stock and hold it 'til it goes up, and then sell it. If it don't go up, don't buy it.
>
> —Will Rogers
>
> He that shoots best may sometimes miss the mark; but he that shoots not at all can never hit it.
>
> —Owen Felltham

Investing in Citigroup through the Years

I n 1972, my wife Beverly started working for Citigroup as a manager in the credit department.

Her pension plan was vested in the company's stock plan. She phoned me very excitedly one day in October 1990 and said that the bank was going to go bankrupt.

"What is the problem?" I asked.

She said, "The Mexican government is going to default on millions of dollars in bonds that Citicorp has loaned to them."

"Do not panic; I will research the Mexican debt and get back to you." As an investment adviser, I am used to dealing with financial news good and bad, real and innuendo, true and false.

After doing my diligent research, I found out that the faith and integrity of the United States Treasury would make good on the bonds if Mexico defaulted. You could not lose—if the Mexican government would not pay, the United States would. Needless to say, I bought Citigroup stock at $10.23 a share. I also encouraged the members of the Contrarian Investment Club to do the same.

CITICORP: A FINANCIAL HISTORY

In 1812, a group of merchants founded the City Bank of New York as a replacement for the First Bank of the United States, whose charter Congress had allowed to expire. The First Bank (FNB) was formed right after the Revolutionary War as the central bank for the new country. Citigroup for many years used the ticker symbol FNB after it became Citicorp. In the Panic of 1837, the bank nearly failed but was rescued by the country's richest man, fur magnate John Jacob Astor. Citicorp was a banking leader of sound finance, large capital reserves, and miserly lending principles. Citicorp financed the Union during the Civil War and easily survived the first postwar economic panic in 1873.

Citicorp began a pattern of conservatism and risk taking, success and near failure, which has marked the banking business enterprise now known as Citigroup. In 1891, James Stillman became the bank's president and combined discretion with great objectives. Citicorp made it through the Panic of 1893, thanks in part to the huge stash of gold that the bank had acquired, gold being the backing for credit then. The bank joined with J. P. Morgan in financing the nearly bankrupt U.S. government in 1895—how about that? It soon grew to be the country's biggest bank, and in 1914 Citicorp started opening branches abroad.

With that expansion came near ruin, as big loans to Cuban sugar farmers went bad.

Charles E. Mitchell, head of Citicorp's securities arm, repackaged the bad Cuban debt and continued to find creative ways to sell securities and lend to the growing middle class. In 1921 he became president of the bank, and built it into the first financial superstore.

In the1930s, when everything monetary turned bad, he became the main target of the Pecora hearings in Congress, was arrested but not convicted of tax evasion, and resigned in disgrace.

The Glass-Steagall Act of 1933 put an end to the joining together of banking and securities businesses that Mitchell had advocated. Citicorp lived on as a much smaller bank.

By the mid-1940s, more than half of Citicorp's assets were in U.S. government bonds and this led the way to a new time of growth in the 1950s. Walter Wriston, the bank's CEO from 1967 to 1984, instituted international expansion and domestic expansion. After years of great success, he left the bank with billions in bad loans to Latin America. Profits generated by the U.S. retail banking and credit card business built by John Reed, combined with forbearance by bank regulators and a lot of cash from Saudi Arabia, enabled the bank to survive. Reed then agreed to a merger in 1998 with Travelers Group, which established Citigroup as the greatest financial superstore in the world.

Citigroup is now on life support, owing its continued survival to $45 billion (thus far) in federal aid. Its stressed top management team is trying to undo most of the 1998 merger with Travelers. The Obama Administration is faced with the inconsistent priorities of trying to avert a depression, nurse the banking industry back to health, and prevent future excesses of the sort that led to today's troubles.

Citigroup's history shows these are not new problems, and that they have not been resolved. Banks and financial systems are flimsy, and tend to zigzag from greed and back to conservatism. We are deep in the fear part of the cycle right now. So what should the government do?

In the past, the government stood by while banks failed. This is not a real option today. The modern world is not prepared to survive a financial shutdown. What is needed is a new start, new management, new investors, and new boards of directors—and in some cases, new institutions. That is how Citigroup and the financial system returned to health in the past.

CONTRARIAN INVESTMENT CLUB HISTORY

Abbreviations used:

STO = sold to open
BTC = buy to close

The newly formed club made our first investment in Citicorp:

- Sep 1989, buy 100 shares @ $31.08 STO (1 contract) April 35 for $164.00, our first option to open
- Jan 1990, BTC 1 contract (100 shares) @ $48.50, net option gain $115.50, our first completed gain
- Jan 1990 (the same day), STO Jul $25 @ $189.00
- May 1990, BTC Jul $25 @ $67.25, an option gain $121.75
- May 1990 (same day), buy an additional (new) 100 shares @ $24.10, totaling 200 shares
- Jul 1990, buy 100 shares @ $20.85 (300 shares total), Jul $25 expired, a gain of $189.00
- Jul 1990, STO 3 contracts, Jan $20 @ $672.32
- Sep 1990, BTC 3 (contracts), Jan 20 @ $189.50 gain $482.82
- Oct 1990, buy 200 shares @ $12.75 (total 500 @ $10,220.35)
- Oct 1990, STO 5 (contracts), Jan 1991 $10 @ $955.21
- Jan 1991, assigned on 5 contracts (500 shares), Jan 1991 @ $10: ($4,919.08 + 955.21 [premium] = $5,874.29 net stock loss [$4,346.06]). Stock cost 500 shares ($10,220.35 – $5,874.29 = $4,346.06), a net stock loss
- Jan 1991, bought 500 new shares, Citicorp stock @ $13.50 ($6,750.00 + $89.00 commission = $6,839.00) new cost ($6,839.00 ÷ 500 shares) = $13.678 per share
- Jan 1991, STO 5 Jul $12\frac{1}{2}$ @ $2.25 = $1,078.21 ($1,125 – $46.79 commission = $1,078.21)

At this point, we have a lower cost basis in Citicorp 500 shares ($6,839.00 instead of our original cost basis of $10,220.35). We have a tax loss of $4,346.06. We have an option gain of $1,864.28 and an open option position 5 July 1991 $12.50 for $1,078.21.

- Jun 1991, BTC 5 Jul 1991, $12.50 @ $1,489.25 (1,489.25 − 1,078.21 = $411.04) net option loss
  - STO 5 Jan 1992, $15 @ $831.97
- Oct 1991, BTC 5 Jan 1992, $15 @ $98.50 = $733.47 net option gain
  - STO 5 Apr 1992, $12.50 @ $456.98
- Dec 1991, BTC 5 Apr 1992, $12.50 @ $324.25 = net option gain $132.73
- Dec 1991, STO 5 Jul 1992 $10 @ $862.96

As you know, when the options are bought to close, new ones are then resold the same day and at a strike price determined by the market. We are realists as to the strike prices sold. No wishing, hoping, or praying, as these will not help. What the ticker shows is what we choose to do.

I will now prove how valuable selling covered call options using this investment philosophy over a long term can be. (See Figures A.1 and A.2.)

The Realized Yearly Net Option Premiums Received

1990	$909.07
1991	$2,319.44
1992	$1,268.17
1993	$0.00
1994	$909.94
1995	$7,267.25
1996	$0.00
1997	$8,335.96
1998	$25,647.06
1999	$8,458.24
2000	$10,240.58
2001	$21,560.29
2002	$13,840.63
2003	$14,571.16
2004	$3,045.37
2005	$10,241.17
2006	$11,437.63
2007	$12,019.96
2008	$34,327.33

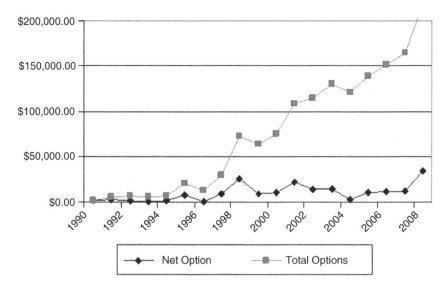

FIGURE A.1 "C" Citigroup Option Premiums

Options Premiums received $186,399.25
+ Dividends $37,306.15   = $223,705.40
2,800 shares Citigroup cost basis   −12,113.75
Total Gain $211,591.79

Stock Split Gains:

2,800 shares? We started with 500 shares. As you know, we received cash dividends of $37,306.15. We also received stock dividends as well.

- On October 8, 1998, there was a stock split of 2.5 shares for 1. Our 500 shares were now 1,250 shares, and our cost basis per share went from $13.678 a share to $5.471 a share ($6,839 ÷ 1,250 = $5.471).
- On June 1, 1999, there was a 3-for-2 stock split. Our 1,250 shares were now 1,800 shares. Our cost basis per share went from $5.471 a share to $3.799 a share ($6,839 ÷ 1,800 = $3.799).
- On August 8, 2000, there was a 4-for-3 stock split. Our 1,800 shares were now 2,400 shares. Our cost basis per share went from $3.799 to $2.849 a share ($6,839 ÷ 2,400 = $2.849).
- On December 4, 2000, there was a stock merger. We owned in the portfolio 600 shares of Associates First Capital, given to us as a spinoff from Ford Motor Co. on April 8, 1999. The 600 shares had a cost basis

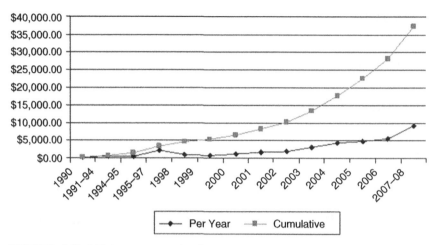

FIGURE A.2 "C" Citigroup Dividend Chart

of $17.53, or $10,514.95. Our 600 shares were merged into Citicorp for 440 shares and $1.99 cash. We now had 2,840 shares of Citicorp and a new cost basis of $14,264.95 or $6.01 per share.

- On January 11, 2001, we sold the 40 shares of Citigroup @ $53.78 = $2,151.20 ($14,264.95 − $2,151.20 = $12,113.75), giving us a new cost basis of Citicorp stock $12,113.75 or $4.326 per share for 2,800 shares. We sold the 40 shares, as you need 100 shares to do an option contract, and we did not want to add more shares.

As I write this, Citigroup is trading at $1.80 a share. The monies received with options $186,399.25 and dividends received $37,306.15 total $223,705.40. The cost basis is ($223,705.40 ÷ $12,113.75) = 18.46 times over our cost. The portfolio today is valued at: 2,800 shares @ $1.80 = $5,040.00. Even if Citigroup should fail and become worthless, did we really lose? This proves my point: Invest for the long term, use covered call options, and collect dividends.

Resources

T here is a wealth of information written about stocks and options. The following list contains the books and information links that I have found the most timeless and useful. There are two categories: general investing information and in-depth studies of options.

INVESTING BOOKS

The Essays of Warren Buffett: Lessons for Corporate America by Warren E. Buffett with Lawrence A. Cunningham (Cunningham Group, 2001)

  The definitive work concerning Warren Buffett and intelligent investment philosophy, this is a collection of the letters Buffett wrote to the shareholders of Berkshire Hathaway over the past few decades. Together, these furnish an enormously valuable informal education. The letters distill in plain words all the basic principles of sound business practices. They are arranged and introduced by leading apostle of the value school and noted author Lawrence Cunningham. Here in one place are priceless pearls of business and investment wisdom, woven into a delightful narrative on the major topics concerning both managers and investors.

Sell & Sell Short by Dr. Alexander Elder (John Wiley & Sons, 2008)

  Dr. Elder asserts that many investors approach selling in a vague and indecisive manner. Selling is the hard part of trading. If the stock we buy rises, when do we take profits? If our stock falls, when do we bite the bullet and exit the trade? If our stock stagnates, when do we say enough is enough and move on to another opportunity? *Sell & Sell Short* offers the essential lessons, rules, and instructions all traders need to look for market tops and jump onto a downtrend.

Against the Gods: The Remarkable Story of Risk by Peter L. Bernstein (John Wiley & Sons, 1996)

"Peter Bernstein has written a comprehensive history of man's efforts to understand risk and probability, beginning with early gamblers in ancient Greece, continuing through the seventeenth century French mathematicians Pascal and Fermat and up to modern chaos theory. Along the way he demonstrates that understanding risk underlies everything from game theory to bridge-building to winemaking."

The Prudent Speculator: Al Frank on Investing by Al Frank (Dow Jones-Irwin, 1990)

One of Wall Street's successful investment gurus shows you how to consistently make money in the stock market. Both part-time and seasoned investors will find a unique but proven approach in Frank's investment strategy. Based on systematic, fundamental principles and the use of margin, his system for finding undervalued investment opportunities will help you make more informed and profitable money management decisions.

Fooled by Randomness: The Hidden Role of Chance in Life and in the Markets by Nassim Nicholas Taleb (Random House, 2001)

In *Fooled by Randomness*, Nassim Nicholas Taleb, a professional trader and mathematics professor, examines what randomness means in business and in life and why human beings are so prone to mistake dumb luck for complete skill. This eccentric and highly personal exploration of the nature of randomness wanders from the court of Croesus and trading rooms in New York and London to Russian roulette, the Monte Carlo engines, and the philosophy of Karl Popper.

The Intelligent Investor: The Classic Text on Value Investing by Benjamin Graham (HarperBusiness, 2005)

This classic best seller by Benjamin Graham, perhaps the greatest investment adviser of the twentieth century, has taught and inspired hundreds of thousands of people worldwide. Since its original publication in 1949, Benjamin Graham's book has remained the most respected guide to investing, due to his timeless philosophy of value investing, which helps protect investors against the areas of possible substantial error and teaches them to develop long-term strategies with which they will be comfortable down the road.

Reminiscences of a Stock Operator by Edwin Lefèvre (George H. Duran & Co., 1923)

Reminiscences of a Stock Operator is the thinly disguised biography of Jesse Livermore, a remarkable character who first started speculating in New England bucket shops at the turn of the twentieth century. Livermore, who was banned from these shady operations because of his winning ways, soon moved to Wall Street, where he made and lost his fortune several times over. What make this book so valuable are the observations that Lefèvre records about investing, speculating, and the nature of the market itself.

Extraordinary Popular Delusions and the Madness of Crowds by Charles Mackay (Wilder Publications, 2008)

Why do otherwise intelligent individuals form seething masses of idiocy when they engage in collective action? Why do financially sensible people jump lemming-like into harebrained speculative frenzies—only to jump, broker-like, out of windows when their fantasies dissolve? We may think that the great crash of 1929, junk bonds of the 1980s, and overvalued high-tech stocks of the 1990s are peculiarly twentieth-century aberrations, but Mackay's classic, first published in 1841, shows that the madness and confusion of crowds knows no limits and has no worldly bounds.

OPTION BOOKS

Getting Started in Options by Michael C. Thomsett (John Wiley & Sons, 2007)

Investing in options sounds so risky that many people fail to capitalize on this potentially lucrative opportunity. In nontechnical, easy-to-follow terms, this book thoroughly demystifies the options markets, distinguishes the imagined risks from the real ones, and arms investors with the facts they need to make informed decisions.

Options for the Stock Investor by James Bittman (McGraw Hill, 2005)

This book includes basic to intermediate strategies for conservative investors and active traders.

New Insights on Covered Call Writing: The Powerful Technique That Enhances Return and Lowers Risk in Stock Investing by Richard Lehman and Lawrence McMillan (Bloomberg Press, 2003)

This book presents an investment approach that, though it has been used by some traders for 30 years, is largely unknown or misunderstood by active investors and traders. This book shows how to use this powerful investment technique for success in today's and tomorrow's markets. It gives a complete guide to the increased control and lowered risk this technique offers active investors and traders, and takes the approach of writing covered calls out from under the general umbrella of options, making it accessible to a broader range of the investing public.

Options as a Strategic Investment by Lawrence G. McMillan (Prentice Hall, 2002)

This blockbuster best seller—more than 100,000 copies sold—is considered the bible of options trading. Now completely revised and updated to encompass all the latest options trading vehicles, it supplies traders and serious investors with an abundance of new strategic opportunities for managing their investments.

Options: Essential Concepts by The Options Institute (McGraw-Hill, 1999)

This latest edition remains the state-of-the-art guidebook for getting started in options trading—and for understanding the motives and objectives of each player. Up-to-the minute research findings and strategic insights outline a practical, hands-on approach to trading options, helping traders of all experience levels master the basics as they make more tactically sound, intuitive, and profitable decisions.

The New Options Market (fourth edition) by Max Ansbacher (John Wiley & Sons, 2000)

With the help of numerous real-world illustrations, appendixes with more than 30 web site suggestions for options traders, and specific advice on option picks, Max Ansbacher explains the basics of trading theory and practice. In easy-to-understand, nonmathematical language, *The New Options Market* is a highly personal, newly updated guide that is specifically aimed at options traders in need of knowledge that will lead them to success.

The Short Book on Options: A Conservative Strategy for the Buy and Hold Investor by Mark Wolfinger (AuthorHouse, 2002)

A concise, easy-to-understand primer that first teaches the basics of stock options and then offers a hands-on approach to using options in a conservative manner. Beginning with a description of what an option is and how an option works, the book takes the reader on a journey from learning the language of options to being prepared to trade. The book is especially useful for long-term buy-and-hold investors, owners of self-directed retirement plans, investment club members, or anyone who wants to increase the performance and safety of their portfolio.

INFORMATION LINKS

Quotes, News, and Research

BusinessWeek	businessweek.com
EdgarOnline	edgar-online.com
Forbes	forbes.com
Fox Business	foxbusiness.com
MarketWatch	marketwatch.com
MSN Money Central	moneycentral.msn.com
TheStreet.com	thestreet.com
Wall Street Journal	www.wsj.com
Yahoo! Finance	www.yahoo.com

Stock and Options Exchanges

American Stock Exchange, LLC	1-800-THE-AMEX	amex.com
Boston Options Exchange	1-866-768-8845	bostonoptions.com
Chicago Board Options Exchange	1-877-THE-CBOE	cboe.com
International Securities Exchange, LLC	1-212-943-2400	iseoptions.com
New York Stock Exchange	1-212-656-3999	nyse.com
The Options Clearing Corp	1-888-OPTIONS	optionsclearing.com
The Options Industry Council	1-888-OPTIONS	optionseducation.org

About the Author

Harvey Conrad Friedentag is a Registered Investment Advisor (RIA) with the United States Securities and Exchange Commission and has been managing personal portfolios professionally since 1986. Mr. Friedentag has been certified as a United States Federal Court expert witness on stock trading, is an acknowledged expert on stock renting the use of derivatives (exchange-traded equity call options), and serves as president of the Contrarian Investment Club in Denver, Colorado. He is also author of *Investing without Fear—Options* (Chicago: International Publishing Corp., 1995) and *Stocks for Options Trading* (Boca Raton, FL: CRC Press LLC, 2000).

Index

Printed and bound by CPI Group (UK) Ltd, Croydon, CR0 4YY

16/04/2025

14658510-0003